Stephen Pálffy · The first thousand years

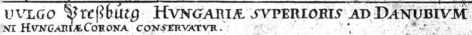

UVLGO Preßburg HVNGARIÆ SVPERIORIS AD DANVBIVM
NI HVNGARIÆ CORONA CONSERVATVR.

.	*Domus Senatoria*	7.	*Porta S. Laurenty.*
6.	*Claustrui Sanctimonialium.*	8.	*Danubius fluuius.*

The first thousand years

*A brief family history
as told for his grandchildren*

by

Stephen Pálffy

BALASSI

For
the memory
of all Pálffys who
lived, and died, to serve
their—*our*—country:
Hungary

Contents

Illustrations & Maps

Picture credits
Vöröskő by courtesy of Count Miklós Pálffy; Nicholas Pálffy (Palatine) and Leopold Pálffy from the portrait collection of the Hungarian National Museum (Magyar Nemzeti Múzeum); all others in the author's possession.

Maps by Dimap Bt.

By way of preface

☎ *(+36 1) 326 5871* 📱 *+36 70 244 0900*   *Cimbalom utca 5/a*
palffy.pista@t-online.hu   *(H-)1025 Budapest*

13 May 2008

Dear Ludo, Spike, Franzi and Coco,

All of you were born at the dawn of the third millennium, the very first years of the 21st century, in distant and remote New Zealand. Your earliest identifiable putative ancestor in the direct male line arrived in Hungary at the end of the first millennium, the closing years of the 10th century. During the thousand years and more in between, a good half of the Christian Era, many of his descendants, not a few of them your direct ancestors, left their mark on the history of Hungary.

It is the pleasing duty of grandparents to pass on knowledge and tradition; indeed, I have read somewhere (in a book by Jarred Diamond, I think) that the advance of Homo Sapiens commenced in earnest only when early humans began to live long enough to tell their children's children about what had gone on in earlier times. You too should know something about who your forebears, whose genes you also carry, were and what they did. You will, I trust, forgive me if, to tell their story in a way that makes sense, I have also included accounts of the main historical events and trends of their times to give their lives and actions context.

It will be some years yet before you can read this, but when you do you will, I very much hope, find it interesting.

Your loving Nagypapa,

Foreword

The persons of whom I write lived, the events and actions they were involved in occurred, in the main in Hungary; the text is in English. This raises the issue of proper names, of people as of places.

In some cases there is no choice in the matter: *Árpád, Géza, Béla*, like *Pest, Buda, Vöröskő*, have no English equivalents, but *István, Miklós, János*, and many more, are precisely equivalent to English *Stephen, Nicholas, John*, and so forth, while among place names *Pozsony*, for instance, has been known to generations of historians—from the peace there signed with Napoleon in 1805—as *Pressburg* (*vulgo*, says of this the Latin caption, which names it as *Poson*, on a seventeenth century print of the town that hangs before me as I write).*

Rightly or wrongly, I have opted for the English versions of Christian names where such exist: this makes the text easier to read, with no need to wonder how the Hungarian might be pronounced. Moreover, in their lifetimes most of those written about would have used the Hungarian form when talking or writing in Hungarian (as, on the evidence of extant correspondence, they certainly did amongst one another), the Latin form in Latin documents—which means virtually all formal documents to the first half of the nineteenth century—and as likely as not the German form when communicating with court and officialdom at Vienna. A Christian name refers, after all, to the same patron saint in whatever language.

As to place names: it has for long been quite common for towns in Central Europe to be designated differently in different languages, thus many Hungarian ones have German names too (*Buda*, for example, is called *Ofen* in German, *Győr Raab*, and so on) and to an extent *vice versa* as well (Austrian *Wien*, for instance, is known as *Bécs* in Hungarian). In the case of places within historic Hungary—the entire Carpathian Basin—I have stuck to their Hungarian names, except for such as *Pozsony/Pressburg* where the German version is already commonly known and accepted in Western Europe; the names of places elsewhere are written, unless there is a generally accepted English form (*Vienna, Prague*, and so forth), in their native form.

---

* *See* endpaper.

A detailed genealogy (albeit still lacking a few dates) is appended, together with some statistics relating to the family: relevant excerpts from this genealogy are included in the text too, to make it easier to follow the narrative (on occasion apparently confusing owing to the frequent re-appearance of the same Christian names). In all of these, those who are the ancestors of all Pálffys alive today are shown in **bold.**

A Glossary seeks to give brief explanations of various terms and concepts, concerning Hungarian offices of state but also other matters, with which the reader might be unfamiliar; the Select Bibliography lists some of the key works consulted.

Finally, since end-notes, unless limited to identifying sources, are an abominable nuisance, the text is accompanied by footnotes that contain expansions, elucidations and other matter that might render the context richer.

Prologue—1943: the last "normal" year

I still remember the deep embarrassment of that morning with acute discomfort. It was September 1943, I had turned ten in May, and was now facing my first day in a new school, the Érseki Katholikus Gimnázium.[1] Not particularly venerable—founded but a decade before the First World War it was so named only because the then Archbishop of Esztergom, Primate of Hungary, had accepted *ex officio* chairmanship of the trustees on behalf of himself and his successors—it nevertheless had a good reputation. It was, moreover, only a brisk fifteen minutes walk, less on a bicycle, from where we lived: when my secondary schooling had been discussed earlier that year I had resolutely resisted all suggestions that I might be sent away to a boarding school.

The academic and personal standing of the masters, perhaps half of them in holy orders, was in general high—not a few left over the years to take up university appointments, and by the cut of their suits (even cassocks), manner of speech, and general demeanour I instinctively judged many of them to be gentlemen whom I could envisage in my mother's drawing room—only a few recent additions did not conform to this pattern: there was a war on and, I suppose, the school had to take whom it could get. But that morning such knowledge and insights were still beyond me.

Some thirty of us sat in two rows of ink-stained wooden double desks, the schoolroom's windows behind us, facing the blackboard and the masters' desk on its slightly raised dais. I knew but one other boy, with whom I had shared four years of elementary schooling, and awaited what might happen next with some trepidation. Up by the blackboard stood a young master, his hair untidy, his suit unsmart, the big black register-book of Form I/B, our collective identity, open before him.

He introduced himself as János Hajdók, told us that in addition to being our form master he would also be taking us in Latin and Hungarian (I think, or was it History and Geography? He only taught us that one year). Next he read out our surnames—Christian names were left behind in elementary school: here we

---

[1] *Archiepiscopal Catholic Gymnasium:* the last term indicates not physical exercises but a type of school not unlike a French *lycée* (albeit, at that time, single-sex).

even addressed one another by surname—one by one. Each boy rose as he was called, was asked a few simple questions—which elementary school had he been at? did he already know anyone else in the class? that sort of thing—while Hajdók made some notes, then the next name was read out. Eventually it was my turn:

"Pálffy!"

As I stood up he eyed me looking vaguely ill at ease, then came out with a question as unexpected as it was embarrassing:

"Tell me, do I address you as *Count* Pálffy?"

The class tittered,[2] I muttered something to squash that preposterous idea, and wished I could slink away. It was unspeakably awful.

⚜

With hindsight I realise that, plainly one of the recent intake of masters, our form master was at that moment probably as uncertain of himself as I was. None of the experienced masters would have raised the matter, least of all in this form. Of course they all knew (the title appeared on all official forms, from birth certificate on, as a matter of course), but only an inexperienced master, quite likely from a 'humble' background, would have asked a pupil such an embarrassingly silly question on coming face to face, possibly for the first time in his life, with a genuine *count*, and a Pálffy at that—a name he had previously often encountered while learning history.[3]

Only ten at the time I had not yet learnt much history beyond the broad outlines I had absorbed from what my mother had read to me of a Sunday morning in pre-school days, my father had occasionally briefly mentioned, and I had later been taught at elementary school. Even so I was aware that *we*—yes, first person plural: I knew myself to be a member of a family that stretched back a long way, in the same way that I knew myself to be a Hungarian, a Catholic—had played quite an important role in Hungary's history (and I was also beginning to notice that not a few other relatives, and also friends of my parents, had names that kept cropping up even in the little history I already knew). This, however, seemed to be just another given fact of life, no more to be made an issue of, let alone to be shown off with, than one's nationality or religion.

And of course I also knew that I was a count[4]—it was, for instance, written on the envelopes of letters addressed to me (including the wrappers of catalogues that Mr Liebner, owner of Budapest's best toy-shop, good at marketing and an assiduous reader of births columns, sent me every year a short while before my birth-

---

[2] But none of them ever made an issue of my titled background at any later time.

[3] Even the Index of the 1982—still Communist days!—edition of the *Historical Chronology of Hungary*, merely a sequence of dates with events that occurred on them, lists no less than thirteen distinct Pálffys associated with, between them, events mentioned on well above thirty different pages.

[4] In Hungary, unlike England, *every member* of a titled family bore its title from birth.

2

day)—but made nothing of it. We and most of our relatives were, others we knew were not, but this really only affected how domestics addressed people and whether or not a nine-pointed coronet was embroidered on their handkerchiefs and shirts above their initials (laundry-marks, of course)—not me and mine, at that age, but those of adults. Otherwise one paid little attention to the thing, even played it down: a year or two earlier I had been taken to some exhibition with a friend of the same age, there was a visitors' book, I signed it just *Pista Pálffy* but he *Count X Y* (no names: he is still around, still a friend), and I clearly recall finding this rather bad form at the time.

True, looking back now I realise that those of us with titles—by then a closed and completed set that would never be added to: Hungary was still a kingdom but, since the death of Charles IV in exile in 1921, it had no reigning monarch, and no one but the crowned king could bestow new titles—and some others without one, but nevertheless quite like us,[5] *were* subtly different from the rest.

However, in the imagination of the rest that difference was magnified. My cousin (his grandmother had been an Apponyi) Dicki Liechtenstein, for example, recounts inviting one of his school friends—we attended the same school, he a few years above me— to spend some of the summer vacation at their country place, Hőgyész in County Tolna. Knowing that Dicki was a *prince* Liechtenstein, the school friend was, as he later admitted, thoroughly disappointed: he had expected a fairy-tale castle with flunkies in knee-breeches and powdered wigs at every door, only to find that the family lived in a comparatively modest late eighteenth-century house, originally built for the estate manager (the large foursquare country house, *château*, on the site of an old fortified castle—of late turned into a de luxe country hotel—had long stood empty even then), with but a manservant or two and a few maids.

Domestic servants were a feature of life that one took for granted. I lived with my mother—my parents had long been divorced—in the street end of her parents' house. By the standards of the day our household was modest: Kati, her maid, did all the cleaning; Ágnes the cook (Kati was her cousin), assisted by a succession of scullery maids, shopped and cooked (for my grandmother too until her death in 1942).

There was also Mr Bilicz—whom, to my mother's amusement, I always so addressed, since that was what I heard the other domestics do, while he blithely called me *Pista* (just *Bilicz* but *Count Pista* would have been the appropriate forms)— who had been my grandfather's man, lived in the porter's quarters next the arched gateway with his wife, and served at table for my grandmother (food rose from the ground-floor kitchen in a hand-pulled lift, which much intrigued me when I was little, to a first floor serving pantry located between my grandmother's and mother's dining rooms; here he also polished the silver, using corks and a pink powder obtained from England).

---

[5] Many families whose pedigree, wealth and role in history could have earned them a title in earlier centuries never got one, generally either because they had been Protestants or for some other reason out of favour with the Habsburgs, or else did not deign to accept one from them.

A maid called Eszter looked after the rooms and laundry of my mother's brother Uncle George Apponyi—known to family and friends as Tóbiás: the reference was not Biblical but to an ill-mannered hog in one of the *Maczkó Muki* books (about the adventures of an anthropomorphic bear), read as avidly by my mother and her sister when they were children as later by me—who lived, by then also divorced, at the other end of the house, in what had been my grandfather's rooms. Finally, my grandmother's old maid, Gusti, had a room at the top of the house, where she told me scary horror-stories about ghosts and country graveyards. In addition Mariska the washerwoman came once a week to launder and iron the household linen—the former in a huge copper kettle, the latter with flat-irons heated on gas jets.

But domestic servants were family—indeed, the Hungarian word for them, *cseléd*, is but a variant of *család* which means *family*—addressed by their Christian names[6] using the familiar *te* form. My mother frequently asked Ágnes, while discussing the following day's menu, to interpret her dreams for her; and if they had any personal problems they were helped and advised—even I became aware that Kati, who was young and pretty, frequently sought my mother's advice about boyfriend matters, and when she did eventually marry, well into the war, my mother saw to it that her husband got a "military service exempt" job at the Weiss Manfréd heavy engineering works so he would not be sent to the Russian front—and they always had their piles of gifts under the Christmas tree next to mine.

They may have performed the household chores but, more by example than instruction, I had learnt that they were to be treated with consideration. So I still smart at the memory of the occasion—then aged perhaps five—when, having been given a small tortoise and told that they eat lettuce, I rang the bell and asked Kati to bring some from the kitchen. My mother, as soon as she became aware of what I had done, gave me a mighty dressing down, told me that if my tortoise needed lettuce I could go and get it from the kitchen myself, made me apologise to Kati, and meted out an appropriate punishment (the nature of which I forget, but in all probability standing in the corner for what seemed a very long period).

On the other hand, from the time when I had learnt to 'behave' and use my knife and fork properly—certainly well before I was five—I joined my grandmother for lunch, until her death (when I was nine): this meant that, as a matter of course, I too helped myself from the serving dish that Mr Bilicz held out to me, in white cotton gloves, standing behind my chair. How superior I felt to my cousins Karli and Albert Rohan, one and two years younger than I, when they came to stay with their mother, Aunt Marika my mother's sister: an adult had to put the food on their plates, cut up the meat for them *and* they still needed a little silver "pusher" to get it onto their fork!

---

[6] Only Bilicz was the exception, so I never knew the surnames of any, except for Kati's: Engelhard.

My maternal grandmother, Clothilde Apponyi
née Mensdorff-Pouilly-Dietrichstein,
with whom I had lunch every day, in the 1930s

Until the war started (for the Reich, not us: Hungary managed to remain neu-tral well into 1941) Great-uncle Albert Mensdorff, my grandmother's youngest brother, also came to visit regularly from Vienna. A rotund, balding, elderly bach-elor, he had been Austro-Hungarian ambassador to the Court of St James from the last years of Queen Victoria's reign to the outbreak of the First World War, a posting he owed in no small measure to the fact that his Coburg grandmother had been sister to the mother of Queen Victoria and the father of Prince Albert. Queen Victoria, who had been very fond of their father her first cousin Alexan-der Mensdorff, treated Uncle Albert like a relative too: according to family leg-end his first despatch from London, reporting on the audience to present his let-ters of credence to the Queen, started with the words *"Du", sagte mir Ihre Majestät...* making the point that she had addressed him (in German) using the familiar form; Edward VII continued this tradition of German *tutoyer* talk with him. Poor Uncle Albert, reputed to be unable even to get dressed without the assistance of a valet, was quite unable to fend for himself in the mounting chaos

5

My great uncle Albert Mensdorff-Pouilly-Dietrichstein as depicted
in a Spy cartoon when Austro-Hungarian Ambassador to the Court of St James

of the Second World War's closing months: in the winter of 1944/45 he effectively starved to death in Vienna.

Aunt Stephanie, whose visits I found rather boring, usually only came to take
tea with my grandmother, but I was trundled in to be shown off. At the time the

significance of her past passed me by: a daughter of Leopold II of Belgium (the same Coburg connection as to Queen Victoria, which made her too a second cousin of my grandmother's), she was the widow of the unfortunate Archduke Rudolph, one-time heir to the throne of Austria-Hungary, but by then long married again to a Count Lónyay (who had been raised to prince on marrying her, since she could not drop to becoming a mere countess[7]). In 1945 the Red Army, almost incidentally, destroyed their country house as it swept across Hungary: she and her husband managed to escape and make their way to the Benedictine Abbey of Pannonhalma, where they both died soon after.

Uncle George Apponyi, my mother's brother, often also had lunch with his mother, would fulminate against Hitler, the Nazis, and their Hungarian adherents, the Arrow-Cross Party: he sat in Parliament for the small but violently anti-Nazi Liberal Radical Party, and his political enemies contemptuously called him *that Jew-hireling*. Indeed, my earliest political memory is of Uncle George bursting into my nursery on a spring morning, to announce to my mother: *"Those **swine** are now marching into Austria! I shan't talk German again while they last!"*—not yet five I did not understand that this was the *Anschluss*, but the emotional intensity of that moment has stayed with me.

Other, non-family, guests, whose names I have long forgotten, frequently came too, exposing me to the talk of adults from an early age. In my memory lunchtime conversation—whose language depended upon who was present: not all guests had Hungarian[8] and the whole table would switch to German, English or French (which last I barely understood) to accommodate their handicap—was, politics apart, mainly about books recently read, plays, concerts and opera performances attended of late. Much of its detail still above my head, I nevertheless absorbed the idea that an interest in literature, music[9] and the performing arts was part of life.

⚜

Table manners were, however, not without their problems. My maternal grandmother's ideas on this were rooted in English practice, which included keeping my hands invisible when not in use; my paternal grandmother, in contrast, adhered to the French approach, berating me for *not* keeping my hands visibly on the table

---

[7] In Hungarian law and practice, on marriage women acquired the title, if any, and status of their husband—none of that English *Mr John & Lady Mary Smith*.

[8] My grandmother had learnt and become fluent in Hungarian on marrying my grandfather.

[9] My grandfather (whose maiden speech in Parliament had been in support of funding for the Budapest Music Academy) had been a friend of Liszt as a young man, and musicians still came to my grandmother's house. I distinctly remember a soprano (whose name I forget) coming for lunch one day: having a short time before heard her sing the leading female role in the Hungarian fairy-tale opera *János vitéz*, I was much put out by how deep her voice was in conversation; I also remember being allowed to attend a recital by a pianist called, I think, Weingarten (a Jewish refugee from Austria, I now realize) on the Bösendorfer grand in my grandmother's drawing room.

My paternal grandmother Yannina Pálffy née Suchodolska,
some months after the birth of my father in 1898

throughout the meal. That had been earlier: by that summer of 1943, when I stayed with them again as I did every year, I had long learnt to switch the position of my hands during meals depending on where I was. But I still failed to overcome her resolute refusal to let me eat melons, despite pleading that at home and elsewhere I was allowed to: having grown up in Constantinople in the 1880s and 1890s, she was firmly convinced that melons were dangerously unhealthy for children, and I had to watch adults eat theirs without getting any myself.

My paternal grandparents—Maurice, generally known as Morkó, and Yannina—lived in a rented house in the village of Cziffer in County Nyitra located,

My paternal grandfather Maurice (Morkó) Pálffy as a young attaché in Hungarian gala-dress (worn in place of diplomatic uniform by Hungarian diplomats) in the 1890s

since the end of the First World War, variously in Czechoslovakia and Slovakia. It was a sprawling, dusty (in winter probably muddy, but I was never there at that season) village in flat country that grew maize and sugar-beet. Up the broad main street, on a corner of which their house stood, was the large, whitewashed parish church; at the far end of the village, in a neglected park, stood an ochre-yellow country mansion, a Zichy property but at that time uninhabited, its white shutters permanently closed.

In the garden behind my grandparents' house—where my grandfather had grown flowers, and I had toddled when little (and had pulled up the seedlings he had just planted, by way of helping him weed)—potatoes and vegetables were now grown and I read voraciously, hidden in a shrubbery: the "Western" stories of Karl May and James Fenimore Cooper (in German and English, respectively), also Zsiga Széchenyi's accounts of his big-game hunting forays to Africa, India, and Alaska.[10] In the cool of the evening we generally went for a walk, in my re-collection almost invariably along the dusty road that lead to the railway station, a short distance from the village itself. By then electricity, and with it a pump and running water, had come to the house, but at the time of my early visits it had been paraffin lamps in the drawing room and candles to go to bed with, water in large lidded metal jugs next the bedroom washbasin, and a tin "sit-up" bathtub, for which jugs of hot water were brought up from the kitchen (all living and bed-rooms were on the first floor) for one's evening bath.

It must have been a dreary place to live in, especially in winter, but at the time I accepted it as merely one more fact of life, never questioning why my grand-parents had settled just there. I now suspect that lack of money had something to do with it (but of course they too employed a cook, Marie, probably a scullery-maid, a maid, and a manservant). My grandfather had been the youngest of three sons (and several sisters). His father my great-grandfather, also Maurice and a ca-valry general (indeed: retired as a field marshal), had arranged for the bulk of his estates to go to the eldest, "Old" Uncle Józsi, with sufficient carved out for the second, Uncle Hans, to support a gentleman in comfort. But, wealthy as he was in land and forests, nothing went to his third son my grandfather, lest the estate become "too fragmented". Instead, my grandfather was ordered (at that time sons did as their fathers commanded) to become a diplomat—which suggests that he must have been given *something*, since in those days aspirant diplomats had to show private means sufficient to support the life-style that the K.u.K (Imperial & Royal) foreign service expected of them but to maintain which it paid them far too lit-tle—and also to join the Sovereign Military Order of the Knights of Malta: the idea was that in due course he would rise to a senior position in the order, possi-bly even to grand master, and thus, the order being extremely wealthy in those days, his comfort and welfare would be assured.

The rub in this scheme was that for this he had to become a professed knight who, as opposed to a mere knight of honour, had to take vows not only of obe-dience but also of personal poverty and, in particular, celibacy. During his first foreign posting, as an attaché at the Austro-Hungarian Embassy in Constantinople, my grandfather met my grandmother. Both of her grandfathers—Suchodolski and Chaikovski—had participated in the Polish anti-Czarist rising of 1830 and, following its defeat, both had been forced to flee abroad, eventually winding up

---

[10] Persecuted as a "class enemy" after the war, in the early 1960s he was then sent on safari to Africa, accom-panied by Party watchdogs, to shoot replacements for the stuffed animals in the Natural History Muse-um that Soviet soldiery had destroyed in 1956: to his glee the "boys" on safari treated him like the lord he was and neglected the apparatchiks meant to keep an eye on him.

in Turkey, where her maternal grandfather rose to the rank of pasha in the Ottoman army.

In Constantinople the young Hungarian attaché (who, like all his compatriots, wore Hungarian national gala-dress for diplomatic uniform) and the young Polish émigrée met, fell in love and—in defiance of my great-grandfather, who could not impede it but was furious—married (but why at Trieste?). As a result my grandfather inherited nothing when my great-grandfather died a short while later, aged eighty-five, and had to make do with his salary and whatever he had already received.

Gradually advancing in the diplomatic service, after increasingly senior postings to Munich (where my father was born), Bern, then Rome (where he was number two at the Embassy to the Holy See), interspersed with spells at the *Ballhausplatz*, Austro-Hungary's joint foreign ministry in Vienna, his first posting as head of mission, to Bern, came in 1916. I regret that he neither wrote his memoirs nor did I at that age think to question him about what it was like to be in that post at that time: during 1916–1918 Bern was the place through which the spies, clandestine agents and secret emissaries of all the warring powers passed, the neutral ground where representatives of countries at war with one another could meet in secret,[11] the node through which information, rumour, and gossip flowed from opposite sides of the front lines.

With the collapse of the Austro-Hungarian Monarchy at the end of 1918 the diplomatic service he had joined—and where he could have gone further: he was barely fifty at the time—also vanished. Fortunately the *successor states* to the old Dual Monarchy—Austria, Hungary, the newfangled Czechoslovak Republic—paid those who had been in its common foreign service appropriate pensions, in his case an ambassador's, for it is my retrospective impression that most of whatever private money he may have had was lost at the time, in unredeemed war bonds, invested in Russian railways and the like, and due to the inflation that followed the war.

That they chose to settle in what became Czechoslovakia rather than in what remained of Hungary was doubtless due to the family's long-standing links with the region, the counties of Nyitra and Pressburg, where most of the family estates lay, either side of the mountain range known as the Small Carpathians.[12] My grandfather had spent some of his youth in those parts, but not much: sent to board in the Jesuit school at Kalksburg as soon as possible, from the nursery so to speak, he thereafter never had a room of his own at home, but had to make do with any guest-room that was going during summer vacations. Also, although the new Czechoslovak state had trimmed the estates of Hungarian landowners considerably, there were still landed relatives in the vicinity who invited him to stalk deer in their forests, one of his passions (the other was photography: he developed and

---

[11] As did, for instance, great-uncle Albert, mentioned earlier, with Jan Smuts in an attempt to negotiate a separate peace between Austria-Hungary and the Allies; alas! he did not write his memoirs either.

[12] For their extent before the First World War: *see* map in the appendix *Pálffy estates in counties Pressburg & Nyitra about 1905*.

printed his own pictures, a process I watched with fascination when allowed to join him in his dark-room at Cziffer).

That summer, like always when staying with them, my grandparents took me to stay with some of these uncles and aunts (one never addressed, or referred to, relatives of one's parents' generation or older otherwise). The journeys were made by train: few people, my grandparents certainly not among them, had cars, and as the war went on even those who had used them less and less owing to petrol shortages. At Cziffer a local horse-drawn cab would take us and our luggage to the station which, in the way of such country stations then, had no proper platforms: one had to scramble up the steep steps of the coach from ground level, a station porter heaving the luggage aboard. Sometimes we had to change to another local train at the county town, Nagyszombat, place of excellent ice-creams if we had time between trains. Awaiting us at the station nearest our destination would be a carriage sent by our host: I always asked to sit up next the coachman, and would sometimes be allowed to drive the horses that sped us along largely deserted dusty country roads at a brisk trot (*never* cantering: directors of costume films just don't know about such things).

Uncle Józsi (Joseph), my grandfather's nephew and ultimate inheritor of most of my great-grandfather's estates, lived at Szomolány, in an unpretentious L-shaped, whitewashed building in the village. Szomolány *had* had a proper fortified hilltop castle too, but this had burnt down some centuries earlier, crumbling to ruin since; in the late nineteenth century "Old" Uncle Józsi had embarked on having it rebuilt, perhaps under the influence of his uncle and father-in-law (he had married a first cousin) Count Hans Wilczek, a dedicated restorer of things mediæval, but the First World War had intervened and at the time of my visits the castle was merely an empty stone and concrete shell.[13]

Uncle Józsi was still a bachelor at the time (he only married Aunt Gabrielle, Martin's mother, at the very end of the Second World War); Uncle Pali on the other hand, who lived at Pudmericz not far from Szomolány, was just getting divorced from his fifth wife, Louise de Vilmorin (who had found it most convenient to sit on the fence away from Paris until it became clear who was going to win the war). The Viennese architect who had designed the house for Uncle Pali's father, Uncle Hans, towards the end of the nineteenth century had intended it to look like a Loire château, if on a reduced scale—an ambition the house did, does, not quite live up to.

I had been given my first firearm, a *Flobert* (what would be known as a *point-two-two* in England), for my tenth birthday, and with this I had been reducing the sparrow population in my grandparents' garden that summer. It also came with me to Pudmericz, and Uncle Pali let me go sparrow-shooting in the yard of the

---

[13] Later, in Communist days, it was rendered habitable, to serve as a place of recuperation for politically reliable scientists and artists dedicated to Socialist-Realism.

12

Myself aged ten, with my Flobert,
that summer of 1943 in my grandparents's garden

home farm, supervised by a gamekeeper: to my great shame I shot a swallow too by mistake, which earned me a well deserved ticking off from Uncle Pali.

Less frequently we also went to Vöröskő—*Redstone*, but called Biebersburg, *Beavercastle*, in German—the family's main seat. Less frequently, because it had been inherited from a childless relative by Uncle Carl (he always spelt it like that), youngest brother of Uncle Józsi with whom he, as their middle brother Uncle Peter, had had a quarrel about some matters related to estates, since when they refused to speak to each other (in 1969 all three came to my father's funeral, and that was the first time they exchanged words again since the 1930s.) So, although Vöröskő is no great distance from Szomolány, it was 'difficult' to go on from one to the other, although my grandparents and father had avoided taking sides in that quarrel. (I was not really aware of these details then, but have pieced them together since.)

Vöröskő was, and is, a massive and very plain foursquare castle atop a steep spur of the Small Carpathians, whence it overlooks the countryside below; from near-

13

Vöröskő, the family's main seat from the 1580s to 1945

by, except for a moat on the side towards the plateau, it is more reminiscent of a huge barracks than of Disneyland, because that is what castles were. Acquired for the family in the second half of the sixteenth century by Nicholas Pálffy (the first *count*, of whom more in Chapter II), most of this vast edifice stood empty apart from a small number of comfortably furnished rooms on the first floor of the south-east corner, where Uncle Carl and his mother Aunt Yetta lived. But while there I was taken to see the huge cellars, with their gun-emplacements (cellars from inside, they were high up from outside) and dungeons, the deep well which provided water in times of siege—the place had last been invested in the early eighteenth century—and the intact early baroque pharmacy; I was also shown the carefully preserved wooden boat alleged to have been used by an ancestor, captured by the Turks in the seventeenth century, to make his escape from the notorious Seven Towers prison in Constantinople on the Sea of Marmara, but I have failed to identify such a forebear since then.[14]

But the quarrel between Uncle Józsi and his brothers was a side-show next the family quarrel that had been going on since the death of János (John) Pálffy in 1908, at the time of those visits still a frequent topic of heated discussions

---

[14] The castle is now open to the public as a museum, filled with objects that never used to be there, except for the pharmacy, and shown by ignorant guides who parrot inaccurate "explanations" of its past; the cellars are much in demand for the shooting of films set in a vaguely mediaeval period.

among the various uncles we stayed with. A bachelor and extremely wealthy, in his will he left some hundred-odd Old Masters, as also his two country houses and town house at Pressburg (each exquisitely furnished in a different style) to the state; the balance of his considerable estate he left, in complex entails, *to the family*.[15] His only sister, married to an Andrássy, claimed that this meant her; but numerous Pálffys insisted that "the family" could only mean one or more of them, however distant the kinship (the lines of János and the rest had diverged around 1700). So they all went to law, and the lawsuits continued for some thirty years before matters were sorted out more amicably, on the eve of the Second World War, most adult Pálffys receiving something. (Much later my father once mentioned, casually and in passing, that he too had been awarded a few hundred acres of forest in this share-out, but he never said where or whether he had ever taken possession.)

And of course we spent time, as we always did, with my father's sister Aunt Therese and her husband Uncle István Mailáth—tall, broad, moustachioed and with a deep booming voice, he had been awarded top decorations for distinguished bravery in the First World War—whose nearby estate and country house was at Pečenadi (I think it had been called Petőfalva in Hungarian, but they always used its Slovak name). Built in the style that would be called Georgian in England, it stood at the end of the village, the home farm across the road from it, the Corinthian (I think they were) pillars of the portico, of a size to take a coach, rising to a triangular tympanum at roof level. On the other side a shady terrace ran the length of the house, overlooking a park laid out very much in the English style, carefully grouped clumps of trees and shrubs bordering the broad lawn that sloped down to a small lake at its far end— but I remember this as rather neglected: perhaps gardeners were scarce during the war. Aunt Therese, who drove herself round the countryside in a pony-trap, kept an excellent cook and a couple of pugs; by that time she had "come off" Hitler, whom she had initially thought highly of. Their sadness, I now realise, was that they had no children, so they lavished a lot of love on me.

My parents had in a sense "always" known each other. Éberhard, the country estate of my maternal grandfather Count Albert Apponyi, lay less then twenty kilometres east of Pressburg, next the Little Danube that branches out of the main river just below that town to rejoin it again (having picked up the waters of the Vág on the way) at Komárom, thus forming the large and fertile island called Csallóköz: in the Middle Ages the *château* at Éberhard had been a moated foursquare castle guarding one of the fords across the Little Danube. Nearby Pressburg was the place to go shopping in the area, as also the scene of many social events, so the

---

[15] For more about this John Pálffy *see* the Comparative decline.

several young Pálffys—my father Francis (Ferenc, generally known as "Franzi"), his sister Aunt Therese, and their contemporaries Uncles Józsi and Peter— and the young Apponyis—notably Uncle George and Aunt Marika, who were the same ages as those Pálffys—had ample opportunity to meet; my mother Julia, five years her brother's and four her sister's junior (to the end of their days they always called her, and addressed her in letters as, *gyerek*, 'child'), would have tagged along.

That said, my father's first conscious memory of the young Apponyis was from Vienna. Aged perhaps five or six they all attended the same dancing classes—such instruction, which included deportment and social graces in general, was started early in life in those days—in the *Palais*[16] Dietrichstein, the town house of my maternal grandmother's family. Uncle George, so my father recalled, was pushing Aunt Marika around on a chair on the highly polished parquet floor, announcing that the two of them were now skating. Obviously, my mother had still been too young to have been present.

My Apponyi grandfather, who died a few months before I was born, had gone into politics in 1871, as soon as he was of an age to sit in Parliament: he had to make a start in the Upper Chamber, there being no election pending just then, but found a constituency to elect him to the Lower Chamber[17] at the first opportunity; that constituency did not last, but the second—Jászberény—he then represented in Parliament for over fifty years. While it was common knowledge in the family that he was not averse to women (even I knew at a comparatively tender age, though probably not yet when I was ten, that he had acknowledged the paternity of at least one bastard son) he seemed set to remain a bachelor all his life. Until, that is, chance in the guise of a society hostess placed him, aged fifty, next my future grandmother—by then also considered stuck in permanent spinsterhood: she was past twenty-eight—at a wedding breakfast in Vienna.

They should have had little in common. He was a serious-minded politician, teaching himself economics (his university degree was in Law) and dedicated to advancing Hungarian interests within the Dual Monarchy, if need be to the detriment of the monarch's prerogatives. She, who had the reputation of being the best dancer and one of the best horsewomen in Austrian society, came of French émigré ancestry—Mensdorff-Pouilly[18]—grafted onto the Moravian Dietrichstein family, which had for centuries supported the Habsburgs unquestioningly. Yet they

---

[16] Madly Francophile since the seventeenth century, the Austrian aristocracy thus designated its town houses, never mind that in Paris the French made do with *hôtel*.

[17] In Hungary, unlike England, those entitled to a seat in the Upper Chamber by hereditary right could also stand for election to the Lower, merely waiving their right to sit in the Upper for the duration of the Parliament for which they were so elected.

[18] While fleeing east from revolutionary Paris the Comte de Pouilly's son realised that his name could attract attention so, remembering that by virtue of a property near Luxembourg he was also Sieur de Mensdorff, he used the latter—less the *Sieur de*—during his journey; thereafter he and his descendants used both names, hyphenated together.

My maternal grandfather Albert Apponyi in his eighties,
about 1930

got engaged, then married (at much the same time as my paternal grandparents), and for thirty-five years lived in the closest and happiest marital harmony imaginable: not a day ended, when they were apart, until each had written the other a long letter with a full account of that day. Alas! the large cabin-trunk that contained these carefully preserved letters was lost, like much else, after the Second World War, to the regret of historians too: he knew and met all leading personalities of the period, in Europe as the United States (where Theodore Roosevelt became a particular friend), describing them, the meetings, and the matters discussed candidly in his letters.

Almost always in opposition—the one time Francis Joseph invited him to form a government in the 1890s this foundered on his refusal to accept the king's condition that he drop certain points from his programme (such as use of Hungarian as the language of command in Hungarian regiments of the Austro-Hungarian army); later he was minister of education on two occasions for a few years—he was, nevertheless, the Grand Old Man of Hungarian politics by the time of the

First World War.[19] Into his seventies when it ended, and Hungary in chaos—in December 1918 Count Michael Károlyi, the last prime minister to have been invited to form a government by the king, declared a republic, whose president he soon became until it was overthrown, a few months later, by Béla Kun's Leninist Bolshevik revolution, which instituted a reign of terror that lasted to August—my grandfather decided to retire from politics and write his memoirs.

Instead he was asked, as 1919 turned into 1920, to lead the Hungarian peace delegation to Paris, the Allies having concluded that, Kun gone,[20] Hungary now had a government sufficiently stable to sign a peace treaty. By then the terms had long been settled by the Allies amongst themselves, to an extent by default consequent upon agreements reached the previous year with others (Romania, the new Czechoslovakia, Serbia, and even Austria). So, although my grandfather was allowed to address the Allied leaders—in a brilliant speech that he repeated in fluent idiomatic French, English and Italian, for the benefit of each—he was also informed that there was to be no negotiation. When the Hungarian delegation's written comments and objections were then rejected out of hand, he and the entire delegation[21] resigned rather than sign such shamefully humiliating terms (almost three quarters, 72 per cent, of the country's territory, and near on two thirds of its population, were handed over to other nations). A nonentity, if just then a member of the Hungarian government, was eventually found to sign the Treaty of Trianon—the ceremony took place at Le Petit Trianon, in Versailles—and my grandfather became a hero.

In Hungary, that is. To punish him for his stand Czechoslovakia promptly passed a special *ad hominem* law, compelling him to sell Éberhard, now within that new state, within six months. Since the deadline was common knowledge it went for a pittance. My mother, then seventeen, who had loved her childhood home, vowed never to set foot in Éberhard again: she even refused to go when my grandparents were re-interred in the family crypt there in 1943 (the region had been re-joined to Hungary in 1938).

Retirement still evaded my grandfather. When Hungary joined the League of Nations he became our country's permanent delegate, admired and consulted by many at the League. As one of his fellow-delegates commented at the time: *"Who else among us can preface an intervention with 'As Bismarck said to me at the Congress of Berlin...'?"*; and the political society hostess Princesse Bibescou remarked *"Celui est plutôt une cathédrale qu'un homme!"* He died in harness in February 1933, aged

---

[19] At the outbreak of which he had in Parliament proposed cessation of party strife for the duration (much in the spirit in which Winston Churchill brought opposition leaders into his cabinet during the Second): his fellow parliamentarians applauded this initiative and then disregarded it, those of a radical bent grouped round Count Michael Károlyi in particular.

[20] He sought refuge in the Soviet Union, where Stalin eventually had him liquidated during the purges of the 1930s.

[21] A year earlier the leader of the German delegation at Versailles, Count Ulrich Brockdorff-Rantzau, had also refused to sign, and a nonentity substitute had to be found.

almost eighty-six, having insisted on travelling to Geneva for an emergency session of the League despite having severe influenza, which turned into pneumonia (no antibiotics in those days). He was given a state funeral as grand as Winston Churchill's in London many decades later.

⚜

How and when my parents got engaged I do not know. After the First World War, in which my father had served as a hussar lieutenant—largely in trenches, in the Dolomites and Carpathians: by the time he joined up in 1916 cavalry operations were a thing of the past (although he had still been instructed in fencing on horseback at the Stockerau cavalry officers training establishment, such are army instruction manuals)—he obtained a degree in law largely, I suppose, because that had long been the done thing. By virtue of this he was entitled to call himself *Dr. iuris utriusque* but he certainly never practised as a lawyer, intending to become a painter. My mother—who had seen to it that she was expelled from her school, the *Sacré-Cœur* at Budapest, because in her opinion the good nuns smelled unwashed and their French accent was atrocious (both doubtless true: even boarding pupils had to wear a long night-dress for their weekly bath, and the nuns probably never took one at all; French my mother, unlike those nuns, had spoken like a native from her earliest childhood)—had ambitions to sing.

So they had the makings of a thoroughly bohemian couple when they married in 1924, he almost twenty-six, she twenty, and both comparatively penniless. I have no idea what they lived on (although my mother always kept a personal maid) during their years at Munich and then Paris, where my father pursued artistic studies: alas, being a perfectionist, he was perennially dissatisfied with his paintings and destroyed all of them, so I have never seen any (by the time I knew him he had long given up painting, unlike his cousin Uncle Peter, whom the collapse of the Austro-Hungarian Dual Monarchy had liberated from the military career planned for him by his father, and who eventually made a success of it). A neglected throat infection that played havoc with her vocal cords cut short my mother's singing career.

At some point in the late 1920s or about 1930 they moved back to Budapest —perhaps the great crash of 1929 had reduced what funds they had even further, but this is conjecture—where I was born; not long after they divorced: how and why is a question I have never pursued; indeed, most of the little I know about their married life I had to piece together much later.

⚜

Which is how I came to spend my childhood in my grandmother's house (it always had been hers: acquired with her dowry, my grandfather had paid her rent to provide her with an income of her own, since she had no other private means) in the

19

My parents after their wedding in 1924; the little bridesmaid is Natalie ('Putzi')
Windisch-Graetz, the page Bálint Batthyány

Vár, the Castle Hill, which in those days had the air of a quiet provincial town set
down on its hill within the bustling capital. The earliest memory accessible to my
mind is tied to that quarter: reconstruction of the walled Castle Hill's Vienna
Gate—which I can date precisely to age three: a plaque placed on the gate later

informed me that this work had been completed by September 1936—was in progress, and I particularly remember seeing the white thighs of women, girls, also working above me on the scaffolding.

My mother had by then decided to invest what little capital she had in starting a dress-shop. "Society" disapproved of her going into trade, and to begin with her background worked both for and against the enterprise. *For* because snobs who otherwise stood no chance of meeting her came to buy, *against* because her own circle initially felt too embarrassed to do so. However, in due course she made a great success of it, and it became *the* place from which really elegant women got their clothes, made to measure of course; eventually "the shop" as we always called it—only outsiders talked of her *salon*—employed some one hundred people. Yet, as she told me much later, curiously it never had a bank account: all transactions were in cash, a book-keeper coming once a week to make sense of payments and receipts.[22]

From the summer following my fourth birthday I had been in the care of *Missy:* Miss Rita Bayley, of Irish Catholic descent, who had been a governess in that general region of Europe since before the First World War. She rapidly taught me English—German I had already mastered from her predecessor Martie, an Austrian nursery nurse whom I had outgrown: I believe she only looked after babies and very small children—and introduced me to Beatrix Potter, English nursery rhymes, the *Dr Doolitle* books, and later also to stories about King Alfred and burnt cakes, Robert the Bruce and his spider, and more such, from small, cloth-bound, olive-green readers whose monochrome line-drawing illustrations I can still visualise. She, presumably, also drilled my table-manners into me. She stayed with us until after the war, a picture of Chamberlain, later replaced by Churchill, from the *Illustrated London News* defiantly on the wall of her room until a Russian bomb destroyed that part of the house early in 1945; after the war she then moved to Vienna to her widowed sister, whose husband had been Austrian (and whose son had been killed at Stalingrad, a leave-pass for Christmas in his pocket).

I no longer remember all other places where, besides my paternal grandparents and Pálffy relatives in their vicinity, I spent parts of that summer: most summers I was asked for a few weeks here, a few weeks there to the country houses of relatives or family friends who had children of a roughly comparable age. But I very much remember one place: Csicsó, near the Danube on the southern side of the

---

[22] Jewish, an officer decorated in the First World War, all his spare time was taken up playing bridge; when Eichman descended on Hungary in 1944, after the country's German occupation, he trusted in his war record to save him—it did not, and by the time my mother got wind of this it was too late to hide him in our house.

My mother Julia Apponyi, by then running
a successful dress-shop, in the early 1940s

Csallóköz, where I spent blissful weeks that summer too, as I had every summer
of my childhood.

Uncle Alexander Kálnoky—his mother, a sister of my grandmother's, had
died when he was an infant and my grandmother then largely took her place in
his affections—and Aunt Marie-Therese had seven children, the youngest of
whom, Hézi (from Teréz), was but some months older than I and the next one
up, Louis, only a couple of years so. Aunt Marie-Therese simply absorbed me
into that large brood, extending her love and kindness to me as to an eighth
child;[23] only now, looking at old photographs, do I appreciate how stunningly
attractive she also was.

Csicsó was utter bliss. The only strict rule was to present ourselves on time
—hands and nails clean, hair combed, wearing shirt and sandals too (much of the

---

[23] And, indeed, some of those cousins still keep saying to me *But you were always the eighth to us.*

time we ran about barefoot, just in our shorts)—for lunch, whose imminence was announced by a gong beaten by a manservant, audible far and wide. Otherwise we spent our days as we wished: at the lake-like "dead" branch of the Danube, to which a carriage took all who wished to bathe most mornings, and where Uncle Alexander taught me to swim; roaming the countryside on our bicycles; exploring land-drainage canals in a punt; climbing trees; and occasionally the *big ones* —by then they were teenagers!—would deign to join with us in a game of cockioli among the trees and shrubberies of the well-kept park. We *little ones* also shared a pony called Gyuri, taking it in turns to go for a ride. Louis had, moreover, constituted a gang of estate workers' sons—this was a strictly masculine affair—whose captain he was: although younger and clumsier than they, I was as a matter of course appointed deputy captain.

Csicsó is one of the few happy endings: in the 1990s Louis managed to get the house back, has largely restored it again—it was in near-ruinous condition after fifty years of Communist misrule—and in summer, although part of the park is gone, it is once more filled with the bustle and noise of children, his many grandchildren (fourteen at last count), enjoying themselves, and swimming in the dead branch of the Danube, just like we did all those years ago. And I am yet again always welcome there.

So it was perhaps appropriate that I should have spent the closing days of 1943, the last "normal" year in my life that still conformed to predictable, established patterns and expectations, and the first of 1944, during which the world I had known began to crumble, at Csicsó. Thick snow covered the landscape, we skated and played ice-hockey on the frozen lake in front of the house, everybody joining in, while indoors the large wood-fired porcelain stoves radiated gentle warmth. On New Year's Eve there was a party, to which many neighbours came too, which we *little ones*, unlike our elders not yet in dinner jackets and evening dress, were also allowed to attend: hot punch, party games, then the local gipsy band came and we watched the *big ones*—teenagers, some even in their twenties—dance the *csárdás* into the new year with abandon.[24] It was to be the last such occasion, of a kind that could have occurred at any time during the preceding centuries.

Back in Budapest the house in the Vár, the Castle Hill, with its solid three-foot walls, vaulted ground floor rooms, and broad wooden gate, wide enough to admit a cart and studded with iron nails—over which the coats-of-arms of my grandfa-

---

[24] At a party more than sixty years on a gipsy band played: Alexander Kálnoky (Uncle Alexander's elder son) and my cousin Évi Apponyi (daughter of Uncle George), who had both been of the *big ones* that New Year's Eve, once more danced the *csárdás* together with abandon, both recalling that they had last done so together on that earlier occasion.

23

ther and grandmother, linked by a nine-pointed coronet above, declared whose house it was—still seemed a secure and inviolable haven, those living in it utterly safe, despite the war that was gradually getting closer. But not for long anymore.

&

The government of Hungary, neutral until autumn 1941 but thereafter a reluctant belligerent on the German side, had so far managed to stave off German occupation and was actively pursuing secret contacts with the Western Allies—for no one in Hungary had any illusions about the Soviet Union—who were by now moving up Italy (if temporarily stuck at Cassino). The Germans, however, knew of these contacts, and on 19 March 1944, in a pre-emptive move, they did occupy the country; the SD—*Sicherheitsdienst*, the branch of the Gestapo that operated in occupied countries—arrived too, with a detailed black-list of known anti-Nazis (it was followed by Eichman and his men who specialised in "dealing with" the Jews[25]). Prime Minister Kállay just managed to make it to the Turkish Legation, where he was granted asylum, before they got him; many others also on the SD's black-list were not so lucky.

Two days later, on the twentyfirst, a staff car brought two immaculately turned out SD officers to the house: politely they invited Uncle George, an outspoken critic of Nazi Germany in and out of Parliament, to accompany them to German HQ *for a chat*. Almost as an afterthought they suggested that he might bring overnight essentials: with the curfew then in force, they said, returning home that evening might be difficult. Trusting in his parliamentary immunity he went, with his overnight case: he never needed its contents in Mauthausen KZ (concentration camp), where his journey ended.

Later that year a German officer was billeted in the house, unaware that by then it harboured several Jews with false papers, and that many an evening visitor was a friend or relative in hiding from the SD, just dropping in for a quick bath and change of underwear. Soon after he had moved on, on Christmas Day 1944 Budapest was encircled by the Soviet Army that had by then been approaching across the country for several months and had already been fighting its way into the town's south-eastern suburbs for some weeks. For almost three months thereafter the town was besieged from all sides, the Soviets advancing street by street; all of Pest to the Danube fell to them by 18 January, by which time the Germans had blown all bridges across the river, but the Vár at the centre of Buda only on 13 February 1945. By then the house, in whose mediæval vaulted cellar we had survived shellfire and bombs, was largely in ruins: this did not

---

[25] Although, under German pressure, some discriminatory racial legislation had been introduced this was hardly enforced, enabling Hungary's Jews to lead largely normal lives up to then; it was only the arrival of Eichman and his cohorts that changed all that.

discourage Soviet soldiers from braking in, raping the women, and looting what they could still find.

We survived one more winter in what still stood of the house, then moved away. In the course of the next few years the Communist Party, backed by the Soviet occupiers (and the ÁVO, the local NKVD clone), established itself as the absolute and undisputed master of the country. Where Nazi ideology had stressed the necessity of getting rid of Jews, Communist ideology now insisted upon the need to eliminate *class enemies*, a category that included all those whose forebears had played a role in their country's history, quite especially if they had gained a title by it. A bare five and a half years after I had started there I was forced to leave my school—by then taken over by the state, now Communist dominated, and re-named Rákóczi State Gimnázium—for the selfsame reason that had caused me such acute embarrassment on that first day (if, thanks to the personal decency of the new headmaster, quietly, and 'officially' *at my own request owing to health problems*).

Soon my mother's shop, which she had re-started in 1945, was nationalised (they broke in at night, changed the locks, and when she went in the following morning told her that was that); somewhat later she was arrested, on Christmas night, imprisoned in a labour camp without a charge, then sent into internal exile. I survived as an unskilled labourer on a construction project in the country's north-east corner, was in due course called up, and eventually arrested, interrogated and imprisoned too.

But all of that is another story, told elsewhere.[26] This story is about our forebears—whose lives and deeds resulted both in my early embarrassment and later exposure to hostile discrimination—about who they were and what they had done.

---

[26] *See* the account of my life in Hungary in the 1950s in the Appendix.

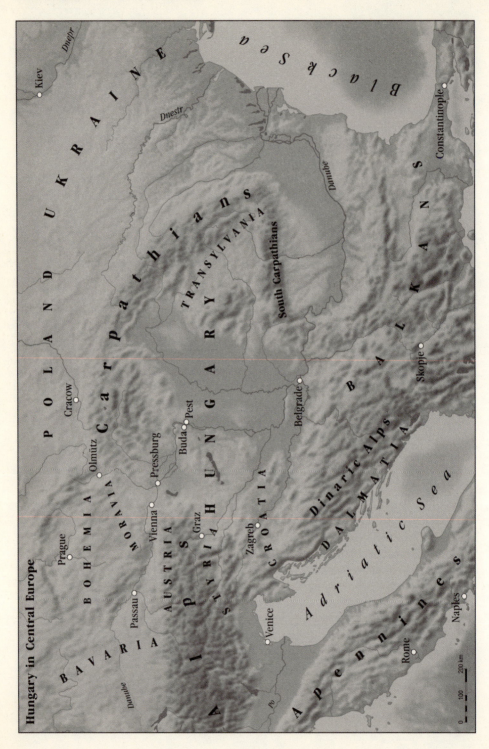

Hungary in Central Europe

Mediæval days (to about 1400)

*B*y Western European standards our title is not very ancient, dating back no further than the end of the sixteenth century—but then, in Hungary *no* hereditary title antedates that century, during which the country's then new, Habsburg, ruling dynasty first introduced them. Which is not to say, however, that Nicholas the first count (of whom more in the next chapter) sprung to prominence from a previously obscure family, as Communist-inspired historiography tried to suggest.[1]

There are gaps in the mediæval documentary evidence—much was lost and destroyed in the course of the Turkish wars and partial occupation of the country during the sixteenth and seventeenth centuries, including the archives of many cathedral chapters and abbeys where documents were generally deposited for authentication and safekeeping—and thus much in this chapter is conjecture. It does, however, seem more than likely that our family's history in Hungary began towards the very end of the tenth century with an immigrant who, and whose descendants, made their mark. But first some historical context.

Europe was a different place from today's when the Hungarians—last of those great waves of peoples from the east to establish a permanent presence in Europe—led by Árpád made their home in the fertile land surrounded by the crescent of the Carpathian Mountains during the years 895–900.

The entire region to their west, north of the Alps, was inhabited by peoples who spoke varieties of Germanic dialects. Since Roman days this region was referred to as *Germania*, but this was a geographical not a political term: at the time Germany, like the rest of the continent, was a hodgepodge of independent

---

[1] For reasons of Marxist–Leninist ideology—according to which no one of a prominent family, a *class enemy*, can nor ever could do anything praiseworthy (any more than a Jew could in Nazi eyes)—even the *Hungarian National Bibliography* published in 1969 (deep in Communist days) downgrades his family background to "petty landowner", thereby making it possible to write of his military successes against the Turks as a positive achievement without offending against ideological correctness.

dukedoms, counties and lordships of varying size, each the territorial base of a powerful family and its retainers. Much the same was true of what is today Denmark, the Netherlands, Belgium, and France (although towards the south of France the populace spoke Latinate dialects, which gradually eclipsed the Germanic ones in its north too). Italy to the south-west of the Hungarians' new home was also fragmented among small states. Finally, the regions to the north-west, north and east of the Hungarians (the later Bohemia, Moravia, Poland, the Ukraine) were still beyond the pale of Christendom, populated by a variety of pagan Slavonic tribes. Only to the south, encompassing most of the Balkan Peninsula (as well as Asia Minor), was there a sizeable and coherent unitary state: the Byzantine Empire, its capital at Constantinople, successor without a break in continuity of the eastern half of the erstwhile Roman Empire.

The Roman Empire had, some five to six centuries earlier, ruled all of Europe, the entire Mediterranean littoral and much of the near Middle East, but in time it was divided into an eastern and western half. The latter (extending from Hadrian's Wall in northern Britain across the Continent, along the lines of the Rhine and Danube, all the way to the Balkans) had during the fifth century collapsed under the impact of attacks by warlike Germanic tribes who had emerged from somewhere to the east: Goths, Vandals, Franks, Lombards, Saxons. Having rapidly overrun all of the western Roman Empire, including Italy itself (as well as the Iberian Peninsula and parts of North Africa), their leading warlords had then —now styling themselves kings, dukes, counts—set up numerous independent territorial states in place of the unified Roman Empire. Adopting Christianity (if often of the heretic Arian persuasion), they gradually transmuted ancient Germanic warrior traditions and tribal loyalties into the beginnings of new institutions that were to dominate the Middle Ages: knighthood and feudal dependency.

Memory of the Roman Empire that had united all of Europe was, however, not dead: in the eighth century Charles king of the Franks, descendant of such warlords, subdued most of the erstwhile Roman provinces north of the Alps, all the way into what is now Hungary, then marched into Italy itself and, at Christmas 800, had the Pope crown him *Holy Roman Emperor of the West* in Rome; his capital he kept, however, at Aachen. Known to posterity as *Charlemagne*, his sons quarrelled, his descendants proved feeble, and the new empire soon fell apart again, the lands of the Franks, the later France, in particular, splitting off from other German lands along and east of the Rhine.

Here by the tenth century the dukes of Saxony had arrogated the title *King of Germany* to themselves, if without effective power over other territorial lords there. But in that century's middle decades Duke Otto, later dubbed *the Great*, established his ascendancy over all other rulers in Germany; next, invading Lombardy, he was also crowned *King of Italy* at Pavia in 951; finally in 962, following in the footsteps of Charlemagne, he too descended on Rome and had the Pope crown him *Holy Roman Emperor*—if with the significant and realistic extension *of the German nation*—claiming to stand in direct line of succession, via Charlemagne, to the Roman Emperors of old. This title was to survive until 1806, although shorn of effective power by the end of the Middle Ages.

Following their arrival in the Carpathian Basin the Hungarians—seven tribes made up of some one hundred clans—had for a good half century indulged in frequent sweeping raids westwards, often invited to do so by one or another local ruler who wished to see his enemies discomfited. Advancing rapidly on their fast-moving ponies—not unlike the Vikings did in their fast ships along the western coasts of Europe—they repeatedly roamed across today's France, and on one occasion even got as far as Andalucia on the Iberian Peninsula. Northern Italy, Lombardy, was every so often raided too, and initially also Byzantine territory, but Byzantium soon negotiated fixed annual payments of gold to keep Hungarian raids away.

Raiding parties heading westwards inevitably had to cross Saxon and Bavarian territory, even if aiming for places further on, and for long the dukes of these proved unable to resist. Until, that is, 955: in that year Otto the Great defeated the largest Hungarian army ever to set out westwards, in the plain by the river Lech near Augsburg. This defeat forced the Hungarians to reconsider their policies, and to withdraw their western border from the river Enns—today the dividing line between Upper and Lower Austria—to the vicinity of the Vienna Woods and then gradually east of today's Vienna.

Not two decades later, in 972, the Hungarians had a new ruler in Duke Géza. As soon as he was firmly in charge, at Easter 973 he sent a numerous embassy to Emperor Otto to offer lasting peace and co-operation, and an agreement to this effect was reached. He also asked that priests be sent to convert all of his people to Christianity and, since at home he was embarking on a policy of asserting his own central authority at the expense of tribal and clan chiefs, he would appear to have let it be known that German knights—not entangled in Hungarian tribal and clan loyalties—willing to enter his service would be welcome too.

Finally, a year before he died, Duke Géza obtained the hand of Gisela of Bavaria, grand-daughter of Otto the Great's brother—and thus a cousin of the then Emperor, Otto's grandson the young Otto III—for his son and heir Stephen.

There is reason to believe that our earliest identifiable ancestor was one of the knights who came to Hungary from Germany, from somewhere in the vicinity of the upper Danube, Bavaria or Svabia, at that time. It would be romantic had he been of the retinue that accompanied Queen Gisela to her wedding at Esztergom[2] in 996, but it is more likely that he had arrived in response to that first invitation.

---

[2] The foundations of the church where she married Stephen, on the castle hill of Esztergom (then the capital), have been carefully exposed in recent times: how tiny it was next the cathedral that has risen there since.

According to chronicles written some centuries later, but which drew on contemporaneous sources since then lost, his name was Hedrik, an early German variant of Henry. Also referred to as *Kundt* and *Poth*, which *could* stem from the roots that gave rise to modern German *die Kunde* ('message') and *der Boote* ('messenger'), he may perhaps have acted as a herald; versions of both names recur among his descendants during the Middle Ages. He was, the chronicles state, of the family of the counts of Hennenburg, but no place of that name can be located.[3] Apparently Hedrik came together with his brother Wolfger and a number of bowmen (one chronicler says forty, another three hundred: the former is more likely).

However that may have been, Hedrik soon had occasion to prove his valour to Stephen, who sorely needed reliably loyal military forces shortly after his marriage. Duke Géza had coerced all tribal and clan chiefs to accept that his son Stephen would succeed him as leader, but their acceptance was reluctant, since up to then the next leader had always been *elected* by the ruling family's adult males from amongst their own number. Thus when Géza died in 997, Koppány, a cousin of Stephen's and master of south-central Transdanubia (to the southeast of Lake Balaton), promptly declared that he, being the elder and more experienced, was better suited to take over, and began to muster followers; moreover, citing ancient custom, he also claimed Géza's widow Sharolt, Stephen's mother, for wife. Just then at Veszprém,[4] slightly to the northwest of Lake Balaton, she was outraged: messengers sped to her son, who happened to be in the vicinity of Esztergom.

Heeding his mother's urgings Stephen moved faster than Koppány had expected: his troops, stiffened by a sizeable contingent of German knights, caught Koppány by surprise, defeated his forces, and soon the rebel's quartered body was exposed above town gates in the vicinity (allegedly at the suggestion of Sharolt). If Hedrik was among the knights who sped to the rescue at Stephen's side it is not improbable that he was also present at Esztergom three years later, on Christmas Day 1000, when the papal legate anointed and crowned Stephen Hungary's first king, with a crown received from Pope Sylvester II. In the decade following his coronation King Stephen had to resort to force of arms against overbearing subjects twice more, to subdue Ajtony, the powerful overlord of southeast Hungary (who had embarked on a private, Byzantine-oriented, foreign policy) and a few years later against his mother's brother the Gyula, master of Transylvania. It is more than likely that Hedrik distinguished himself in both of these campaigns too.

---

[3] However, the gravestone with funerary statue of a count of Henneberg, grand master of the Teutonic knights, from *c.* 1330 is preserved in the Bayerisches Staatsmuseum at Munich—could there be a connection?

[4] Later, from Gisela on, Veszprém became closely linked with Hungary's queens, its bishops entitled to crown them and *ex officio* serving as their chancellor.

More than likely because, although the chronicles are maddeningly vague as to dates, before the end of King Stephen's reign (997–1038) Hedrik already held an estate received from the king along the Danube, a short distance upstream from the town, and by then already a bishopric, of Győr. Here he constructed a castle—not a hill-top eyrie with battlements and soaring turrets as in Disneyland and fairy tale illustrations, just a low structure of earthen ramparts and wooden palisades with a moat: the region is flat and watery—which was named Hedriksburg *(Hedrik's castle)*. Since Hungarian dislikes a succession of hard consonants, his German name soon evolved into Hungarian Héder[ik], and that of his castle into Hédervár *(vár* = 'castle'). The village of that name is still there, and the shape of the nineteenth century country house now in it, last of numerous reconstructions on the site, still suggests the outlines of that early fortified place.

Of Hedrik we hear no more. There was little fighting to do: after those rebels had been put down there was peace within the rapidly Christianised realm, the new Emperor in the west was by now Queen Gisela's brother, relations with Byzantium to the south were amicable too. Nor is it known whom Hedrik married, whether a local girl or a bride from his native Germany, or what his immediate descendants' Christian names were. But he and they settled, appear to have thrived, and took to calling themselves Hédervári *(de Hedervar* in mediæval Latin documents: an *i* suffix attached to a place name is the Hungarian equivalent of Latin *de*, English *of*).

After Hedrik there is a gap of perhaps three generations in the sequence of known names. The principal written sources about persons of that period are official documents granting them land, appointing them to offices, or witnessed by them in some official capacity: perhaps Hedrik's immediate descendants simply sat at home, running their estate and keeping away from all official business—in Hungary the eleventh century was, for the most part, dominated by civil wars fought for the crown and, newcomers that they were, they might have found it prudent to avoid taking sides—thus gaining no mention. Alternatively, the relevant documents may have perished, as did so many others of the period.[5]

Then a document of 1150 explicitly identifies *comes Morus* (Maurice) of Hédervár as Hedrik's direct descendant. *Comes* was at that time not an hereditary feudal-territorial title in Hungary, but the designation applied to governors of counties appointed by the Crown, comparable to English lords lieutenant. That Maurice held this office suggests that the Héderváris had been doing well dur-

---

[5] Including one similar to England's *Doomsday Book*, compiled in about 1056.

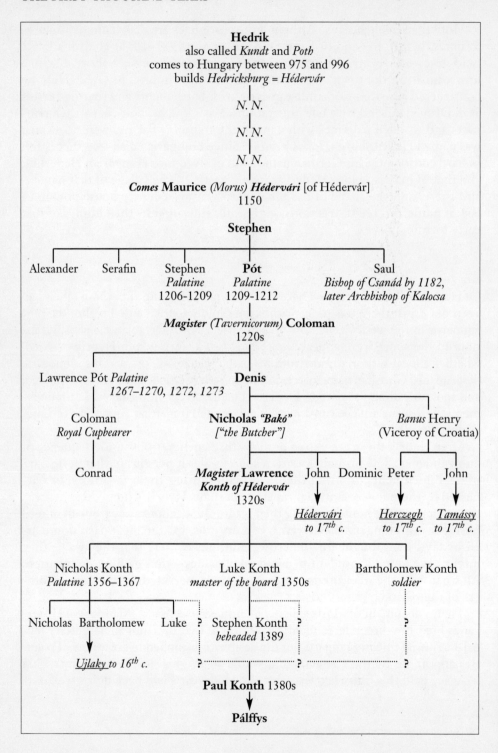

Hedrik
also called *Kundt* and *Poth*
comes to Hungary between 975 and 996
builds *Hedricksburg = Hédervár*

N. N.

N. N.

N. N.

Comes* Maurice** *(Morus)* ***Hédervári [of Hédervár]
1150

Stephen

Alexander	Serafin	Stephen	**Pót**	Saul
		Palatine	*Palatine*	*Bishop of Csanád by 1182,*
		1206-1209	1209-1212	*later Archbishop of Kalocsa*

Magister *(Tavernicorum)* **Coloman**
1220s

Lawrence Pót *Palatine* **Denis**
1267–1270, 1272, 1273

Coloman	**Nicholas** *"Bakó"*	*Banus* Henry
Royal Cupbearer	[*"the Butcher"*]	(Viceroy of Croatia)

Conrad	***Magister* Lawrence**	John	Dominic	Peter	John
	Konth of Hédervár				
	1320s				

Hédervári *Herczegh* *Tamássy*
to 17th c. *to 17th c.* *to 17th c.*

Nicholas Konth	Luke Konth	Bartholomew Konth
Palatine 1356–1367	*master of the board* 1350s	*soldier*

Nicholas Bartholomew Luke **?** Stephen Konth **?** **?**
beheaded 1389

Ujlaky to 16th c. **?** **?** **?**

Paul Konth 1380s

Pálffys

ing the intervening period: the office entitled its holder to a seat in the Greater Royal Council, and only persons of some wealth and standing were appointed to it. But how many generations of Héderváris intervened between Old Hedrik and *comes Morus?*[6]

The duties of the office—economic, judicial and military—called for a mature but physically fit man, so Maurice is likely to have been at least about thirty but short of sixty at the time. Not much above thirty years later the *youngest* of his grandsons was already a bishop, so perhaps thirty years old: to father him Maurice's son must have been born not later than in the 1120s.

Between them these observations suggest that Maurice might have been born around 1100, some hundred and twenty-five years after the earliest, and about a hundred years after the latest, time at which Hedrik would have come to Hungary as, presumably, a young man. This, in turn, makes three generations—whose names are not known—between the two of them likely.[7]

From this *comes* Maurice onwards the names, and increasingly also some of the deeds, of successive members of the family can be traced with reasonable accuracy from generation to generation, as they advance to ever more and higher offices (terminating, as you will see, in an enigma). An account of all of them in Old Testament style—*and Maurice begat Stephen, and Stephen begat... etc.*—would be tedious to read: they are all are shown in the genealogical table above, to which you might wish to refer as you read on; the text is limited to thumbnail sketches of the more notable among them.

From the late eleventh to the end of the twelfth century competent monarchs, internal peace, and abstention from crusades, made Hungary the wealthiest and most powerful kingdom in Central Europe. Nor was learning absent: increasingly clergymen who advanced to senior positions in the Church had studied at Paris, then the top university, especially after the visit of Louis VII of France and his queen, Eleanor of Aquitaine, in 1147 (when they stood godparents to the future king Stephen III). Unfortunately we do not know whether the youngest grandson of *comes* Maurice, Saul—by 1182, at the latest, Bishop of Csanád in eastern Hungary, from 1183 to 1185 Chancellor, i.e. responsible for all royal documents and paperwork, and ultimately, from 1192, Archbishop of Kalocsa, second only

---

[6] Some historians suggest that Hedrik arrived not at the time of Duke Géza (r. 972–997) but almost a century later, during the reign of King Géza I (1074–1077), in which case no generations would need to have intervened.

[7] Three intervening generations per century does, in fact, appear to have been the approximate norm in the family since then too; most recently, for instance, three generations (my father, myself, and my son Alexander) have come between my grandfather Maurice, born in 1869, and my grandson Ludo, born in 2001—a timespan comparable to that between old Hedrik and *comes* Maurice.

to the Archbishop of Esztergom Primate of Hungary—had been one of their number, but it is not unlikely.[8]

However, from 1296 when King Imre came to the throne, the situation in the country began to deteriorate: the king's younger brother, Prince Andrew, demanded a share of the country for himself and instigated repeated armed rebellions to obtain it. These were defeated, but to secure followers Andrew made extravagant promises should he win, which the king had to counter with gifts and grants. In the event King Imre died after a reign of but eight years, the infant son who succeeded him a few months later, and in 1305 the rebellious prince came to the throne as Andrew II. Now promises made earlier had to be honoured.

It would seem that two of archbishop Saul's elder brothers, Stephen (in some instances written *Chepan*) and Pót our ancestor, whose name harks back to Old Hedrik's *Poth*, had been among Andrew's supporters in his rebellious days,[9] for within a year of his coronation he appointed first Stephen, and three years on Pót in his place, to the highest secular office and dignity of the realm, Palatine. Neither is known to have held any senior office (beyond a lord lieutenancy each), as was more usual, before being so promoted—somewhat like becoming prime minister without any previous ministerial, let alone cabinet, experience—making it likely that these appointments were rewards for earlier support (which would also explain why they had not been given senior appointments by King Imre). While in office they jointly founded and endowed a monastery at Lébény, not far to the south of Hédervár, whose church, dated to 1208 (if somewhat restored in the nineteenth century), now serves as the parish church of the village.[10]

Neither held any high office again, but they must have kept on good terms with the king: Pót's son Coloman (*Kemen* in sources, which reads like a corrupt spelling of *Kelemen* that so translates into English) is known as *magister*, suggesting that he would have been among the first to have held—on the evidence probably some time in the 1220s—the then recently created high-ranking office of *magister tavernicorum* (Master of the Treasury), at the time generally abbreviated to just *magister*[11] (much as in modern English just *the Chancellor* is often used for *the Chancellor of the Exchequer*). His task would not have been an easy one: Andrew II had given away much of the royal lands and other sources of revenue, and had squandered money he did not have on pointless military campaigns (including participation in the Fifth Crusade in 1217, the first and only king of Hungary to

---

[8] We do know that his ecclesiastical superior, archbishop Lucas of Esztergom, had studied in Paris with the same masters, albeit a few years later than, Thomas à Beckett.

[9] A supposition further supported by the documented fact that in 1208 Andrew II formally raised the idea of Saul's (who seems to have died in 1202 or 1203) canonisation with the Holy See.

[10] Were endowment and completion in 1208 (*see* previous footnote) pure coincidences? But a couple of miles off the Budapest–Vienna motorway, with an exit for the village, it is still well worth a visit.

[11] *Magister* was also applied to clerics who had acquired this degree at Paris, Padua or Bologna, but Coloman, who had at least two legitimate sons, was certainly no cleric.

have done so, during which he bought vast numbers of relics in the Holy Land), to pay for all of which the coinage was depreciated and new taxes, promptly borrowed against from tax-farmers, had to be invented. [12]

It is not clear just how long Coloman remained in office, but probably not for long: senior office holders seldom did during the reign of Andrew II. The three years each of Coloman's father and uncle as Palatine was not bad going: during the thirty-year reign there were fourteen Palatines and fifteen each of the two next-highest ranking dignities, Governors of Transylvania and Justices of the Realm, some lasting but a few months in office.

In the next generation—having fought valiantly against the Mongols, who invaded and largely destroyed Hungary in 1241–1242, during the early years of King Béla IV's reign—the younger of Coloman's sons, Denis, our ancestor, seems to have concentrated upon consolidating and rounding off his estates, leaving it to his elder brother Lawrence Pót (the double Christian name would appear to honour his grandfather) to advance in office: appointed Justice of the Realm in 1261, then the most senior judicial office, he was promoted to Palatine in 1267, to so remain until the king's death in 1270; he was Palatine twice more, for brief periods, in 1272 and again in 1273. All these offices came to him at exceptionally difficult times: from the 1260s the heir, Prince Stephen, had split the country into opposing camps, most of the time waging open war on the king his father; then, having finally succeeded his father on the throne, Stephen IV died two years into his reign in 1272, and the crown passed to his son László IV aged but ten: Lawrence Pót, an experienced elder statesman, would have been appointed Palatine again at that time to hold the fort while competing factions manoeuvred to gain the upper hand during the king's minority. But his line died out in his grandson, Conrad.

So it was the sons of Denis, Nicholas and Henry, who carried on the family into the reign of a new dynasty, choosing, it would appear, the right side at the right time.

⚜

The last king of the Árpád Dynasty Andrew III—who had inherited a country riven by factional infighting between overmighty barons—died in January 1301, in his early thirties, leaving no son to succeed him on the throne. At this Wenceslaw of Bohemia (who later ceded his claim to Otto of Bavaria) claimed the throne of Hungary for himself, citing descent from the House of Árpád in the female line; but so also did Charles [-Robert] of Anjou-Sicily, whose grandmother Mary was the daughter of the late King Stephen IV. It took until 1310 before Charles

---

[12] The seething discontent due to all of this had in 1222 forced Andrew II to issue a charter of the freemen's rights and liberties—not unlike England's *Magna Carta* of 1215—known as the *Golden Bull.*

(he dropped the Robert on coming to Hungary) finally gained the upper hand, to be confirmed on the throne by Parliament and be duly and legally crowned. The country's fragmentation had meanwhile continued apace, and it took Charles another ten years to subdue all his overmighty subjects and restore central authority and order.

At some stage during these turbulent events Henry, the younger son of Denis, was Viceroy of Croatia and Slavonia. This makes it likely that he, and in all probability the family as a whole, backed the Anjou claims from early on, since support for them came mainly from the country's southern regions, including Croatia and Slavonia. The fact that the family did well during the century of Anjou reign also suggests this, since Charles methodically reduced and sidelined families that had supported other claimants. But the descendants of Henry's sons Peter and John adopted the surnames Herczegh and Tamássy respectively,[13] to fade out of our story (both families died out by the seventeenth century).

Denis' elder son Nicholas, who continued to call himself Hédervári, acquired the sobriquet *Bakó*, which at that time meant *butcher* (its current meaning, *executioner*, only came into use, by extension, some centuries later): it is not known why, but since his lifetime coincided with a bloody period of internal and civil wars in Hungary's history he may have perpetrated some nasty deeds. Of his three sons Lawrence the eldest, in a throwback to old Hedrik's *Kundt*, expanded his surname to *Konth of Hédervár*; John, the second, and his descendants continued to call themselves just plain Hédervári until their line died out in the mid-seventeenth century, while Dominic the youngest appears to have had no issue.

In the 1320s Lawrence Konth of Hédervár was *magister*, Master of the Treasury. As such he would have played an active part in the consolidation the country's finances initiated by King Charles: complete reorganisation of the country's mints—after the Mongol invasion Béla IV had leased their operation to (it so happens: Jewish) entrepreneurs, Charles now reverted to direct management of the relocated mints[14]—in 1323, and the concurrent introduction of new reliable silver coinage, made possible by a new royal monopoly in precious metals. In 1325 these measures were followed by the first issue of Hungarian gold florins, *forint*, modelled on the gold coins, *fiorini*, of Florence (the minting of these Hungarian coins was to continue, at much the same weight and purity, until the nineteenth century).

Lawrence Konth of Hédervár the *magister* had three sons, the youngest of whom, Bartholomew, was killed early in life soldiering in Dalmatia; the other two, Nicholas and Luke Konth, made careers in royal service. During the 1340s

---

[13] Surnames, which had only recently come into general fashion, were still frequently adopted, discarded and changed at personal whim at that time.

[14] Minting was profitable: the coins' face value was somewhat above that of the metal that went into them and, moreover, coins in circulation had to be exchanged for new ones, at a discount, at regular intervals.

Nicholas took part in the Neapolitan campaigns of Charles' son Louis[15] (the only Hungarian king to become known as *the Great*) and then some minor ones in north Italy, next undertook several diplomatic missions to the papal court at Avignon and to Italy. Finally in 1351, following some less senior appointments, he was made Governor *(voivode)* of Transylvania and five years later moved up to become Palatine, remaining in this office until his death in 1367.

Luke's career was less spectacular but also assured him a position of influence at court: in the 1350s he was *Master of the Board*, with an important say in the running of the royal household. Of his son Stephen, who died on the scaffold, more below.

⚓

At this point we come to an enigma: our descent from Paul Konth, active in the 1380s, is fully documented but, although genealogists have been teasing away at this for some centuries, nobody has been able to establish which of those three Konths of the previous generation, Nicholas the Palatine, Luke, or Bartholomew, was his father.

Three sons of Nicholas are known; the eldest and youngest appear to have had no issue, while the middle one's two sons, grandson (in particular) and great-grandson played significant roles in historical events for another century and more, firmly calling themselves Ujlaky. Could this, so well known and documented, branch harbour a fourth unrecorded son?

Lawrence's second son Luke had a son Stephen who is well enough known from history. In a nutshell: following the death of Louis the Great in 1382 the crown passed to his teenage daughter Mary; in 1385 she married Sigismund of Luxembourg, who in 1387 became joint monarch with her. But some would have preferred to see Charles of Naples, a *male* Anjou cousin, on the throne and conspired to place him there. In 1388 Stephen Konth, leader of such a conspiracy, and some thirty of his co-conspirators had the misfortune to be captured together, almost inadvertently: tried for high treason and sentenced to death, they were offered a royal pardon if they did homage to Sigismund. They refused, and were beheaded. Was Paul Konth a shadowy younger brother of this Stephen, careful to stay out of conspiracies and, in particular, keen to play down that family link after the traitor's execution?

As to Lawrence's youngest son, Bartholomew: there is no record of his having married and fathered a son before he was killed at war, but the possibility cannot

---

[15] His younger brother Andrew had married their cousin Joanna, heiress to the Kingdom of Naples; when she came to the throne she refused to share it with him despite an earlier contract to this effect, and then—when the Pope, who had been appealed to, eventually ruled in Andrew's favour—she connived at his assassination: the campaigns were to avenge this foul deed.

37

be excluded, especially if his son was, as he would have been, an infant at the time of Bartolomew's death. If there was such a boy, he too would have wished to play down family links with the cousin executed for high treason.

So the enigma remains. And if genealogists working when many family and other archives were still intact across Hungary—the Soviet occupation, in particular, destroyed much that had survived earlier depredations—failed to solve it, then there is little likelihood that it will be solved in the future. Yet not only tradition but also heraldic evidence supports the descent of Paul Konth from the Konths of Hédervár: when in about 1510 one of our ancestors, yet another Paul, adopted the coat of arms we use to this day he retained the ancient Hédervári device, vertical "wavy" blue stripes on silver, in the little pennants he incorporated with the new arms.

Finally, there is one further option that none of those genealogists, constrained perhaps by nineteenth century prudery, seem to have suggested: Paul Konth may have been a bastard (or, in that quaint phrase, natural) son of one of those three Konths—so not recorded in "official" family trees but recognised by his father and quite properly using his surname. Bastards recognised by their fathers were far from uncommon in those days even, or especially, at the highest levels of society: a generation or two before Paul Konth's birth King Charles I had obtained papal dispensation from the stigma of bastardy, which excluded from higher clerical office, for one of his own illegitimate sons so he could become a bishop. Why not, then, recognised bastards in the Konth family too?

Coming of the Turks (15th–16th centuries)

*I*t is likely to remain an enigma forever which of the three Konths of the right age and generation—Nicholas the Palatine, Luke, or Bartholomew—was the father of Paul Konth, who appears in documents at the time Queen Mary (r. 1382–1395) followed her father Louis *the Great* on the throne and then married Sigismund of Luxembourg. But with him and beyond him we are on firm genealogical, and soon historical, ground, document-

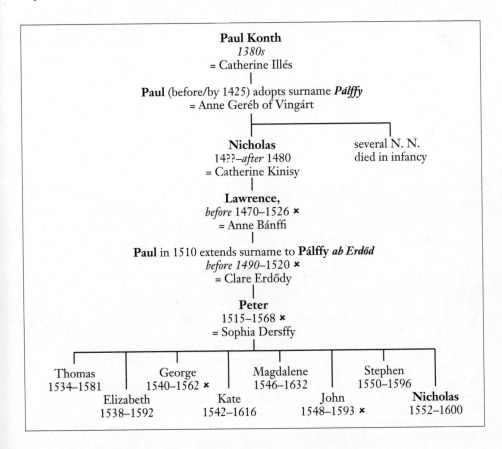

Paul Konth
1380s
= Catherine Illés

Paul (before/by 1425) adopts surname *Pálffy*
= Anne Geréb of Vingárt

Nicholas
14??–*after* 1480
= Catherine Kinisy

several N. N.
died in infancy

Lawrence,
before 1470–1526 ✗
= Anne Bánffi

Paul in 1510 extends surname to **Pálffy** *ab Erdőd*
before 1490–1520 ✗
= Clare Erdődy

Peter
1515–1568 ✗
= Sophia Dersffy

| Thomas 1534–1581 | | George 1540–1562 ✗ | | Magdalene 1546–1632 | | Stephen 1550–1596 | |
| Elizabeth 1538–1592 | | Kate 1542–1616 | | John 1548–1593 ✗ | | Nicholas 1552–1600 | |

ed with sufficient reliability to have satisfied the exacting editors of the publication commonly, if somewhat incorrectly, known as the *Almanach de Gotha*. The family's descent from here to our ancestor Nicholas is shown below.

Paul Konth's wife Catherine Illés was almost certainly, but this cannot be proved for sure, of the family that later called itself Illésházy.[1] She bore him a son, baptised Paul too who, presumably to distance himself from Stephen Konth executed for high treason in 1389, made a point of stressing that he was the *son of Paul*—in Hungarian: *Pál fia* or, more succinctly, *Pálfi* (much as a king's son, *király fia*, is referred to as *királyfi*)—and then soon dropped the tainted name Konth altogether[2] to call himself, by 1425 at the latest, just *Pálffy* (spelling was variable at the time), equivalent to *Paulson* or *Fitzpaul*. And thus we have called ourselves ever since.

He would seem to have kept away from prominence and office. However, he too married well, taking for his wife Anne Geréb of Vingárth, whose family was prominent in Transylvania and closely related by marriage to Elizabeth Szilágyi, wife of the Regent (1445–1451) John Hunyadi and mother of King Matthias *Corvinus* (r. 1458–1490). Of their several children only one, Nicholas, survived into adulthood; by the 1480s he was writing himself Pálffy *of Dercsika & Ráró* (two estates, one in County Pressburg, the other across the Danube in County Győr). It is unclear from the sources how his wife Catherine Kinisy was related to Paul Kinisy (also spelt Kinizsy), the foremost military commander of King Matthias: she may have been a niece but, since Paul Kinisy had risen to prominence from very modest origins—tradition has him a miller's lad—and left no descendants, no details of the Kinisy family at large are on record.

Nicholas' son Lawrence, just to confuse matters, took to writing himself Pálffy *of Kápolna & Cseleszteö* (two other estates): such qualifiers eventually became permanently attached to the names of families, but at that time it was still usual to change them at will with the acquisition of new estates.[3] Firmly ensconced in County Pressburg, he married Anne, daughter of John Bánffi, Lord Lieutenant of that county and principal chamberlain (*praefectus*) of the court of the boy-king Louis II (r. 1516–1526). A family tradition, passed to me by my father, holds that by his time the Pálffys, which would mean Lawrence, were already associated with the profitable business of the Hungarian Thurzós and the Fuggers of Augsburg, who were by then coming to jointly control the mining, refining and export of metals—copper, silver and gold—from Hungary's northern Highlands (gold and

---

[1] Of ancient lineage, in the mid-fifteenth century they went by the name **illésházi Illés**—i.e. Illés **of** Illésház *(Illés-house)*, a village they had founded and named for themselves on their estates—but by the early sixteenth century George (an MP for County Pressburg) dropped the *Illés* still used by his father and called himself just *Illésházy:* later Kate Pálffy (in last line of table above) was the second wife of his grandson Stephen, who played a notable role in Hungarian politics.

[2] It is worth noting that at much the same time, and doubtless for similar reasons, the executed Stephen's cousin Bartholomew Konth also dropped that surname completely in favour of Ujlaky, from an estate.

[3] Indeed, even in the twentieth century, there being two Joseph Pálffys, informally they were often distinguished one from the other as the Joseph Pálffy *of Szomolány* or *of Koroncó*, after their country places.

silver was beginning to trickle into Spain from the Americas too, but up to then Hungary had been one of Europe's main sources of these precious metals, and still was of copper).

However that may be, when Suleiman the Magnificent launched a major attack on Hungary in 1526, Lawrence was appointed captain of the contingent sent by the County of Pressburg to join the army being hastily assembled against the Turk: leading his men into battle, he fell at their head at Mohács, on 29 August 1526.

❧

The Ottoman Turks had first emerged as a power to be reckoned with in Asia Minor (today's Turkey) around the turn of the thirteenth to fourteenth centuries. Byzantium, reduced to a shadow of its former self by the destruction the Fourth Crusade of 1204 had wrought, was unable to resist their advance across Anatolia, then over the straits south of the Sea of Marmara into the Balkan Peninsula: by the 1370s Hungarian forces had already encountered advance raiding parties of Turks north of the Danube and south of the Carpathians (in today's Romania). In the course of the fifteenth century they occupied all of the Balkan Peninsula, Constantinople itself falling to them in 1453; by that time they were also pressing hard against Hungary's southern borders, whose defences (reorganised in the early 1400s by King Sigismund) had still held, if only just, while the energetic and effective Matthias *Corvinus* had been king.

He was, however, followed on the throne by Ulászló *(Wladislaw)* II of the house of Jagiello (r. 1490–1516), elected to it—in the absence of a male, or indeed any, legitimate heir—precisely because he was dithering and lackadaisical: this suited many a magnate who had chaffed under the firm hand of King Matthias. During the latter reign monies intended for the Treasury increasingly found their way into private pockets and the southern defences were neglected: neither the money nor the leadership needed to keep these up to scratch was forthcoming. There was even less leadership when the crown passed to Louis II (r. 1516–1526), a spoilt child not even in his teens yet. Sultan Suleiman, not dubbed *the Magnificent* in vain, saw his opportunity. Gradually he eroded what remained of Hungary's defences, taking Belgrade, linchpin of the whole system, in 1521: it had been its near-miraculous relief by John Hunyadi when the Turk had besieged it in 1456, just three years after Constantinople fell, that had given Hungary somewhat above another half-century's breathing space.

The road into Hungary now stood open, and in 1526, as soon as the harvest was in, Suleiman marched a huge army north. His aim was Vienna, capital of Ferdinand Habsburg, younger brother, and in Germany the representative (as *elected King of the Germans*), of the Emperor Charles V. Much of the Emperor's time and energy was taken up fighting the French: also king of Spain, Duke of Burgundy (which then included all of today's Netherlands, Belgium and French Flanders, as well as Burgundy proper), and claiming large swathes of northern Italy

41

too, his realms surrounded France. This the French resented, and it gave them reason to encourage Suleiman to attack Habsburg possessions from the east. Meanwhile Germany itself, the Empire, was increasingly divided by the unfolding Reformation and, in consequence, incapable of concerted action. All of this suggested to Suleiman—rightly, as it proved—that only enfeebled Hungary stood between him and Vienna.

What few professional troops—soldiering had become a job for professionals—Hungary still had were, in contrast to the days of King Matthias who had maintained a strong standing army, rarely paid on time or in full. Moreover, by way of compromise between court factions, overall command had been entrusted to Paul Tomory, Archbishop of Kalocsa, a Franciscan better versed in administrative procedures than military matters (to give him his due, he did repeatedly try to resign, but was each time prevailed upon to stay on). On news of Suleiman's approach urgent calls went out for fighting men to join the army being hastily assembled south of Buda: the contingent captained by Lawrence Pálffy had been mustered in response to that call. The army thus thrown together, some twenty-eight thousand men in all, then marched south along the right bank of the Danube, the king, just turned twenty, and his entourage catching up with it at Szekszárd, from where they all moved on to the vicinity of the market town of Mohács. One notable absentee was John Szapolyai, Governor of Transylvania, who was still at Szeged with an army some ten thousand strong that he was bringing from Transylvania and the eastern parts of the country.

Suleiman—whose army was not only about three times the size of the Hungarian but also disciplined, battle-hardened, and well lead—decided to leave the initiative to his opponents: screening his cannon, placed at the foot of a low rise, with unimpressive rag-tag auxiliary troops, he concealed the main body of his formidable janissaries behind that rise, and then waited; the Hungarian army deployed facing what they could see of the Turkish forces. Becoming bored and impatient when nothing much seemed to happen all morning, Francis Batthyány, Viceroy of Croatia in command of the right wing, foolishly decided to charge; the rest rapidly followed his example. The screen of Turkish auxiliaries was, as Suleiman had intended, soon scattered, giving his cannon a clear field of fire: their effect at close range was devastating. Then the Janissaries moved forward from their concealed position: the rout was complete, the battle over within less than two hours. Most of the Hungarians who had not fallen fighting—the majority of senior dignitaries, including bishops, and other leading men present (among them Lawrence Pálffy) had been so killed—were then rounded up and put to death on the spot: best estimates put the number of Hungarian dead at some twenty-four thousand.

The young king, who had watched but not participated, and his bodyguard galloped off northwards to avoid capture. A few miles on they reached the Csele brook that flows into the Danube from the west along a shallow, marshy valley: the king's horse slipped as he tried to ford it and threw him. Falling face down encased in heavy armour and helmet he was unable to rise; by the time his attendants became aware of what had happened and hurried to his rescue he had drowned.[4] Suleiman went on to loot Buda[5] and burn Pest, then decided that it was too late in the year to attempt Vienna and took his army home to winter quarters.

Hungary just might have recovered from that defeat had a firm hand been in charge;[6] but as it was, the king dead without an heir, that autumn two separate and equally incomplete Parliaments elected two kings to the vacant throne.[7] First John Szapolyai—who had failed to arrive at Mohács in time (possibly on purpose, but his apologists claim that he had received contradictory orders) and thus still had an intact army—got himself elected King John by a Parliament he had no right to call; then another Parliament, legally called by the Palatine, who had survived Mohács, elected Ferdinand of Habsburg, the late king's brother-in-law twice over (his sister Mary was the widow of Louis II, his wife the sister Louis II), in the hope that he would mobilise the resources of the Empire against the Turks, which he promised to do.

John, in possession of the Holy Crown, had himself crowned, settled into despoilt Buda, and held the country east of the Danube; Ferdinand hung on to the west and north, for the next decade making sporadic war on John for the rest of the country rather than strenuously fighting the Turks (whom John dared not offend, lest he be caught between two fires). The winner was Suleiman; Hungary was never to recover completely.

Initially loyalties were split, many uncertain which king to accept and support, but the Turk remained a menace and it soon became apparent that John was in no position to resist the Ottoman threat—indeed, in 1529 Suleiman marched an army across Hungary to besiege Vienna with John's agreement—so those who wished to see the Turks held back increasingly gave their allegiance to Ferdinand, trusting that he would, as he had promised, mobilise the Empire against them. In the longer run he and his Habsburg successors failed to act effectively, but this could not be predicted at the time.[8]

---

[4] Having inspected the region, the folly of the Hungarian strategy becomes even more apparent: their only hope, knowing they were outnumbered, would have been to deploy in a defensive position atop the low ridge to the north of the Csele brook's marshy valley (north of which there are more low ridges down to the Danube), forcing Suleiman to attack across this natural obstacle and uphill.

[5] Carrying off not only many of the splendid volumes of the great library Matthias had created, but also the main chandeliers from the Church of our Lady—colloquially known as the Matthias Church—in Buda, which can be seen to this day in the Hagia Sophia mosque at Istanbul.

[6] Of, at least, four million inhabitants but twenty-four thousand fighting men had been lost at Mohács.

[7] Parliament's right to fill the throne in the absence of a legitimate male heir was by now well established: it had had to do so repeatedly during the preceding two centuries, since from 1301 to 1526 only three of Hungary's eight kings had left male heirs to succeed them.

[8] In all fairness it must be added that had not Szapolyai's questionably legal parallel election to the throne deprived Ferdinand of most of the country he might have acted more firmly against the Turks: for the next few years there were no Ottomans north of Belgrade and had he been undisputed master of all of Hungary from 1526–1527 on he just might have rallied the nation and organized more effective resistance against their next onslaught. And later on his successors might have taken a firmer stand too had such early action resulted in all, or at least most, of Hungary remaining theirs.

Meanwhile Kings Ferdinand and John concluded a secret treaty—secret, since John was fearful of Suleiman's response should he become aware of it—by the terms of which John's part of Hungary was to revert to Ferdinand on his, John's, death. Alas, late in life he married the ambitious Isabella Jagiello (first cousin to Ferdinand's queen): shortly before he died in 1540 she gave birth to a healthy son, baptised John Sigismund. Following her husband's death she soon repudiated the secret treaty and had the baby crowned King John-Sigismund. In 1541 a badly led army sent by Ferdinand tried, but failed, to dislodge her from Buda; then Suleiman arrived there with a sizeable Turkish army "to protect the infant king". Next Suleiman gave a banquet for members of the regency council, during which Buda was taken by stealth and at the end of which they were arrested.[9] A few days later young John Sigismund and his mother were sent to Transylvania, which Suleiman permitted them to keep on condition of paying an annual tribute.

Thereafter the Turks rapidly occupied most of the central plains, as well as the eastern portion of Transdanubia, roughly to the line of Lake Balaton. For the next century and a bit Hungary remained divided into three parts: the Turkish occupation in the centre, so-called Royal Hungary to its west and north, and Transylvania to its east. The offices of state and Parliament had, meanwhile, moved to Pressburg, the Archbishop of Esztergom to Nagyszombat. But as the wars dragged on and the Turkish presence seemed ever likelier to last for a while, policy and strategic decisions, especially in military matters, were increasingly made in Vienna.

This is the general background against which the story of the next several generations of our forebears—firmly in the camp of Ferdinand from the outset, both because they had confidence in his, and the Empire's, ability to see off the Turks as also because their estates lay in the country's northwest, mainly counties Pressburg and Nyitra, a region that was always under his and his descendants' control—must be seen.

Fortunately for us—for otherwise we would not be here—well before he was killed at the battle of Mohács Lawrence had had a son, Paul. Styled *magnificus*, which indicated that his standing was that of a magnate, in 1510 he married Claire Erdődy, a relative of Cardinal Thomas Bakócz of Erdőd, Archbishop of Esztergom, Primate of Hungary, and titular Latin Patriarch of Constantinople (and runner-up in the first ballot at the conclave of 1513, which finally elected the Medici Leo X as Pope), who had amassed a considerable private fortune that he left to relatives.[10]

---

[9] All of this giving rise to the Hungarian saying *the black soup* [i.e. coffee] *is yet to come*—meaning *the worst is yet ahead*—allegedly Suleiman's rejoinder when members of the regency council wished to leave early and return to Buda castle.

[10] She also had an uncle who was Bishop of Zagreb; the precise degree of relationship between the archbishop, the bishop and Claire's father Peter is not entirely clarified.

There is little reason to doubt that her dowry was more than satisfactory and, on marrying her, Paul both added *ab Erdőd* to our surname and adopted her family's coat of arms,[11] both of which we have been using ever since. Like his father (if before him, in 1520) Paul too fell fighting the Turks, at a place that sources name as Kocsina.[12]

He did, however, leave a son, Peter, who was also determined to fight the Turk, and did so to such good effect that in 1535 he was granted the estates of a family that had died out without issue (under the law as it then stood, the Crown inherited in the absence of direct heirs or near kin) in recognition of his military prowess; a decade later he also inherited the estates of his maternal uncle, Simon Erdődy Bishop of Zagreb (and there is evidence that he added to his estates by direct acquisition too). And, besides whatever dowry his wife Sophia Dersffy, whose family was well established (and fighting the Turks too), might have brought—under Hungarian law she remained its legal owner, but her husband would have managed and administered, and her children would inherit, it—he was, of course, heir of his grandfather Lawrence's estates as well, so with him the family was becoming ever wealthier. This did not, however, stop Peter continuing to fight the Turks: in 1568 he too was killed in a skirmish, near Vellicza in Slavonia.

By then wealth was certainly needed: unlike the five generations preceding them, Peter and Sophia had lots of children who all survived into adulthood (perhaps because they were reasonably spaced, possibly owing to Peter's frequent absences at war): three daughters, who married into distinguished and wealthy families (the two younger a second time too when widowed), and five sons, all soldiers, two of whom also fell fighting the Turks (one of them barely into his twenties).

Thomas the eldest was for long captain of the castle of Várpalota,[13] by that time a border-fort facing the Turks, from where he fought the troops of the pasha of Székesfehérvár (and kept complaining to the high command, *Hofkriegsrath*, in Vienna that money for his soldiers' pay was always in arrears, forcing him to pay them from his own pocket). Fighting at times elsewhere too, in 1562 he was captured by the Turks near Szécsény, north of Pest, but was ransomed: both sides were in the habit of selling back senior captives. In 1581, shortly before his death, Thomas

---

[11] These arms were confirmed to Bishop (as he then was) Thomas Bakócz in 1474; on the evidence of one of the still extant *Corvina Codices*, where it is depicted in colour, *we* still use the original colours—stag *or* in field *azure*—while the Erdődy family, curiously, uses these arms with stag *argent* in field *gules* (red).

[12] Difficult to identify. A small village called Kocsin in County Nyitra lies too far north for even a stray raiding party of Turks to have got that far at that time, a year before they captured Belgrade and were still probing the southern defences of Hungary, but the Kocsina named in sources might have been the Croatian village now called Konjščina—phonetically not unlike Kocsina—some way north of Zagreb, a region Turkish raids could have got to in 1520.

[13] In the vicinity of which there was in the 1950s a coal-mining forced labour camp where I spent some time (*see* Appendix).

was made a *baron of the Holy Roman Empire*—far less costly than repaying him money he had spent on his soldiers' pay[14]—and along with him his brothers John, Stephen and Nicholas too.

Thomas's only son, of the same name, hardly outlived him; Stephen had one daughter only; John's line died out in his grandsons, one of them, Thomas, a bishop, ultimately of Nyitra and famous for his sermons, another one, Andrew, a colonel who, in the next century, appears to have served in the Thirty Years War for a while under the great Imperial commander Wallenstein.[15]

But it was Nicholas, the baby of the family and ancestor of us all, who was to achieve the fame and wealth that thereafter secured the family's standing and role in Hungary.

⚜

By the time Nicholas was born in 1552 his eldest brother Thomas, eighteen years his senior, would have been riding out on his first sorties against the Turks, but there were still plenty of other children in the house: his brothers Stephen and John, aged two and four, as well as his sisters Magdalene aged six and Kate all of ten, who doubtless played with and mothered their baby brother (he and Kate were for long close, but later in their lives there was an unexplained cooling off between them; however, twice married but childless, Kate willed most of her estate to his sons). Beyond such conjecture nothing is known of the first ten or so years of his life: we know that a tutor *(pedagogus)* — who, in keeping with the period's preferences, used the Latin name Valentinus Literatus (but was known in Hungarian as *Bálint deák*, i.e. Valentine the clerk)—was employed by their father; one can assume that he taught the children to read and write, Latin and German too (the latter increasingly necessary in order to communicate with court and imperial bureaucracy at Vienna), and other basic skills, while riding, fencing, hunting, and listening to stories of warlike exploits against the Turk would have been natural pastimes.

When about eleven—the exact date does not seem to be known—Nicholas was sent to court, to serve as page and companion to his exact contemporary the Archduke Rudolph, grandson of Ferdinand I and soon, following the accession of his father Maximillian I (r. 1564–1576, II as Emperor), heir apparent. To prepare him for his future role, and to meet and learn from his uncle who reigned the other

---

[14] Just as the Fuggers of Augsburg, whose banking house had lent the Habsburgs vast amounts during the fifteenth and sixteenth centuries, were eventually, if gradually, elevated to *Fürst—prince*—in lieu of being repaid the money owing them.

[15] This may account for Schiller having a Count Pálffy—by the time he wrote all Pálffys were counts, so he had little reason to be aware that the colonel was merely a baron—present at Wallenstein's headquarters in *Die Piccolomini*, one of the *Wallenstein Trilogy* of plays, which contains the immortal line *Graf Pálffy hat ein leeres Glas vor sich! (Count Pálffy has an empty glass before him!)*.

1646. COLONELLVS · ANDREAS PALEFI L. BARO CROATORVM · S.C.R⁹.M.

VIRTVS IN ACTIONE.

E.Widman sculpsit.

Colonel Andrew Pálffy, probably the Pálffy mentioned
by Friedrich Schiller in his play *Die Piccolomini*

side of Europe—his mother, a sister of Philip II of Spain (and thus her husband's
first cousin), feared that otherwise he might grow up to adopt his father's lax attitude towards Protestant "heretics"— Rudolph was sent on travels: across Germany, on to the Spanish Netherlands, then down across France to Spain, where

he remained at the court of Philip II until 1571.[16] Nicholas went with the heir, absorbing new impressions, getting to know Europe, learning languages and the ways of a wider world (including, one must assume, being in attendance on Rudolph at the single *auto da fé*, the ceremonial burning at the stake of unrepentant heretics, that his uncle forced Rudolph to attend). They finally returned to Vienna by way of the Mediterranean, just rendered safe again by Don Juan of Austria's naval victory over the Turks at Lepanto, even stopping off at some Greek islands on their way up the Adriatic.

Neither of them later made any public reference to those years spent together but—great as their difference in standing was, especially by sixteenth century standards, with Rudolph to become king of Hungary as of Bohemia, and Holy Roman Emperor, Nicholas always but a subject—this shared boyhood away from home, teens, onset of puberty, must have forged a special link of some kind between them: to the end of his life Nicholas always seems to have had ready access to Rudolph, increasingly a recluse, whom he visited quite regularly at Prague. During those early years he must also have got to know well Rudolph's next younger brother, Archduke Ernest, who had been sent to Spain along with them: in later years, when Rudolph had made Ernest supreme in military matters in Hungary and Nicholas had become an effective senior military commander there, relations between them were often tense—what boyhood offences, real or imagined, might Ernest have held against Nicholas?

On their return to Vienna, both almost twenty, Nicholas remained at Rudolph's side, no longer his page but his Master of the Board, responsible for the heir's physical comforts. This is when he must have got to know Rudolph's other brothers, born while they were in Spain, and Archduke Matthias in particular, who played an increasing role in Hungarian affairs by the 1590s, with whom he seems to have been on exceptionally good and confidential terms: their later correspondence is marked by a tone of brisk cordiality that would otherwise be unusual, and Matthias always supported Nicholas in disputes with officialdom at Vienna and the court at Prague.

In 1580, not content with life at court as a career—and perhaps also because Rudolph (r. 1576–1608) was moving his court from nearby Vienna to Prague—Nicholas returned to Hungary to look after his estates (in whose management and profitability he always took a keen interest, keeping in touch with his estate managers by a stream of letters wherever he was) and to take up the family tradition of soldiering. As a parting gift Rudolph appointed the twenty-eight year old Nicholas Lord Lieutenant of the County of Pressburg and captain of the Royal Castle there (both offices to become hereditary in the family later on; in time the county even adopted our coat-of-arms). Soon thereafter he was also appointed to the captaincy of the key fortress of Komárom, at the confluence of the Vág and

---

[16] The tutor who accompanied Rudolph was a Dietrichstein, ancestor of my maternal grandmother.

48

Danube: Pressburg was largely honorific but Komárom, lower down the Danube, was a fighting forward outpost against the Turks.

Following the death of Suleiman *the Magnificent* in 1566—under the walls of Szigetvár in southern Hungary, which only fell because neither its defenders, commanded by Count Nicholas Zrinyi, who ended their lives in a suicidal final sally, nor the besieging Turkish army knew that the Sultan had just died in his tent— the Ottoman advance lost its impetus. But, since Hungary's Habsburg monarchs, elected to its throne in the expectation that they would mobilise the resources of the Empire to help dislodge the Turks from all of Hungary signally failed to do so, indeed negotiated truce after truce and, from 1547, even agreed to pay the Sublime Porte an annual tribute of thirty thousand florins for what of Hungary remained to them, the situation had become an uneasy stalemate.[17]

The Turks held numerous fortified places along the periphery of the region they had occupied, the Hungarians others facing them (known as *végvár*: 'end-fort'), which could range in size from walled towns with sizeable garrisons down to hilltop stockades manned by but a few dozen soldiers. North of the Danube the hinges of Hungarian positions were Komárom and, somewhat to its north, Érsekújvár on the Nyitra stream (whose Captain Nicholas eventually also became, despite Archduke Ernest's resistance to this appointment); south of the Danube Győr was the largest and strongest Hungarian stronghold. Further downstream the Turks held Esztergom, and Párkány across the river from it: that they might construct a bridge between these two, which would enable them to move troops from one side of the Danube to the other with ease, was a constant preoccupation of Nicholas'; further to the south and west, on the western slopes of the forested Vértes and Bakony hill-country, their line of forts hinged on Tata and Pápa (the days when Thomas still held Várpalota, on the eastern slopes of this country, were long gone). These fortifications defined a broad fighting zone—nowhere was there a continuous front-line, such as became established on the Western Front during the First World War—into and across which, sometimes far and deep into regions beyond, both sides launched fast-moving sorties and raids, occasionally taking or re-taking a minor fort, but mostly just capturing a few of the enemy (the more prominent of whom would then be sold back for a ransom, as Thomas had been) and driving off pasturing horses and cattle.

---

[17] In fact the *Holy Roman Empire of the German Nation* was, since the Reformation had swept across it, far too divided against itself to act effectively against *any* external threat, even had its Emperors—this dignity by now in fact, if not law, hereditary in the House of Habsburg—wanted to do so; they were, moreover, reluctant to risk what military forces they could muster (the backbone of these usually Spanish troops made available by their Iberian cousins) in serious offensive warfare in Hungary, preferring a passive strategy limited to keeping the Turk out of their Austrian lands.

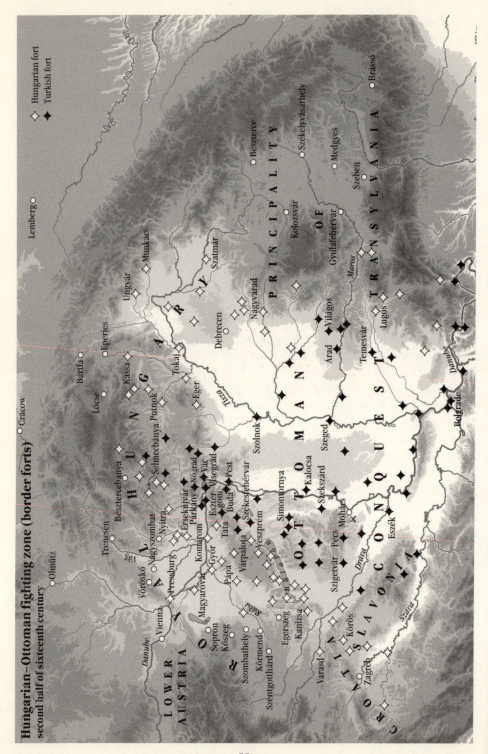

Hungarian–Ottoman fighting zone (border forts)
second half of sixteenth century

◇ Hungarian fort
◆ Turkish fort

In the intervals between such raids commanders of forts, Hungarian as Turkish, would every so often issue the enemy garrison opposite a formal challenge to single combat by chosen champions: an agreed number of Turks and Hungarians would then meet at a mutually appointed time and place to watch their champions slog it out (but not to death: this, known in Hungarian as *koplyatörés*, 'lance-breaking', was more like a formal tourney); on one such occasion combat was terminated by mutual agreement because the Turk had failed to observe accepted rules: he had trained his horse to bite and kick his opponent, considered unsporting by both sides. And, when not fighting, both sides made a point of punctilious politeness: thus, for instance, the Pasha of Buda sent Nicholas a letter of congratulations on his appointment (in Hungarian: the Turks employed Hungarian clerks and scribes for purposes of correspondence with Hungarian commanders and also, to the Habsburg bureaucracy's annoyance, with Vienna—the Turks, at least, appreciated that here they were dealing with the king of Hungary).[18]

For the next decade or so Nicholas sporadically fought the Turks in minor sorties and raids in the regions outlined above—in 1586 penetrating, with Francis Nádasdy, as far as Székesfehérvár, there inflicting a defeat on the Turks in the field but unable to take the town—and was eventually appointed captain-general in Transdanubia. The Treasury's tardiness in providing the money needed to pay, feed and equip his soldiers, money he frequently had to find and advance from his own resources, was a constant worry, as was also the incessant niggling interference by letter of Archduke Ernest. All of this necessitated frequent trips to Vienna, and occasional ones to Prague (where, he had made sure, he had friends at court who kept him informed of what intrigues were going on there).

In his private life, meanwhile, Nicholas set about buying Vöröskő from the Fuggers of Augsburg, who had acquired it from the Thurzós earlier in the century and with whom the family had had business associations for some generations. The hilltop castle had been the Fuggers' principal transit *dépot* for metal-exports from the Highlands but, that trade by now in decline, they were happy to sell.[19] However, since it was owned jointly by several Fuggers, some of them minors, he had to buy them out one by one: by 1582 he had acquired but four-tenths, although the purchase of even this much was a serious strain on his finances.[20] But by then

---

[18] This period also saw the emergence of the earliest Hungarian vernacular poetry that is enjoyable to this day, especially that about love and war and religious devotion, in equal measure, by Bálint (Valentine) Balassa, also written Balassi—into whose family one of Nicholas' sisters and one of his daughters married—which far surpasses the epic poetry, in a late Homeric tradition if not in verse as splendid, of his contemporary Sebastian Tinódi "the Luteplayer" that recount events in this warfare.

[19] A sizeable estate—getting on for 30 thousand acres and some dozen villages—went with the castle.

[20] By the time he had acquired eight tenths it had cost him 87,173 Rhine Florins (I have failed to discover the value of these in comparison to Hungarian Florins).

he was courting Mary Fugger, busily corresponding and exchanging portraits with her and—wise groom—corresponding with her mother too; the following year they were married at Augsburg. Since, on the evidence of later correspondence between them, it was a mutually very happy marriage, it is unlikely to have been dictated merely by financial considerations, but her dowry did help complete the purchase of Vöröskő, from then until 1945 the principal family seat, where he soon put much reconstruction (including some "secret rooms"—what were they?) and embellishments in hand.[21]

During the following years he acquired further estates too, in part as royal grants to recompense him for money of his own that he had spent on his soldiers' pay and other military expenditures, in part by complex "leveraged" deals with owners of estates in debt.[22] By 1590 he was building model villages on his estates, where he settled peasant families imported from Germany: during six decades of continuous, if often piecemeal, warfare many a peasant lad had concluded that a soldier's life had more to offer than working a lord's land.

And every year or two a child was born, eight in all (of whom only the first, Marc, died in infancy: his mother had gone down with the smallpox while carrying him). Nicholas was an exceptional father for the sixteenth century: on each occasion when yet another delivery was imminent he fretted, chivvied his household staff to ensure that the services of the best midwife and wet-nurse available be retained; and despite his military (and other) duties he seems to have managed to spend much time with his family: if he could not join them at Vöröskő they would join him in one of the forts he commanded and, when unavoidably absent on campaigns, he expected regular news by letter of how his children were doing (of their education more in the next chapter).

In the public sphere honours came his way: Principal Chamberlain for Hungary, privy councillor (the title baron had already been conferred on him, along with his brothers, in 1581). But Archduke Ernest's constant niggling interference[23] and the perennial delays in receiving the amounts needed to pay his soldiers—time and again he had to dip into his own pocket, often causing him severe financial embarrassment, to the point of having to pawn all of his silverware on one occasion[24]—repeatedly induced him to tender his resignation from military command.

---

[21] Formally confirmed in its possession by a royal charter of 1592, in 1598 he founded, and funded, an alsmhouse in the village of Cseszte that lies at the foot of the castle: it continued to function as such until the First World War.

[22] There is a PhD in the latter for a student of economics well versed in sixteenth century Hungarian property law, or one of history well versed in modern economic practices (and equally fluent in sixteenth century Hungarian, German and Latin).

[23] For instance, he repeatedly berated Nicholas, who was trying to concentrate on fighting the Turk effectively, for failing to put a stop to the open preaching of Protestant divines in fortified towns under his command; the repetition of such complaints suggests that Nicholas disregarded them.

[24] On another occasion he approached his father-in-law for a loan who, however, replied that he could not help because *the king of Spain has sucked me dry*—the Fuggers were still the principal bankers of the Habsburgs, for whom the gold and silver of the Americas was not enough.

Time and again it took the persuasive powers of Archduke Matthias—by about 1590 also actively involved in Hungarian matters—or Rudolph himself, whom he visited every so often at Prague, to dissuade him from retiring to private life.

By now tensions with the Turk were mounting and, indeed, soon the small-scale raids of the recent past developed into full open warfare. In 1594 Nicholas' initial successes north of the Danube, where he retook a number of forts that the Turks had held for several decades (notably Nógrád, whence he could threaten Vác), were more than counterbalanced by the Turk taking Győr. Back at Vienna the despondent *Hofkriegsrath*, the main military decision-making body, was now all for a defensive strategy, its foremost concern preparing Vienna for a possible siege. However, after considerable argument Nicholas, supported by other Hungarian commanders and backed by Archduke Matthias (about to step into the place of Archduke Ernest, who was dying), managed to get it to reverse this passive strategy. So, after yet another visit to Prague to obtain royal backing, in the summer and autumn of 1595 Nicholas, as captain-general in Transdanubia, launched an offensive. Esztergom was retaken from the Turk,[25] then Visegrád further downstream, as were Tata and then Pápa to its southwest; by the next year also Vác on the left bank of the Danube not far above Pest, then Hatvan further to the east on the edge of the Great Plains.

Despite such successes—or because of them? some self-important courtiers on the *Hofkriegsrath* had been proved wrong—it took the personal intervention of Archduke Matthias while on a visit to Prague to neutralise intrigues at court against Nicholas, who the following year then deemed it wise to visit Prague in person too in order to wait on Rudolph. While there he also took part in discussions with Sigismund Báthory, Prince of Transylvania,[26] about co-operation against the Turk (the possibility of re-joining Transylvania to Royal Hungary was also floated at these discussions).

Spring 1598 saw the event for which Nicholas is still best remembered, and for which he acquired the epithet *the hero of Győr*: the re-taking of that town from the Turk, which might well have failed but for his personal bravery and determination. Using a tactic he had developed earlier, one of the gates was successfully blown with petards and foot-soldiers rushed in immediately after their explosion. However, outnumbered by the defenders, who may well have expected and prepared against just this tactic, these advance troops were soon being pushed out again. Seeing this adverse development, Nicholas ordered the cavalry stationed outside the gate to dismount and go to the infantry's assistance, but the cavalrymen demurred, considering it below their dignity to fight on foot. Furious at them, Nicholas himself now dismounted and rushed through the gate brandishing his sabre: this sight finally shamed the cavalrymen into dismounting too and following

---

[25] The soldier-poet Bálint (Valentine) Balassa, mentioned earlier, was killed during this siege.

[26] By the Treaty of Speyer of 1571 Transylvania had been recognised as an independent principality; its ruling prince was elected for life by its Parliament.

Nicholas Pálffy in a print celebrating his recapture of Győr in 1598

him. The attack now led by Nicholas in person swept all before it, Turkish resistance crumbled, and by nightfall town and citadel had been taken.

Buoyed by this success Nicholas then swept across much of Transdanubia, retaking Veszprém and Várpalota (and all the smaller forts in between) from the Turks, then attempting Buda itself. Here the Turkish outpost on the Gellért Hill, which commands the southern approaches to the Castle Hill, was taken, and the guns there captured, but torrential autumn rains then set in eventually making continuation of the siege impossible. The next year Buda was unsuccessfully attempted again; then Székesfehérvár taken, but found to lie too deep within territory controlled by the Turks to be held. Nevertheless, by late autumn 1599 the Turks were, in effect, suing for peace or at least an extended truce, and Nicholas was playing a key role in preliminary negotiations with their Ambassador Paleologue (a renegade Greek).

This time recognition was forthcoming. Parliament passed Act XLVIII of 1599, devoted entirely to the praise of Nicholas[27] and a request that the monarch confer the title *count* on him, to which request Rudolph promptly acceded as soon as the Act had received his royal assent: thus, uniquely, we owe our title to an Act of Parliament not mere royal favour; the hereditary Lord Lieutenancy of County Pressburg and title Count of Pressburg,[28] as well as captaincy of its castle, came to the family at the same time and in the same way. Rudolph also offered Nicholas, as a personal gift, a reward of several thousand gold ducats: this he haughtily refused with the rejoinder that he *fought for his country, not for money.*[29] And the Estates of Lower Austria, relieved that the Turkish threat had been pushed back, presented him with a huge gold cup, richly (for modern tastes: too richly) decorated in enamel-work, which weighs some 8 lbs together with its lid. (But is it all gold?)

The following spring—while being pressed by Archduke Matthias to accompany him to his cousin Ferdinand's (the later King Ferdinand II) wedding at Graz, during which trip he (Matthias) wished to consult him privately on *important matters*[30]—Nicholas fell ill, and died. He was only forty-eight: had he lived a few decades longer, into the reign of his friend Matthias II, he might have achieved even more. As it was, the war against the Turk was pursued with some vigour, but

---

[27] Much in the way that Nelson was to be lauded by Westminster some centuries later.

[28] Up to then Count of Pressburg—as some others, e.g. Count of Temes, Count of Szepes—had been *not* an hereditary title but the designation of an office, governor of a specific region: Pressburg (like the others) lay near the borders of Hungary, calling for firmer regional control than the counties could provide; in Werbőczy's summary of Hungarian public law completed in 1514, known as the *Tripartitum*, the *comes Posoniensis* is listed among the *veri barones regni*, the term he applied to holders of senior offices of state.

[29] Unlike the Austrian General Schwarzenberg who, having also distinguished himself at Győr and in those campaigns, had no such misgivings about accepting a similar cash reward.

[30] Eight years later Archduke Matthias engineered the abdication of his brother Rudolph, whose mental health, undermined by syphilis, had been deteriorating for years, to succeed him on the throne: it is impossible to tell whether the *important matters* about which he wished to consult Nicholas in private—too delicate to be committed to paper—were the beginnings of his plans to replace his brother on the throne.

perhaps less effective generalship, for another couple of years before it gradually petered out (to an extent, it must be admitted, owing to factional strife and a short-lived civil war[31] within and between Hungary and Transylvania), to be formally terminated with a peace, signed at Zsitvatorok in 1606, based on the new territorial *status quo* and to last twenty years; this peace also absolved the king of Hungary from the annual tribute of 30 thousand gold ducats, paid to the Sultan since 1547, for a single payment of 200 thousand then and there.

Nicholas Pálffy's sabre—possibly that which he brandished at Győr—and helmet, as also that cup, are now prominently displayed, labelled as such, in the National Museum at Budapest.[32] But of a group of four statues depicting persons who had distinguished themselves fighting the Turkish invaders in the sixteenth century the Communists removed his alone[33] (perhaps because of those four only he still had and has living descendants) from the public square—now Kodály körönd—where it had stood in Budapest. It has not been re-erected anywhere since then, although a poor quality, vaguely "socialist-realist", statue has been erected to him at Győr on the quatercentenary of that town's reconquest from the Turks. Nor has what used to be Pálffy Square in Buda regained that name.

---

[31] Key details, too complex to summarise here, are briefly discussed in the next chapter.

[32] They were presented to the museum a short time before the outbreak of the Second World War by László Pálffy, the last prince, of whom more in the Comparative decline.

[33] To replace it, ironically, with a statue (inferior in artistic quality, and not matching the other three in style) of his kinsman-by-marriage, the fighting poet Bálint (Valentine) Balassa.

Soldiers and statesmen (17th century, first half)

*O*n Nicholas Pálffy's unexpected death at only forty-eight his widow Maria, thirty-four at the time, was faced with managing all his considerable estates—by a will he had drawn up in 1596 (a year of intensive warfare: in those days commanders were as likely to be killed fighting as common soldiers) she inherited a life interest in all of them *so long as she shall continue to bear the name Pálffy,* i.e. not remarry—and bringing up their seven children, Stephen the eldest (from whom we all descend) pushing fifteen and Magdalene the youngest barely out of the nursery.

A singularly competent woman, she not only saw to it that the estates continued to be run as efficiently and profitably as in the lifetime of her husband (who had learnt about double-entry book-keeping from the Fuggers and made sure it was used for his estate accounts too), but also successfully completed some of the complex acquisitive transactions he had initiated, most notably the transfer into her name of the debt-ridden estate of Borostyánkő.[1] Only in 1619 did she then share out the landed estates among her sons—the three daughters received dowries of 20,000 gold florins[2] each—to live on at Vöröskő until her death, aged eighty, which occurred on the very same day as that of her sons Stephen and John, 29 May, 1646.[3]

While little explicit detail is known of Nicholas' own childhood and youth, there is ample information concerning that of his sons Stephen, John, Paul and Nicholas, fifteen, thirteen, eleven and seven[4] years old when their father died. In 1598 he had retained the services of one Stephen Körmendy as their tutor *(praeceptor)*, who continued in this office until all had left the school-room, from 1600 reporting on their

---

[1] Today *Bernstein* (both names mean 'amber') in Burgenland, the chunk of Hungary given to Austria after the First World War; when Nicholas started its "leveraged" acquisition it was encumbered with a debt of 84,156 gold florins.

[2] Legislation of 1524 had re-standardised the Hungarian gold florin at just over 3.24 grams of 18 1/2 carat gold (by way of comparison: nineteenth century English sovereigns were just under 8 grams of 22 carat gold).

[3] By one of those weird coincidences, my maternal grandfather Albert Apponyi was born *exactly* two-hundred years later, on 29 May 1846.

[4] Sources disagree about young Nicholas' year of birth: I incline to accept 1593 rather than 1599.

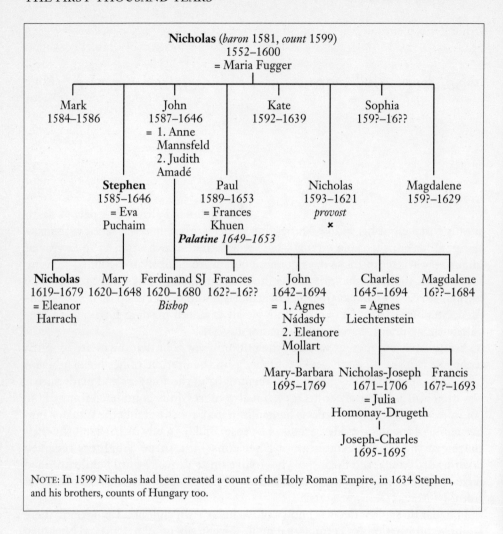

Nicholas (*baron* 1581, *count* 1599)
1552–1600
= Maria Fugger

Mark	John	Kate	Sophia
1584–1586	1587–1646	1592–1639	159?–16??
	= 1. Anne		
	Mannsfeld		
	2. Judith		
	Amadé		

Stephen	Paul	Nicholas	Magdalene
1585–1646	1589–1653	1593–1621	159?–1629
= Eva	= Frances	*provost*	
Puchaim	Khuen	✗	
	Palatine 1649–1653		

Nicholas	Mary	Ferdinand SJ	Frances	John	Charles	Magdalene
1619–1679	1620–1648	1620–1680	162?–16??	1642–1694	1645–1694	16??–1684
= Eleanor		*Bishop*		= 1. Agnes	= Agnes	
Harrach				Nádasdy	Liechtenstein	
				2. Eleanore		
				Mollart		

Mary-Barbara   Nicholas-Joseph   Francis
1695–1769   1671–1706   167?–1693
= Julia
Homonay-Drugeth

Joseph-Charles
1695-1695

NOTE: In 1599 Nicholas had been created a count of the Holy Roman Empire, in 1634 Stephen, and his brothers, counts of Hungary too.

progress to the boys' mother (in German). Many of the regular financial accounts he also submitted survive and give an insight into their school-days.

Lodging under Körmendy's supervision in the house of a Mr and Mrs Haberstock in Vienna (at a rent of 220 florins a year), they attended school there. I have been unable to identify the school, which must have been a public establishment since *gold paint wherewith to write [their] names in the school* (perhaps on lockers?) is an annually recurring expense item, but it also transpires from the accounts that four lads *(die Jungen)* were being educated there alongside the Pálffy boys *(die Junge Herren)* at the family's expense. Expenditure on books—many not identified, but volumes of Cicero, Ovid, Horace, Julius Caesar and Sallustius are named, as are Latin (Rudimenta, Syntaxis, Prosodia) and German grammars—as well as on student needs such as pens, inkwells, and paper to write on, is regularly recorded.

Other items mentioned in the accounts include *paints and brushes for Master Stephen* and *lute-strings for Master John*—indicating that they were inclined or encouraged to practice these arts—as also cages and seeds for pet birds, a dog, cakes of soap, going to baths, having haircuts, doctor's visits (Stephen, in particular, was prone to illness), shoes and other items of clothing, balls (for what game?), and cash spent at fairs, for alms, and to tip messengers, stable-boys and the like, as also to buy wine and cakes to entertain friends (and, on one occasion, their visiting sister Kate, between her brothers Paul and Nicholas in age). No Christmas or Easter holidays, but every summer they went home to Vöröskő, journeys that called for six horses (riding them? or in a coach-and-six?). Their school-days patently gave them a reasonably all-round classical education and would appear to have been pleasant enough.[5]

Some months after his father's death Stephen the eldest travelled to Prague (under the supervision of a Mr Schnitter) to wait on King Rudolph; then, too young to get involved in any of the political upheavals of the century's early years (*see* below), he continued his studies. Four years later, by now nineteen, he received a formal summons to attend the Parliament[6] called for January 1605, as did his mother (being a woman she could not, however, attend in person, only send a male representative), and similarly with the next Parliament two years on, without, as far as one can tell, making any particular impact at either: only in and from 1608—when Archduke Matthias became king (*see* below)—did his public role take off.

Unlike his father Maximillian I, Rudolph was intolerant of Protestants (an attitude engendered or sharpened, perhaps, by those years at the court of Spain when an impressionable teenager). The majority of his Hungarian subjects—including most of the country's wealthiest, and by now generally titled, leading families (the Catholic Pálffys were almost an exception)—were Protestants, mainly Calvinists,[7] but Lutherans in the towns whose burghers had many family and commercial ties to their counterparts in Germany. The Hungarians themselves, more concerned with the Turkish danger common to all Christians than with doctrinal differences,

---

[5] Three centuries on my father and two of his cousins, my Uncles Józsi and Peter, were similarly lodged together under the supervision of a tutor, in Pressburg where they all attended the same school (*gimná-zium*); from the year-books of that school, which Unce Józsi preserved and I now have, it appears that the Latin curriculum had not changed much in between.

[6] Only in 1608 (*see* below) was a second chamber of those with hereditary titles (as well as bishops and holders of certain senior offices and dignities) formally established, but the heads, and other weighty members, of the wealthiest and most influential families were traditionally summoned by the monarch to attend Parliament in person.

[7] Which made it all the worse: the Religious Peace of Augsburg (1555), which had conceded the presence of Protestants in the Empire, recognised Lutherans but not Calvinists; although it had no legal standing in Hungary, it inevitably influenced the attitudes of Rudolph and his court.

rubbed along happily whatever their denomination (although they did argue, from pulpits and in a flood of printed tracts, in attempts to convert one another) and were much offended by Rudolph's anti-Protestant stance, which gave rise to many grievances. Traditionally, grievances arising from royal policy were raised in Parliament: Rudolph, however, repeatedly made it clear that he objected to the discussion of any, and quite especially religious, grievances by Parliament (many of whose members were, of course, Protestants) and that he would withhold his royal assent from *all* legislation if such were raised. Finally, in 1604 he went further: on giving his formal royal assent to the twenty-one Acts that had been passed by that year's Parliament he also, arbitrarily and unconstitutionally, added an extra twenty-second one, not passed or even discussed by Parliament, that reconfirmed and demanded strict adherence to all anti-Protestant legislation ever adopted—all of which, starting with an Act of 1515, was generally considered effectively defunct, since never enforced.

Moreover, ruling Hungary by remote control from Prague Rudolph preferred to do so exclusively through the imperial bureaucracy at Vienna—besides the *Hofkriegsrath* for military matters, there was by now also an *Ungarische Hofkanzlei* (Hungarian Court Chancellery) alongside similar bodies for the Austrian lands[8] and for Bohemia—and to discuss and be advised on policy by the mainly German courtier-councillors who surrounded him (Cardinal Khlesl, who achieved the establishment of an archbishopric at Vienna, foremost among them). Yet the Kingdom of Hungary had well-established senior dignities and offices, evolved since the Middle Ages precisely for the purpose of advising the monarch on policy and of controlling its execution. Since Rudolph did not wish to consult them, he simply failed to replace incumbents when they died: thus, for instance, there had been no Palatine, previously the head of the king's government in Hungary, since 1562 and even the Primatial See of Esztergom, whose incumbent had always had a weighty voice in matters of state too, had been left vacant[9] for twenty-four years, from 1573 to 1597.

Furthermore, Rudolph kept the Holy Crown—symbol of Hungary's statehood—and other regalia at Prague, as just a few more pretty artefacts in his great

---

[8] Austria as a "nation" is a recent invention: the Habsburgs had acquired and ruled—as their archduke, duke, prince or count—a number of historically distinct German lands, including Upper- and Lower-Austria, Styria, Carinthia, Tyrol and Vorarlberg (today provinces, *Länder*, of the Republic of Austria constituted after the First World War), and several more; what these had in common was that the Habsburgs considered all of them to be their *hereditary property*—landed estates writ large—and for this reason best administered by a single central body. Hungary, as Bohemia with Moravia, had, in contrast, been distinct kingdoms long before the rise of the Habsburgs.

[9] The Crown had always had a say in senior ecclesiastical appointments; by a concession King Sigismund had wrung from the Papacy—being in a strong position on termination of the great schism of the Church and as the mastermind behind the Councils of Constance and Basel—all senior clerical appointments in Hungary were thereafter explicitly in the gift of the Crown (much as a parish living might be in the gift of the lord of the manor).

collection of *objets d'art*. True, it was not entirely his fault that they were not in Hungary: when the country had split in two after Mohács (*see* previous chapter) Szapolyai had been in their physical possession; in 1541 his widow Isabella had then taken them with her to Transylvania when Suleiman sent her packing from Buda, but had in 1551 finally surrendered them to Ferdinand I. Thereafter he, and Maximillian I, had kept the Holy Crown and other regalia in Vienna, where they seemed safer from the Turks but were close to nearby Pressburg for coronations; removing them to Prague was, however, felt as an affront to Hungary.

All these grievances had contributed to the success of, although they had not directly caused, the brief civil war of 1604-5—notionally over the status of Transylvania, which had around the turn of the century flirted with formal reunification with Royal Hungary—that had rapidly spread to much of the northern Highlands. Known from its, initially reluctant, leader as the *Bocskai*[10] *Rising*, it was terminated in 1606 by an agreement known as the Peace of Zsitvatorok (its Turkish aspect already mentioned in the previous chapter), by which— Stephen Illésházy, the late Nicholas Pálffy's brother-in-law, acting as the principal "rebel" negotiator—Rudolph made some concessions (notably rescinding that arbitrarily inserted Act XXII of 1604). A twenty-year peace, or more properly truce, with the Turk was also concluded alongside, bringing to an end the war with the Ottomans that had began in 1590.

But discontent with Rudolph and his rule kept simmering under the surface. It was in these circumstances that, in 1608, Archduke Matthias—who knew and liked Hungary, where he had been acting as his brother's representative, and who was easygoing in religious matters, both of which made him popular—persuaded Rudolph (with a show of armed force, and some tacit backing from his younger brother and archduke cousins) to abdicate in his favour, letting Rudolph keep only Bohemia, Tyrol, and the, effectively vacuous, imperial dignity.

There were two Parliaments that year, the first principally to approve the succession and coronation, a constitutional requirement, of Matthias II (r. 1608–1619). But a valid coronation also required the Holy Crown and other regalia, still at Prague: Matthias—who had all along watched over the interests of, and kept in touch with, his late friend's widow and sons—now nominated,

---

[10] Wealthy, and for long a loyal servant of the Crown, he turned against it when imperial troops attempted to seize a castle and property he held from the Crown as surety against loans made to it; Vienna then got wind of tentative feelers he had, as a result of this, put out to the Turks, rather forcing his hand; next Transylvania elected him its prince. Nationalist sentiment sees a hero in him, and a form of dress —black suit with stand-up collar and black frogging—that became popular a good century ago (and is now becoming so again, in some circles) was named after him and adopted by numerous boys' schools as their uniform.

Stephen Pálffy the Crown Guardian

and Parliament duly elected, the twenty-three year old Stephen to the long vacant office of Crown Guardian. In this capacity he then hastened to Prague, retrieved the Holy Crown (did he wait on Rudolph on this occasion too?), and delivered it to Pressburg for Matthias' coronation,[11] amongst much pubic jubilation at its return to Hungarian soil. Crown and regalia were thereafter kept in Pressburg Castle, whose hereditary Captaincy Stephen had inherited from his father, under his guardianship.

The second, post-coronation, Parliament of that year put through much legislation that righted wrongs, plugged gaps, and fitted the mood of the country. In particular—with far-reaching and unforeseen consequences—Act I established legal equality between Catholics, Calvinists and Lutherans (Transylvania had already got there in 1568, including Unitarians too), if not lesser denominations such as Anabaptists. In the same spirit it enacted not only that henceforth the Holy Crown and regalia were to be kept at Pressburg but also that there should always be *two* Crown Guardians, one a Catholic the other a Protestant, an arrangement that lasted until 1945; Stephen was confirmed as the Catholic, and Baron Peter Révay (to whom we owe the earliest detailed description, stone by stone, of the Holy Crown as it then was) as the Protestant. It also legislated, besides many other matters that do not affect our narrative directly,[12] that all vacant high offices and dignities should be filled, exclusively by Hungarians. In the case of the Palatine it further laid down that henceforth the Crown was to propose two Catholics and two Protestants from among whom Parliament was then to choose and elect one to that office; then and there the result was that Stephen Illésházy, a Protestant and few years back a leader in the Bocskai Rising, was elected Palatine. All other offices and dignities that had long stood vacant were also filled.[13]

⚜

Few historians seem to have spotted the direct links from the Hungarian Parliament's legislation of 1608 to the Thirty Years War, which began to engulf all of Germany a decade later.

---

[11] Interestingly, it appears to have been at this coronation that the red-white-and-green Hungarian national colours were first used as such, for the drapery of the throne; the Great Seal of Matthias II was also the first such on which an image of the Holy Crown is shown above the country's coat-of-arms, as it still is to this day.

[12] Such as the formal division of Parliament, hitherto in principle a unitary body, into a Lower Chamber for the elected county members (two per county) and representatives of the Royal Free Cities, and an Upper (or Magnates') Chamber for the bishops, senior dignitaries and office-holders, and those with an hereditary title (who, however, never constituted a distinct "peerage").

[13] Stephen's aunt Kate was married to Illésházy; the father of Peter Révay was first cousin to the husband of Stephen's aunt Elizabeth; another vacant dignity was filled by Francis Dersffy, a nephew of Stephen's grandmother Sophia: it was a small world, with most of those at the centre of affairs linked by blood or marriage.

Rudolph's Bohemian subjects had also long fretted at their lack of religious liberty. Now, aware of and doubtless encouraged by that Hungarian legislation, they were becoming ever more restive: in 1609 Rudolph, or his advisers, felt constrained to grant them a degree of religious freedom too, if but by an "act of royal grace". When Rudolph died in 1612 Matthias came to the throne of Bohemia as well (and to the Imperial dignity), but by 1618 he too was approaching death: his cousin Ferdinand, a known bigot in matters religious (he was already busy getting rid of Protestants in Styria, his personal inheritance), and thus expected to cancel that "royal act of grace", was eagerly waiting in the wings to take over, in Bohemia as elsewhere (Matthias was childless). That year the Bohemians, sensing the first signs of a coming crack-down on their fragile religious liberty, chucked a number of senior officials, whom they (rightly) suspected of planning to suppress it, out of the windows of the Hradzyn Palace: the famous *Prague Defenestration*. On Matthias' death Ferdinand made his intentions explicitly clear, whereat the Bohemians hastily invited the Protestant (Calvinist, to boot) Frederick, Prince-Elector of the Palatinate[14] and son-in-law of James I of England, to their throne in place of Ferdinand Habsburg. The rest—Ferdinand's armed invasion of Bohemia to assert his claimed hereditary rights, culminating in the Battle of the White Mountain (1620) where what spirit of independence Bohemia had had was for centuries broken, the flight of Frederick, and the savage war across Germany that followed—is history. But would any of this have been set in train had the Bohemians not had the example of that Hungarian legislation of 1608, and quite especially the religious liberty afforded by Act I, before their eyes?

That little excursion into general history is not without relevance to our story: observing events in Bohemia, in 1618 Gabriel Bethlen, Prince of Transylvania and a staunch Protestant, launched an attack from the east across Hungary's Highlands in support of his Bohemian co-religionists. Since Ferdinand's troops were tied down dealing with those, Bethlen's forces rapidly overran northern Royal Hungary all the way to Pressburg, from where he launched raids as far as Vienna to harass Ferdinand. In 1619 he then convened a Parliament at Nagyszombat,[15] and demanded that the Holy Crown be handed over to him. Stephen,

---

[14] Head of the branch of the Wittelsbach family that ruled the Rhine-Palatinate *(Rheinpfalz)*—the other, Catholic, branch ruled Bavaria—and as such one of the seven Electors *(Churfürst)* who chose the *Holy Roman Emperor of the German Nation:* had he maintained himself on the throne of Bohemia he would have had two of the seven votes in the Electoral College, resulting in a Protestant majority in that body.

[15] Technically this Parliament was convened by the Palatine (who in the king's absence was entitled to do so), Forgách, in effect in Bethlen's power since holed up in Pressburg castle.

faced by an overwhelming force—he had less than two-hundred men in Pressburg Castle—but by his office responsible for the Holy Crown's safety, was in a quandary: he extricated himself from it by insisting that, since the Holy Crown was where it was pursuant to an Act of Parliament, only a new Act of Parliament could authorise its removal. That Parliament, and its successor in 1621 (which Stephen briefly attended), both perhaps suspicious of Bethlen's intentions and ambitions,[16] let the matter rest there, and the Holy Crown remained in Pressburg Castle.

However, by summer 1621—when, Bohemia having been dealt with, military resources for action in Hungary became available—Ferdinand II (r. 1619–1637) broke off negotiations with Bethlen and the process of pushing back his forces began. Stephen was given command; his youngest brother Nicholas, by now in his late twenties, joined him.

Nicholas had for a while been destined for the Church (his cousin Thomas had, and his nephew Ferdinand was to, enter it: both rose to become bishops) and, indeed, had been appointed provost[17] of St Martin's church at Pressburg, with special papal dispensation since he was only just in his teens, and not in holy orders, at the time. Indeed, in a very ambitious scheme the family (which probably meant his mother) had even tried to secure the archbishopric of Esztergom for him when it fell vacant in 1615—once he had reached the canonical age required of a bishop, of course, and taken holy orders—lobbying at court that no appointment be made until he could be enthroned, but this came to nothing.[18] Despite such beginnings Nicholas knew himself to be unsuited for the Church, did nothing to be ordained, and took up soldiering instead (while doubtless continuing to receive the revenues due to the provost); by now he was a colonel. Which is how he found himself riding with his brother against Bethlen's forces. In July they got embroiled in an armed clash, not quite a battle but more than a skirmish, under Fülek and young Nicholas was killed in it (fighting, alas, fellow Hungarians rather than Turks).

That armed clash also resulted in another blow to the family: Stephen himself was wounded, and then captured by Bethlen's men. A prisoner of his standing was important enough to be rapidly passed up the line to Bethlen himself, who treated him with courtesy while trying to win him over to the Transylvanian anti-

---

[16] On the principle that "my enemy's enemy is my friend" had had obtained Ottoman backing for his fight against Ferdinand, and the Sublime Porte had even encouraged him to make himself King of Hungary.

[17] The equivalent of an Anglican dean.

[18] In the event Peter Pázmány—a convert from Calvinism, a Jesuit, and one of Hungary's greatest churchmen—was promoted to the Primatial See; correspondence between him and sundry Pálffys indicates that they were on excellent terms, and in his last jocular letter to Stephen's wife, written not much above a week before he died in 1637, he asks her to recommend *pills that retard the onset of old age by twenty years.*

Nicholas Pálffy the Provost who fell fighting Gábor Bethlen's troops

Habsburg cause. But Stephen refused to even consider changing loyalties, and finally the exasperated Bethlen—with whom that earlier refusal to hand over the Holy Crown probably still rankled too—demanded a ransom of 24,500 gold florins for him, meanwhile holding him in honourable captivity. That amount was so large

66

that the family had great difficulty finding it at short notice: by November they had still not scraped together more than 10 thousand florins in coin, but Bethlen then agreed to accept a selection of jewellery and other objects of value—including the enamelled gold cup that Nicholas had received after retaking Győr—for the balance.[19] The ransom paid, Stephen was released at the end of the year when Ferdinand and Bethlen finally concluded a formal peace—very favourable to the latter personally, but also advantageous to Hungary at large, since by it Ferdinand bound himself to respect the religious liberties enacted in 1608—at Nikolsburg in Moravia.[20]

By the time of these events Stephen had already married (in 1618) Eva Susannah Puchaim—whose father Count Christopher, as also grandfather Count Wolfgang, had soldiered in Hungary against the Turk—and their two children, Nicholas (of whom more in the next chapter) and Mary, must have been born not long after;[21] it seems far from unlikely that Stephen's mother parcelled out the family estates among her sons in 1619 because the eldest, the head of the family, was by now married (and possibly the father of an heir).

In 1625 Stephen was followed as Crown Guardian by his brother John.[22] Having began as a chamberlain at the court of Matthias II, he had then turned to full-time soldiering: the bravery and dash with which he fought were recognised, but he never rose to any senior command. His only son Ferdinand (named for his godfather, King Ferdinand II) insisted, much to John's chagrin, on joining the Society of Jesus: following studies at Rome and elsewhere he was then sent to teach at the Jesuit College at Nagyszombat, but obtained his release from the Society to pursue lawsuits over landed properties in which he got embroiled with some of his cousins (as his father had also been in the habit of doing); later he was named Bishop of Csanád, a diocese largely occupied by the Turk or in Transylvanian hands, and thereafter of Eger, whose episcopal seat itself was also held by the Turk but most of the diocese not.

In 1626—not only was the twenty-year truce of 1606 with the Turk about to expire, but Gabriel Bethlen had also launched a new attack, co-ordinated with the military actions of anti-Imperialist commanders in Germany, from Transylvania that year—Stephen was appointed captain-general of Érsekújvár (once his father's command) and of all northern border-forts, and not long thereafter also captain-general in Transdanubia, the command his father had held three decades earlier; here his brother John served under him as captain of the caval-

---

[19] Bethlen's receipt for all of this has survived.

[20] The family seat of my maternal grandmother's Dietrichstein forebears.

[21] The sources are unclear as to their years of birth, but Nicholas, certainly the elder of the two, was at Vienna University from 1636 and married in 1646, which makes it likely that he was born well before the year 1634 claimed by several sources.

[22] Whose motto ♀ *Hunc refer principium et finem* ☌ (the figure at the end is a tiny *homunculus*) suggests some involvement with or links to alchemy and secret learning, but I have so far failed to find any other reference to this.

John Pálffy who might have been an alchemist or the like

ry. But this time there was no all-out war as there had been in the 1590s, only perpetual cross-border raiding attacks that, nevertheless, gave Stephen ample opportunity to prove himself as a commander in the field and acquire the sobriquet *terror of the Turks*.

Honours—imperial & royal chamberlain, privy councillor—had already come his way, and in 1634 Ferdinand II created him, along with his brothers, counts of Hungary too in addition to the Imperial title that had been bestowed on their father in 1599.[23] And in 1639 he was appointed, in addition to all his other commands, general of all cavalry forces. However, a bare five years later he resigned from all of his military commands for reasons of ill-health and, although only in his mid-fifties, infirmity due to age. He does, it is true, appear to have been prone to illness when a boy, and had since led a strenuous campaigning life, but perhaps the death of his wife in 1640 also made him feel old for his years: no more than forty, if that, when she died, and apparently unable to bear any more children after those first two, she may well have been ailing all along. He retired to Vöröskő, where he died two years later (on the same day—as already noted—as his mother and brother John).

Stephen is the ancestor of all Pálffys born in and after the eighteenth century, but his brother Paul deserves a section to himself. Following their joint schooling in Vienna, in 1609 he went on to attend the Jesuit's college at Olmütz for a couple of years.[24] This, like other Jesuit schools of its day, enforced strict discipline and instilled Catholic orthodoxy, but also offered a curriculum then at the forefront of European educational practice, much of it devoted to the latest advances in the natural sciences, to the new geographical knowledge, and to novel political and historical thinking as they were evolving at the time, rather than just to the classical authors of antiquity; innovatively, the Jesuits also encouraged their pupils to stage plays.[25] From here Paul went to Italy, spending a term or so at the University of Perugia, then visiting Naples, Rome and Sienna—he must have passed through other towns too without, however, staying in them any length of time—before he settled to read law at the University of Padua in 1612. Not for him a military career.

Back in Hungary by 1616, for some years he busied himself running, modernising and rounding off his estates. Like his father before him, he kept a watchful eye on the management of his estates all his life, seeing to the introduction of new products and manufactories—such as buffalo-milk processing, saw-mills, even

---

[23] Owing to this doubling of the title we may place above our coat of arms either the strawberry-leaf coronet due to an imperial (*Reichsunmittelbar*, i.e. bestowed directly by the Emperor rather than some lesser king) count—similar to that of an English marquess—or the standard nine-pointed coronet used by counts at large.

[24] Stephen is also listed as a pupil there in that year, but since he had embarked on his public career a year earlier, in 1608, it must have been one of their other brothers, John or Nicholas.

[25] His contemporary Francis Bacon had a high opinion of the schooling offered by the Jesuits, regretting that this was a *popish* accomplishment not matched by any of England's then leading schools (Eton, Westminster, Winchester).

Paul Pálffy who as Palatine aimed to mediate between Crown and Protestants

glass-works—and to the profitability of trading in the produce of his estates (and also of produce, especially cattle, bought from others to sell on when this seemed commercially advantageous), even at those times when he had many time-consuming official duties. Like his father in this too, throughout his life he kept acquiring further estates whenever an opportunity to do so arose,[26] often by methods very similar (going for estates heavily encumbered with debt), and was a keen rebuilder of the castles and mansions he acquired with them.

The first call to public duty came in 1622: an invitation—in effect a command, of course—from Ferdinand II to join the entourage that was to accompany him to the Imperial Diet assembling at Regensburg. This was purely honorific: as a Hungarian Paul had no standing at the Imperial Diet, and his presence would have served merely to boost the size and pomp of Ferdinand's retinue.[27] But during the journey from Vienna Ferdinand himself might have, and members of the court inevitably must have, carried on conversations with Paul, got to know him personally, and may have discussed his approach to managing his estates with him. Whether or not any of this played a part in it, in 1625 he was appointed to head the Hungarian Treasury, which administered all incomes and expenditures of the kingdom. Before the year was out he was also named Principal Royal Cupbearer, by then a purely ceremonial dignity, and a few days later privy councillor: among Hungarians so honoured at the time he alone eventually came to attend *working* meetings of the German-dominated council, and to contribute to its discussions and decisions.

For the next twenty years he managed the finances of the realm with considerable skill and efficiency: the country was perennially at war, which both reduced revenues and increased expenditures, while the imperial bureaucracy also kept trying to siphon off as much of Hungary's revenues as possible. Somehow Paul succeeded in balancing all this without upsetting either Parliament or court circles. Indeed, by an Act of Parliament of 1630, which expressed confidence in his ability and integrity, he was charged with supervising the reconstruction of Pressburg castle; a later Act of Parliament, which lauded his stewardship in general, made especial mention of his management of that reconstruction.

Throughout this period he continued to acquire further estates; on completion of Pressburg castle's reconstruction in 1635 he took into his own service many of the architects and master stone-masons whom he had called to Hungary from Italy for that task, setting them to work on reconstructing castles and mansions he had in the interim acquired (such as Malaczka and Bajmóc, both in the family into the twentieth century). But none of his detractors then or since ever accused him of abusing his position to do so.

Paul's detractors include not a few nineteenth and twentieth century Hungarian historians, not necessarily Marxists only, who reduce the complexities of the peri-

---

[26] Beginning in the year he returned from Italy, when he asked the then new Archbishop of Esztergom, Peter Pázmány, to advise him on how to acquire the castle and estate of Léva; the archbishop mildly replied that this question might be more suitably addressed to his (the archbishop's) estate manager.

[27] With the invitation he was also asked how many horses, servants and other attendants he intended to bring.

od to a vastly simplified black-and-white *we-against-them*, Hungary against the Habsburgs, picture,[28] within which they depict him as a foreign-educated—why should education abroad be considered *ipso facto* damning?— court toady of the Habsburgs, concerned with his own advancement only. This image is false.

When the Habsburgs had come to the throne a century earlier, in the immediate aftermath of the catastrophic defeat at Mohács, they had seemed the best, indeed the only, sensible option in the face of the Turk, rightly seen as the major threat to Hungary. The Habsburgs could call on the resources of the Empire, Germany, against the Ottomans, while a home-grown "national" king could not stand up to them, as was shown by how rapidly John I (Szapolyai) had become the Turk's subservient client. For this reason all the leading men and families of Hungary, not just the Pálffys, remained loyal to the Habsburg dynasty—at least until the reign of Leopold I, of which more in the next chapter—even when it failed to live up to expectations: gaining offices of state offered a better chance of influencing imperial policy in favour of Hungary's interests than turning against and opposing the dynasty.

Unfortunately for Hungary, during most of this period Habsburg policy was dominated by two interrelated issues: religion and Germany; the Turk was considered a troublesome distraction from these, to be dealt with by maintaining the *status quo* in Hungary, beyond the boundaries of the Empire. Following the success of the Reformation in much of Germany, in 1555 the Religious Peace of Augsburg had established the principle of *cuius regio eius religio*—every territory's people were to accept the denomination of its ruler—for the Empire. Events in Bohemia (which, although not German, had always been part of the Holy Roman Empire of the German Nation) in 1618–1620, when the Bohemians had repudiated their Catholic Habsburg ruler in favour of the Protestant Frederick of the Palatine, had upset that compromise arrangement. This was, of course, unacceptable to Ferdinand II and he had successfully crushed the Bohemians—only to find that soon all of Germany was engulfed by an increasingly bitter and bloody war between the rulers of Germany's Protestant lands and the Habsburg-led Catholic "imperialists", which became known as the Thirty Years War.

Throughout the 1620s, 1630s, and most of the 1640s, this war swayed back and forth. Foreign powers intervened: Gustavus Adolphus of Sweden, a brilliant commander and leader of men, took to the field in the Protestant cause (if also to extend Swedish rule to regions of Germany and Poland bordering the Baltic Sea); Catholic France, governed by Cardinal Richelieu and arch-enemy of the Habsburgs, subsidised the Protestant contestants with money. The imperial side had a brilliant commander in Wallenstein,[29] eventually Duke of Friedland, who,

---

[28] England and France also went through court *v.* nation upheavals in that period (the English Civil War, religious wars and the Fronde in France), but their serious historians no longer present these in such starkly partisan black and white.

[29] Actually Waldstein—as such the family is still around—but better known by that name from Schiller's great *Wallenstein Trilogy* of plays.

although Bohemian himself, had gained the final victory over the Bohemians at the White Mountain in 1620; to a large extent the secret of his successes in the Thirty Years War seems to have been that, quite exceptionally for his day, he saw to it that his armies were properly fed, clothed and supplied (if to the profit of his Duchy of Friedland), even if, more in keeping with his times, he also attached great importance to the predictions of astrology. But many thought he was getting too big for his boots: accused, in a whispering campaign, of dealing with the enemy, in 1634 he was assassinated with the court's tacit approval.[30]

But by the mid-1640s—Gustavus Adolphus killed in battle, Wallenstein assassinated, Germany devastated, and both sides increasingly exhausted—that war was beginning to wind down, and it was apparent to all observes that soon a general peace would be agreed, as indeed it was in 1649: the Peace of Westphalia. In these circumstances hopes revived in Hungary that, once that war in Germany was over, the focus of Habsburg policy might be redirected to assist in pushing the Turk out of the country.

⚜

In 1646 Paul relinquished the Treasury to be appointed Justice of the Realm, besides its judicial aspects also the second most senior political office. Having become deeply involved in political developments in Hungary while still running the Treasury—a task that gave him exceptionally detailed insight into the true state of the country—he was by now a prominent member of a small but influential group of Hungarian magnates who shared the common conviction that the Turk could and should be ejected from Hungary, and that the time to do so was fast approaching.[31]

Paul was ideally suited for the task of co-ordinator that he gradually assumed in this group. On the one hand he was trusted at court, where he had excellent connections (including family ties: the imperial minister Maximillian Trautmannsdorf was his brother-in-law) and was thus well informed not only of events[32] but also of shifts in power-play and current thinking among influential court cir-

---

[30] The Irish Butler and Scottish Leslie, both Catholic mercenary officers in imperial service, had a hand in the assassination: rewarded with imperial titles and estates, through my maternal grandmother's mother—whose full surname was Dietrichstein Proskau & Leslie—this Leslie is our ancestor.

[31] Key members of the group were Counts Adam Batthyány, László Esterházy, Adam Forgách and Nicholas Zrínyi, the last the one-man think-tank of the group, writing and publishing politico-strategic appreciations of what actions and how should be undertaken; he wrote, as had Cardinal-Archbishop Péter Pázmány in his theological works, in Hungarian, and they all corresponded amongsts one another in that language, disproving the later view, much touted especially by Austrians, that until the nineteenth century Hungarian was used by peasants only.

[32] On one occasion, for instance, he was able to circulate to others of the group a summary of the latest report received from General Piccolomini, one of the principal imperial commanders in the war in Germany, almost as soon as the court had received it.

cles. On the other hand, as head of the Treasury he had not only acquired very detailed knowledge of the true state of affairs across Hungary, but had also established many friendly contacts in county administrations,[33] which ran the country on the spot and had close links with the members sent to Parliament from their county. Finally, building on initial official contacts, he had developed good personal relations with the ruling Prince of Transylvania George I Rákóczi (and, from 1648, his son George II), always a factor to be considered in Hungary's affairs during that century.

Paul came to the forefront of attention as a member of this group at the Parliament of 1646, the first he attended as Justice of the Realm. Esztergom's archbishop George Lippay—zealously keen to eradicate Protestantism from Hungary, and thus in favour of all court policies in other matters too[34]—and others who shared his views attempted to introduce measures that would have been much to the detriment of the country's Protestants. As the mood sharpened Paul stepped in as Justice of the Realm with interventions aimed at the archbishop's supporters, and with sagacious management of Parliament's mood gradually took the heat out of debates that threatened to get completely out of hand—in a comparable situation in a later Parliament Protestant members withdrew in fury, leaving the field to their opponents—and thus finally succeeded in having the most offensive aspects of Lippay's proposals squashed. Protestant members were not *entirely* satisfied with the outcome—Paul (motto: *tout avec le temps*) was always a good judge of just how far it was sensible to go without risking defeat—but they agreed in their wholehearted appreciation of the role Paul had played.

One of the consequences of this was that Archbishop Lippay began to assemble a group similar to that of which Paul was a leading member, to oppose them and their ideas more methodically. But, although he could always count on the support of the court, most of the Church hierarchy and, behind the scenes, the apostolic nuncio, he failed to construct a political group of quite the same standing: its members were less independent, less weighty, and less committed.[35] For the next few years knowledgeable observers kept watching the power struggle between these two groups—"political parties" if not in the modern sense, to which some contemporaries referred as "factions"—with interest, tracking in particular the course of waverers likely to change sides (which were, in the event, all away from Lippay). Paul, meanwhile, used his new office to protect Hungarian commanders facing the Turks who got embroiled in fighting the enemy despite the court's non-aggression policy, seeing to it that they were neither put on trial nor otherwise punished for their actions.

---

[33] Whose senior officials were elected, usually from among members of the most influential county families.

[34] It must be added, however, that twenty years later events led him too to join those opposing those policies.

[35] Several senior clergymen, two of them future archbishops, and only four leading magnates: Counts Stephen and László Csáky, Francis Nádasdy, and Francis Wesselényi, the last two of whom soon switched sides.

Parliament met again in 1649;[36] since the Palatine had just died the Crown, in accordance with the legislation of 1608, put forward four names for Parliament to select and elect one. Paul was one of those whom the crown proposed; the other three,[37] including the two Protestants, agreed amongst themselves to step down before it came to a vote, and Paul was elected to the office unanimously, receiving the votes of all Protestant members too. His election as Palatine just as the war in Germany was formally terminated, freeing imperial troops, raised high hopes that soon a concerted offensive would be mounted against the Turks.

However, it was not to be: imperial soldiery was indeed moved to Hungary, but kept well away from the front line, largely in order to place the burden of housing and feeding them on Hungary rather than the Hereditary Lands; and in 1650 the court renewed the truce with the Ottomans for another twenty years, without even bothering to inform—let alone consult—the Palatine and other Hungarian dignitaries in advance. This did not stop Hungarian garrisons facing the Turk fighting on for a while, despite Vienna's official disapproval, but even such warfare petered out after 1652, when Ottoman forces inflicted a serious defeat on the Hungarians at Vezerkény (in which action, famously, four Esterházy brothers fell).

During these years Paul and his circle had pinned their hopes on significant military successes against the Turk, which could induce the court to revise its policy. In order to be listened to at court he had to keep on good terms with court circles. Just then this was best achieved by supporting Ferdinand III in his latest pet scheme: having his elder son, also Ferdinand, both elected King of Germany—in effect Emperor-elect—and also crowned "junior king" in Hungary in his father's lifetime.[38] Paul's support in these matters was clearly appreciated at court, and in 1651, while negotiations about all of this were still going on, Ferdinand III saw to it that his cousin Philip IV of Spain invested Paul with the Order of the Golden Fleece, the first of the family to receive it. In 1653—shortly after young Ferdinand was duly crowned junior king as Ferdinand IV (unfortunately dying a year later, so his younger brother Leopold, of whom more in the next chapter, eventually became king)—Paul died. But before his death he made arrangements, some of which lasted until 1918, for the future of his considerable estates: the first to do so in Hungary, he set up, and obtained formal royal approval for, two entails.[39]

The first entail, of the bulk of his estates, was to his sons and their descendants by male primogeniture, to revert, no longer entailed, to his nephews and their

---

[36] This was exceptionally soon after the last one: by earlier legislation, it is true, Parliament should have been called every three years, but neither Ferdinand II nor Ferdinand III did so with any regularity.

[37] They were Adam Forgách, of the group, and the Protestants Sigismund Lónyay and Louis Nyáry.

[38] There were mediæval precedents, the first in the reign of Andrew I (r.1046–1060), for coronation of the heir in his father's lifetime, although the last to be so crowned had been the future Béla IV in the 1210s.

[39] In a sense all Hungarian estates were quasi-entailed since 1351, but only to remain within the family —interpreted to mean all descendants of the first to have owned the estate—giving rise to much litigation when there were no obvious direct heirs; Paul's arrangements, modelled on Ferdinand II's entail in primogeniture of all his Hereditary Lands, went beyond this.

descendants should his descent die out (which happened half a century, and but two generations, after his death). Being by now the hereditary captain of the castle of Pressburg as also Lord Lieutenant of the county, as well as Count of Pressburg, Paul's second entail comprised all the estates that went with the castle—all fortified castles had had estates attached to them, to pay for upkeep and feed the garrison—to pass, along with those titles, to his nephew Nicholas and after him the eldest, for the time being, male of the family, an arrangement know as *senioratus*. Since all later Pálffys are that Nicholas' descendants, by 1918—when such entails were broken up by the new Czechoslovak government, from then possessed of the regions were the estates lay—sixteen of them, from various branches of the family, had enjoyed the comfortable income that the estates thus entailed to the Senior provided. The income is gone, but the Senior is still the head of the family (and, if he chooses to so style himself, Count of Pressburg).[40]

⚜

Paul's descent, as mentioned, soon died out. His elder son John who, although twice married, had one daughter only, does not appear to have done anything noteworthy during his life (beyond becoming the Senior on his cousin Nicholas' death).

In contrast the second son, Charles, embarked on a military career in his twenties, soon raising a regiment of horse and one of foot at his own expense, and was granted the colonelcy of both; the cavalry regiment continued in being until 1918 as the Imperial & Royal 8th Hussars.[41] For the next fifteen years he fought the Turks, being promoted to general of cavalry—in which capacity he served under Charles Duke of Lorraine during the siege and retaking of Buda from the Turks in 1686[42]—and then lieutenant general, and also made captain of the Royal Bodyguard. Then towards the end of 1680s, by which time the Turks were almost completely pushed out of Hungary (*see* next chapter) but renewed war between Louis XIV of France and the Habsburgs was looming again (*see* also next chapter), he was sent on diplomatic missions to the Netherlands, to England, and to Venice (as well as several of Germany's Electors) to discuss joint military action against the French. Following the outbreak of hostilities he joined the armies fighting back the French in Savoy, distinguishing himself, in particular, at the Battle of Pignarolla (1693), during which three mounts were shot out from under him and

---

[40] At the time of writing László is the senior; I am next in line, and after me Franz who lives in the Lungau.

[41] Although, having been the Pálffy Hussars, renamed the Kaiser Wilhelm Hussars when that monarch became the regiment's colonel-in-chief.

[42] His is the only Hungarian name mentioned in a contemporary English account of that siege, *A Journal of the Siege and Taking of Buda...* by Jacob Richards (present as a military engineer sent there as England's contribution), published in London in 1687, a copy of which is on my shelves.

at which his younger son Francis,[43] still in his early twenties but already in command of a regiment, was killed: promotion to commander of that army was scant consolation. His elder son Nicholas-Joseph also became a soldier, but died of a fever while on campaign in Italy a decade later: his only child, a son, had already died very soon after birth.

In consequence the entail Paul had set up for his direct descendants was broken up; the considerable estates it had consisted of went to his great-nephews Nicholas and John (of whom more in the next chapter).

---

[43] Some contemporary sources mention that a young "Count Pálffy" (without giving his Christian name) was in 1686 entrusted with the honour of delivering Turkish standards captured at Buda to Leopold at Vienna: this *might* have been Francis, possibly present—perhaps as a teenage ensign—during the siege with his father, whose standing with the Duke of Lorraine, in overall command, could have enabled him to obtain this honour for his son. But there is no certain way of telling, and it might have been John, also serving in that regiment (of whom more in the next chapter).

Nicholas Pálffy the courtier

More soldier-statesmen (late 17th–18th centuries)

*T*he descent of Stephen's three younger brothers, including that of Paul the Palatine, petered out by the end of the seventeenth century. But the family was carried on towards the eighteenth by Stephen's only son Nicholas, and into it by Nicholas's two sons Nicholas (from whom we all descend) and John. This chapter is largely devoted to them.

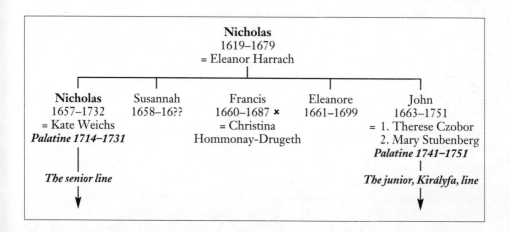

Stephen's son Nicholas was educated at the Jesuit schools at Nagyszombat and Vienna, then studied at the University of Ingolstadt in Bavaria and later in Italy. Thereafter he did not—unlike his cousin Charles (*see* previous chapter)—become a soldier, although he did take to the field against the Turks once, briefly, in 1662, nor did he get involved, as his uncle Paul had, in serious politics and government. He opted, instead, for the life of a courtier in a succession of largely honorific posts: Royal Cupbearer, Principal Janitor, Chamberlain, and the like, none of which entailed any particularly onerous duties. True, he did eventually become one of the two Crown Guardians too, but only when and because he inherited the Pressburg entail set up by his uncle Paul, which included the hereditary captaincy of Pressburg Castle where the Holy Crown was kept. Following his death in

1679 his widow, née Countess Eleonore Harrach, became governess to the children of Leopold I,[1] further underlining their loyal standing at court.

That Nicholas was happy to live out his life as a courtier is doubly disappointing: not only because of the sad contrast to his grandfather's, father's, uncles', and cousins' active involvement in the military and political affairs of their country, but also and in particular because the court at which he served most of his life was that of Leopold I (r. 1657–1705), a disaster as king of Hungary.

⚜

Leopold, originally intended for the Church—where, of course, a rich archbishopric was to be his—not the throne, had been brought up by ultra-bigoted clergymen in the spirit of fervent counter-Reformation zeal. But on the premature death of his elder brother, already crowned "junior king" as Ferdinand IV in his father's lifetime, Leopold suddenly became heir apparent and, a year later aged but seventeen, ruler. By then the two principal notions that were to guide him throughout his long reign had been ineradicably implanted in his mind: that he ruled by Divine Right and was, therefore, entitled to act as he saw fit (guided, at most, by the advice of his confessor), and that it was his sacred duty to extirpate from his lands all traces of Protestant heresy (so effectively kept away from *their* realm by his maternal uncle Philip IV, and then his cousin and brother-in-law Carlos II, of Spain).[2]

Yet his Hungarian subjects, the bulk of whom were heretic Protestants, pretended to have a right to interfere in the running of their country, even to be entitled to approve—or, by implication, disapprove of, if they so chose—his coronation, through their Parliaments in which, *horribile dictu*, Protestant members sat as equals alongside Catholics. At least the Turks, about whose expulsion from their—from *his!*—country they kept whining, were there to keep them in check and put a brake on their wicked pretensions. So his reign, of almost half a century, was marked by repeated royal measures against Hungary's Protestants, by extended periods of unconstitutional direct rule without Parliaments, and by accommodations sought with the Turks, time and again, at any cost to Hungary.

By the 1660s, within but a few years of his coronation, senior Hungarian dignitaries—by and large those referred to as *Paul Pálffy's circle* in the previous chapter, Count Francis Wesselényi, who had succeeded him as Palatine, now at their head—were already seriously discussing how to get rid of Leopold (the example of England, not twenty years back, doubtless in their minds), and were putting out feelers to foreign powers, especially France, in this matter. The budding conspiracy gained in force after 1664: in the wake of an unexpected and signal victo-

---

[1] Possibly the source of later, unsubstantiated, gossip that Leopold had had a Pálffy mistress.
[2] Curiously, he was also a keen musician, in his spare time composing music still quite pleasing to listen to.

ry over the Turks, who had launched the campaign, at Szentgothárd Leopold had promptly, without consulting anybody in Hungary, sent an emissary to conclude a peace with them—the Peace of Vasvár—that was wholly favourable to the Ottomans and much to the detriment of Hungarian interests.[3] But Hungarian objections to its ratification fell on deaf ears in the Hofburg. Now even many of those who had been opposed to the views of Paul's circle, such as Archbishop Lippay, took against Leopold. In the event Wesselényi died (as did Archbishop Lippay) before the conspiracy, still known by his name, turned into a short-lived open rebellion in 1670. It soon collapsed, its main leaders were apprehended, sentenced to death by an *ad hoc* imperial tribunal and executed, in Austria, early in the following year;[4] some thirty lesser participants followed them to the scaffold, in Hungary, also sent there by similarly *ad hoc* imperial tribunals.

Leopold thereafter ruled Hungary by decree through a Governing Council of loyal Germans. Only in 1681 did yet another and rather more successful rebellion in Hungary (*see* below) force him to reconsider, call a Parliament, and make a show of reverting to constitutional rule, also conceding to Protestants some of the rights they were by law—the legislation of 1608—entitled to.

Yet throughout all of this, including those executions, Nicholas Pálffy appears to have had no qualms over continuing to serve as His Majesty's Chamberlain, then Principal Chamberlain, in Vienna.

However, despite his reluctance to fight the Turks, Leopold's hand was eventually forced. The Peace of Vasvár about to expire, and encouraged by developments in Hungary (an armed rising against Leopold's arbitrary rule, led by Count Imre Thökölyi, was achieving considerable successes), the Turks launched their last grand offensive, which in 1683 carried them to the walls of Vienna. Jan Sobiesky, King of Poland, and his army arrived just in time to help beat them off; this time, although Leopold again inclined to offer them a hasty and advantageous peace, pressure orchestrated by Pope Innocent XI compelled him to continue fighting to push the Turks out of all of Hungary. Stiffened with additional contingents from most of Europe the imperial army led by Prince Eugene of Savoy advanced, Buda was retaken in 1686, and by the end of the century the Ottomans were left with but a small south-eastern corner of Hungary, the region of Temesvár, still in their possession.

Concurrently with that successful campaign against the Turks war was looming in the West too. For centuries France had resented Habsburg power, and had fought many wars (on occasion even concluding formal alliances with the Turks) against them, in Italy, in Germany, and elsewhere; in the second half of the

---

[3] By its most objectionable clause the Emperor, who was after all also King of Hungary, and the Sultan agreed to abstain from aiding the Hungarians against the other.

[4] They were Counts Peter Zrínyi (Viceroy of Croatia), Francis Frangepán, and Francis Nádasdy (Justice of the Realm).

seventeenth century—*le grand siècle* of Louis XIV, keen on military glory too—these had been renewed as France aggressively pushed its borders towards the Rhine and into Savoy to its east, and in a northerly direction at the expense of the Habsburg Netherlands (roughly into what is today French Flanders).

Now, in the final decades of that century, an additional bone of contention threatened the peace of Europe: the Spanish, senior, branch of the House of Habsburg was patently on the verge of extinction. Carlos II, the last male of that branch, was—although not, according to his wife, devoid of sexual drive—apparently unable to father any children, probably owing to excessive inbreeding in his immediate ancestry: his mother, grandmother and great-grandmother, themselves born from marriages between Habsburg cousins, had been his father', grandfather's and great-grandfather's cousins. So the question that preoccupied the chanceries of Europe was: who would inherit the throne of Spain, and with it much of the Americas, on Carlos' death?

Louis XIV of France and Carlos II were first cousins and brothers-in-law—Louis's mother had been a sister of Carlos' father, his queen a half-sister of Carlos—and on the strength of this he asserted that his grandson the teenage Philip Duke of Anjou was the rightful heir by descent, a view that Carlos himself accepted. But Leopold would have none of this: as far as he was concerned Spain was first and foremost a Habsburg possession, and as such it should, on extinction of the senior branch, revert to his, junior, Austrian branch of the House of Habsburg; his candidate for the throne of Spain was his younger son Charles. Nobody thought to ask the Spaniards, but all European powers were taking sides, in the main against France: united with geographically contiguous Spain by a common ruling dynasty France might become too powerful for comfort (Britain, in particular, was firmly anti-French). Thus, by the end of the century all those previous wars with France were followed by the long-drawn-out War of the Spanish Succession, only terminated in 1713—by which time Leopold was long dead—by the Peace of Utrecht, by which all parties recognised the Bourbon succession in Spain (and Britain gained Gibraltar).

⚜

In these warlike circumstances, in Hungary as elsewhere, it is not to be wondered at that all three of Nicholas' sons— Nicholas, Francis and John, in their twenties when hostilities with the Turks became serious—embarked on military careers as soon as they had completed their education. All three initially attended the Jesuit college at Nagyszombat: earlier and later merely a county town, during those centuries it was the residence of the Archbishop of Esztergom, a focus of not only political but also of cultural activity, home to Hungary's then only university (founded by Cardinal-Archbishop Peter Pázmány; it was to be moved to Pest a century later), and an important publishing centre. From there Nicholas went on to the University of Vienna, Francis was sent on a Grand Tour of the

Netherlands, England and Italy, while John continued his studies at the University of Parma.

The military career, as the life, of Francis the middle son was regrettably brief: returning from his Grand Tour he soon obtained the colonelcy of the regiment of horse founded by his cousin, Paul's son Nicholas-Joseph, only to be killed in 1687, aged twenty-seven and but a few months married, by a stray bullet while pursuing retreating Turkish forces near Eszék, a key bridgehead on the Dráva river. Not so that of the other two, who between them take up the rest of this chapter.

His father had seen to it that his eldest son Nicholas (ancestor of all Pálffys still around) was appointed a court chamberlain at the age of eighteen. But he soon abandoned court service for the military: by the time he was thirty he had been promoted colonel of the regiment in which he had served as lieutenant-colonel and was also appointed captain of the castle of Esztergom (a post his grandfather had occupied almost a century earlier), by now finally and definitely retaken from the Turks. No doubt the fact that in the following year he set up and equipped, at his own expense, a regiment of foot of twelve companies helped accelerate his further promotion: major-general in 1690, lieutenant-general by 1692.

As such he was in summer 1693 sent to join the forces besieging Belgrade without much success, with the brief to resolve quarrels within the command there, the main cause of slow progress, and to restore discipline. However, within weeks of his arrival he ventured too near the Turkish defensive positions his troops were attacking: the Turks, spotting what was obviously a group of senior officers, directed artillery fire at them, an officer standing next to him was killed and a cannonball shattered his leg. He survived, his leg was pieced together again—but for the rest of his life he walked with difficulty and a pronounced limp—and his military career was over.

For the next few years he recuperated on his estates—his then unguessed at and more significant political career a decade and more in the future—surrounded by a growing family: a good dozen years earlier he had married Catherine Weichs, a lady-in-waiting of the empress-queen's, who gave birth to yet another child almost every year, eleven in all, of whom only three boys died in infancy. The eldest (from whom we descend) was born in 1681: that he was baptised Leopold, while all the others were given good traditional names,[5] suggests that Leopold I might have stood godfather to him (as Ferdinand II had to Ferdinand the son of Nicholas' great-uncle John).

Meanwhile Nicholas' surviving brother John had in 1681, by then eighteen, abandoned his studies at Parma to volunteer for service in a regiment of foot in the imperial army; whether at his own initiative or under family pressure, within months he transferred to his cousin's regiment of horse, as a humble ensign. Fighting the Turks under Vienna in 1683 and then into Hungary, promoted captain,

---

[5] John, Francis, Charles; Eleanor (possibly for her grandmother), Mary, Anne, Caroline.

in 1686 he took part in the siege and retaking of Buda, and was soon thereafter appointed adjutant to the commander-in-chief of the forces fighting the Turks, Charles of Lorraine. However, having made his mark at headquarters, he returned to service in the field, joining his Czobor father-in-law's regiment of hussars with, by now, the rank of colonel; on his father-in-law's death he was appointed its commanding officer. Not long after, a mere twelve years since he had been but an ensign, he had become a major-general.

However, his career was soon, in 1693, to be interrupted. Incensed at disparaging remarks about Hungary and Hungarian soldiers that Prince John-Frederick of Würtemberg made in his hearing, he challenged the prince to a duel. The prince, reputedly a crack shot, fired first but his ball only holed John's hat;[6] John's aim was better, and his shot finished off the prince. This may have been an affair between gentlemen, conducted in accordance with all the rules of duelling *politesse* that applied at the time (when duels were, if frowned upon, frequent), but the prince was the scion of a sovereign ruling house connected, moreover, by marital links to the Habsburgs: the court did not look kindly on serving officers killing persons of such exalted standing. John prudently fled to Poland for a while; the rest of the family pleaded for him and eventually, his services required against France in the War of the Spanish Succession, which had just broken out, he was pardoned, sent to the front on the Rhine (where he would have fought alongside, and might have known, Marlborough), and was by 1700 promoted to lieutenant-general.

At this point the story of Nicholas' and John's subsequent careers needs to be interrupted by a summary of the events and context amidst which these unfolded thereafter.

⚜

By 1690, as mentioned earlier, the Turks had been effectively pushed out of Hungary but, to the disgust of his Hungarian subjects, Leopold I declared that he considered all retaken regions new conquests, constituting ownerless land *(terra nullius)* at his personal disposal, without regard to property claims rooted in ownership before the Turks had occupied those areas. Undiluted this attitude proved too extreme, so in 1690 a bureaucratic body, the *Neoacquistica Commissio*, was set up, outside the framework of Hungarian property law, to adjudicate such property claims. Making up its own rules, this body demanded documentary evidence of ancestral ownership to stringent standards—in most cases difficult to provide, following the destruction of many archives during a century and a half of warfare and occupation—and even when it did accept the validity of a claim it demanded a hefty cash payment by way of a *war tax*, ten per cent of the estate's value as assessed by it, before the heirs to the land, often effectively destitute, could gain possession.

---

[6] In the nineteenth century it was still preserved in the family—where can it now be?

In addition, Protestants were also being harassed again, while ill-disciplined and grasping imperial soldiery, no longer fighting the Turk, was quartered on the population. Indeed, in the 1680s already, even while the war against the Turks was still in progress, the imperial general Caraffa had swept across the north and east arresting, torturing, confiscating the property of, and executing wealthy burghers and landed gentry—mainly, but not only, Protestants—on trumped up charges of pro-Thökölyi conspiracy. No wonder, then, that towards the end of the century discontent was mounting in Hungary, especially in the northern regions that had never been under Turkish occupation.

Sporadic local risings became increasingly frequent as the seventeenth century approached its end and then turned into the eighteenth, but were put down with comparative ease. Until, that is, 1703, when Francis II Rákóczi placed himself at the head of what was about to coalesce into a major rebellion, which then rapidly evolved into a full-scale civil war (covertly supported, subsidised with money and French artillery experts, by Louis XIV: the War of the Spanish Succession now in full swing along the Rhine, a diversion to the east of Habsburg heartlands was most welcome).

Rákóczi had personal charisma, and was immensely wealthy: his estates, mainly in the northeast, extended over several counties, above two million acres in all (his great-grandfather and grandfather in turn had married the richest heiresses of their day, Susannah Lórántffy and Sophia Báthory). His father, Francis I, had only escaped execution for involvement in the rebellion of 1670—details of which had been plotted at his wedding—owing to the wealth and connections of his Báthory mother; while the mother of Francis II Rákóczi, Ilona (Helen) Zrínyi, was the daughter of one and the niece of another (Frangepán) of those who had been illegally executed at that time. Widowed she had married Imre Thökölyi, leader of the rebellion of the 1680s already mentioned, and had held the castle of Munkács on his behalf against imperial forces for three years.

When it finally fell young Francis, then fourteen and at his mother's side, was taken to Vienna to be re-educated a loyal subject, created a Prince of the Empire, given the Golden Fleece, and sent on a Grand Tour of Italy; soon thereafter, and against the court's inclinations in this matter, he married a German princess. Having then finally re-visited his estates, by the first years of the eighteenth century he began to dabble in, somewhat amateurish, anti-Leopoldine conspiracy, was betrayed by an *agent provocateur*, and arrested; he managed, however, to escape form the prison in Wiener Neustadt, where his Zrínyi grandfather and Frangepán great-uncle had been executed, and fled to Poland. From there he then slipped into northern Hungary to accept leadership of the budding rebellion.

By 1704 he had formal standing too, as elected Prince of Transylvania. By the end of the 1680s, with the Turks expulsed from Hungary, nothing had stood in the way of re-integrating Transylvania—only separated from the rest of the country, of which it had always been an integral part, from the mid-sixteenth century by the Turkish-occupied regions—with the rest of Hungary. Nothing, that is, except Leopold I, aided and abetted by that principality's leading men (Michael Teleki, chancellor of the last elected prince, Michael Apafi, foremost among them), who preferred to be big fish in a small pool rather than becoming middling fish in a much larger one: between them they had turned Transylvania into an "independent" (from the Crown of Hungary, that is) hereditary Habsburg duchy that, to gain that local support, was, however, allowed rather more control over its own internal affairs (in matters of religion, in particular) than other Habsburg Hereditary Lands. But this new status was very recent, nor was it universally popular; Rákóczi was, moreover, the great-grandson and grandson of two elected Princes of Transylvania, George I and II Rákóczi, the first of whom had been successful and popular, his rule remembered as a golden age. A Transylvanian Parliament met, rescinded the Leopoldine settlement, and elected him ruling prince.

This is not the place for a detailed account of that civil war: in its early years much of the country was repeatedly overrun by Rákóczi's *kurucz*,[7] as they were called, forces, but eventually physical and economic exhaustion began to set in: Hungary was still recovering from the war to oust the Turks, not two decades in the past. His forces were, moreover, badly led volunteers, brilliant at rapid cavalry movements, raids, and harassment of the enemy, but not trained or equipped to fight in the disciplined formations by then common in European warfare,[8] while their inexperienced commanders lacked proper tactical sense, let alone strategic vision: titled amateurs of wealth and standing who had joined the cause—to force the crown to rule constitutionally[9]—had to be given senior commands to keep them committed. Thus in face to face battles imperial forces inferior in number repeatedly beat them.

Leopold I had finally died during the second year of this struggle, at a time when Rákóczi was going from strength to strength. His son Joseph I (r. 1705–1711)—still in his twenties, long at odds with his father's rigid outlook in private life (Joseph was a notorious seducer of ladies at court) as in politics, intent on reforming the government of his realms—inclined to a settlement. He soon let it be known that pardons would be forthcoming for those who submitted, only Rákóczi himself excluded, and in 1708 he called a Parliament, which remained in session, with interruptions, for several years. But it was to take some years more before peace was restored.

Our ancestor Nicholas remained in effective retirement throughout this period, even if appointed Crown Guardian (later confirmed by Parliament), then commander of the foot bodyguard (a purely honorific post), and finally promoted to field marshal. His new, political, career only took off after the events summarised above, and in the following paragraphs, had run their course.

His brother John, however, was a serving officer with the army fighting the French in the west when Rákóczi unfurled his *Pro Patria et Libertate* flags in northern Hungary. As the scale of the rebellion (as it was seen in Vienna) became apparent he was recalled from the western front, initially to be entrusted with organising the defences of Croatia and Slavonia, south of the Dráva, being made Viceroy of Croatia in 1704 to add status to his efforts. For the next several years he moved about Transdanubia, organising and mounting defences against *kurucz* incursions into the region, interrupted with a dash to the north to relieve the family seat of Vöröskő, whose outer defences had been overrun by a fast-moving *kurucz* detachment which, however, withdrew at his approach; he also played subordinate roles in the clashes—they hardly deserve to be called battles—near Pudmericz and Nagymegyer,[10] in the region north and east of Pressburg. In the course of all of this he was promoted to full general and then, before the events described below, to field marshal.

In the autumn of 1710 John finally agreed—at the personal insistence of Joseph I: he had refused to accept this appointment when it was first proposed some time before—to take over as commander-in-chief in Hungary. By now it was clear to all parties to the struggle that, after seven years of fighting, Rákóczi's forces were collapsing: as commander-in-chief John saw it as his principal duty to wind down the war as rapidly, and with as little bloodshed and bitterness, as possible. He cautiously pushed his army east across the plains towards Debrecen, avoiding armed actions, and simultaneously initiated contacts with General Alexander Károlyi, by then Rákóczi's right-hand man and most senior commander,[11] whom he knew personally from earlier times. To cut a long story short: letters were exchanged, then John and Károlyi met, next a temporary armistice was agreed upon, and by late January Károlyi had even arranged a meeting between John and Rákóczi himself,[12]

---

[10] Two centuries and a bit later I occasionally stayed at Pudmericz as a child, with Uncle Pali, and Nagymegyer is only a few kilometres distant from Csicsó of happy childhood memories (*cf. Prologue*).

[11] Károlyi had come to this position on the rebound: in 1703 he had, at his own initiative, defeated an early insurgent force and had then rushed to Vienna, with captured trophies, in the expectation of praise and, in particular, reward; there he was, so to speak, patted on the head but received no further reward for his loyal action—in disgust he rode back east, sought out Rákóczi, and offered his services in the fight against Leopold I.

[12] Looking back on this time in his *Confessions* (written a few years later, in France) Rákóczi comments that *at least he was now dealing with a Hungarian, if a friend of the Germans, whose word he had to trust and believe, although the Germans might try and go back on it* (he consistently referred to the court at Vienna as "the Germans"); in letters they exchanged, in Hungarian, Rákóczi addresses John Pálffy as "dear cousin" *[kedves atyámfia]* although they were not related.

Erdödy

GRÓF PALFFY JÁNOS,

*Magyar orszag Nádor Ispányja,
a' Iászok és kúnok Birája és
Csász. Kir. Gener. Fővezére.
Szület 20 Aug. 1663. meghalt 24 Martz. 1751.*

COMES JOANNES PALFFY

ab Erdöd

*Regni Hungariae Palatinus,
Iudex Cumanorum et Caesareo
Regius Campi Mareschalhis
ect. ect.*

John Pálffy who, by the peace he negotiated with Rákoczi's adherents,
laid the foundations for reconcilliation hetwcn nation
and Crown and became Maria Theresia's paternal Palatine

to discuss as amicably as possible terms and conditions, both general and person-al (by now even Rákóczi could have a pardon), for terminating the war. And, indeed, as a result of that meeting Rákóczi entrusted John with a letter addressed to Joseph I, seeking reconciliation along the lines John had suggested—but spoilt everything by signing it *Franciscus princeps* (i.e. of Transylvania: to sign it as a prince of the Holy Roman Empire the form should have been *princeps Rákóczi*), a style and title totally unacceptable at Vienna: Joseph I was prepared to pardon a rebel-lious subject in the interest of peace, but not to abandon his claim to what was by now the hereditary Habsburg duchy of Transylvania.

Court circles in Vienna—notably the entourage of the dowager empress-queen Eleanore—in large part still imbued with rigid Leopoldine attitudes to Hungary, and thus in favour of crushing those insufferable rebels ruthlessly, were shocked and furious on learning of that meeting: the commander-in-chief had gone too far (up to then they had believed that all he was trying to do was to subvert Károlyi), had exceeded the powers vested in him (which, to an extent, was true: John had a tendency to act first and seek authorisation after the event), and should be instant-ly recalled. Fortunately Joseph I backed John: by a letter despatched in mid-Feb-ruary he formally authorised him to press ahead with negotiations and conclude a peace; to appease the more intransigent elements at court this letter was carried by a reliably loyal German bureaucrat, one Military Councillor Locher, who was to stay at John's side and keep an eye on him. Rákóczi soon departed for Poland, with a view to travelling on to seek the assistance of Czar Peter (later known as *the Great*); from now on John and Károlyi kept acting very much on their own ini-tiative, between them beginning to hammer out an agreement that would restore peace—in a sense broader than just the cessation of hostilities—in Hungary, both straying somewhat beyond what their masters expected (Locher proved less obstructive than had been feared: his Hungarian, if any, may have been too poor to follow and interfere in their discussions).

They were making satisfactory progress when, late in April, the news that Joseph I had unexpectedly died of the smallpox reached them. His successor, his brother Charles, was at the time—being the Habsburg candidate for the throne of Spain—in distant Barcelona. With no ruler in residence Leopold I's widow Eleanore assumed the regency, and with her active support the intransigent faction at court hastily set about undoing John's achievements, ordering him back to Vienna and appointing one General Cusani as commander-in-chief in Hungary in his place. Formally notified of this, John wrote back that as a soldier he would, of course, obey orders but that, since he judged the situation in Hungary too delicate for a handover of his command at just that moment, he would stay on for a while longer.

Then, working at it furiously, he and Károlyi finalised the treaty in time to sign it, as the plenipotentiaries of their respective masters, at Károlyi's headquarters at Szatmár on 30 April. The following day they made it public, John accepted the formal surrender of *kurucz* troops still under arms, and despatched a copy of the treaty to the still distant new King as also to Vienna. Here, while the court dithered, word was soon received from Charles (who had not received his copy of the treaty yet) that he had every confidence in Field Marshal Count Pálffy; thus, on the advice of Prince Eugene of Savoy, chairman of the *Hofkriegsrath* supreme in all matters military, Dowager Empress & Queen Eleanor gritted her teeth and confirmed royal acceptance of the Treaty of Szatmár in her son's name.

It was a remarkably generous conclusion to eight years of bloody civil war. All who had fought against the Crown were granted a full pardon, confirmed in possession of their estates, and permitted to continue carrying such arms as was habitual, subject only to swearing an oath of loyalty to the king within a set period (with the added concession that those who, being out of the country, could not meet the deadline would be permitted to do so later on, provided only that they communicated the reason for their absence to the appropriate authorities as soon as possible). And these terms were to apply to Rákóczi himself too, with the additional proviso that, once he had sworn his oath of loyalty, he would be free to live abroad if he so chose.[13] Further clauses dealt with tidying up other issues arising from the fighting, guaranteed adherence to all past legislation granting rights of religious liberty, in Hungary as in Transylvania, and a final clause left it to the next Parliament to settle any matters not satisfactorily resolved by the treaty.

By the time Charles III (r. 1711–1740) made it to Vienna in the autumn[14] John, who had already had a personal letter of thanks from the new king, and Nicholas were both there to welcome him. Whether or how well they and Charles III knew each other from his earlier youth (born in 1685, he had been in Spain from his late teens, but they might have met at court) is a moot point, but the tone of subsequent personal correspondence between them suggests a relationship as close to easy friendship as was possible between monarch and subjects in the eighteenth century.

Following the outbreak of renewed hostilities with the Turks in 1715 John returned to active soldiering, taking part in several victorious battles against them and crowning his military career by commanding the troops that stormed Belgrade in 1717: although they did not immediately take the town, the impact of this action forced the Turks to abandon Belgrade three days later. But John himself was also wounded, if not as badly as his brother had been there in 1693, and

---

[13] But he refused, choosing penniless exile, first in France—where even Louis XIV would not accord him the title Prince of Transylvania: at Versailles he was officially referred to as *le Comte de Charoch* (French phonetic for *Sáros*)—and finally, after the death of Louis XIV, in Turkey at Rodosto on the Sea of Marmara, where he occupied himself hunting, turning woodwork, and writing his memoirs, until his death in 1735. The *Letters from Turkey* there penned by his faithful page and later factotum Kelemen Mikes of Zágony are a gem of eighteenth century Hungarian literature.

[14] With a delightful Spanish mistress (for form's sake married off to his principal chamberlain Count Althan) in tow, while his wife was left behind in Spain to follow later. The prevalence of extramarital liaisons in court society during Charles' reign is entertainingly described by Lady Mary Wortley-Montagu in letters from Vienna, where she spent much of the autumn and winter of 1716 *en route* to the embassy at Constantinople.

in consequence retired from active military service. Of his subsequent political career more further below.

As to Nicholas: immediately on his return Charles III appointed him Master of the Horse to his mother, the Dowager Empress & Queen, and in the next year bestowed the highest Habsburg accolade, the Order of the Golden Fleece on him. These honorific distinctions were followed by senior political ones: on the office falling vacant in 1713 Nicholas was appointed Justice of the Realm and in 1715, a Parliament having been called, was proposed for and elected to the most senior, that of Palatine, advancing to these offices and dignities in the same sequence as his great-uncle Paul had. The account of the role he then played needs to be preceded by a brief sketch of the political background.

⚜

Charles III (VI as Holy Roman Emperor) had one major preoccupation: the House of Habsburg, so prolific in earlier centuries, was on the verge of dying out—the Spanish branch already gone, the Austrian was threatening to vanish likewise. For, although Leopold I, twice widowed thrice married, had fathered no less than sixteen legitimate children, eleven of these had been girls, several of whom died in infancy, and only two of the five boys had survived into adulthood: Joseph I, who had died young leaving only two daughters (his only son had died a baby), and Charles III himself, now the last surviving male Habsburg.

The possibility that the Habsburg inheritance of numerous titles and considerable territories might have to pass on through the female line had already been foreseen by Leopold I, who had drawn up a formal document regulating the order of succession in this contingency. However, this Leopoldine settlement was not to Charles' liking, since by its terms his surviving sisters, and then his nieces, daughters of his elder brother Joseph I, would take precedence over his daughters in the order of succession should he fail to father any sons. So in 1713 he in turn drew up a new formal document, known as the *Pragmatic Sanction*, by the terms of which, should he have no son, a daughter of *his* (and then her descendants) would inherit all his crowns, other titles, and lands.

At the time this was just a piece of contingency planning: his empress and queen, Elizabeth-Christine of Brunswick-Wolfenbüttel, had just re-joined him from Spain, and now there was no reason why they should not begin to have numerous children, including boys. However, the son actually born in 1716 died that same year, to be followed by two girls, Maria Theresia and Maria-Anna in 1717 and 1718, and somewhat later another girl who, however, died soon. Thereafter no more children were likely: Charles III certainly abounded in sexual energy, so it must have been due to Elizabeth-Christine who, however, unlike the first two wives of Leopold I, did not conveniently die to enable him to re-marry. The Pragmatic Sanction now became of the utmost importance to Charles III and henceforth most of his reign was devoted to gaining acceptance for this disposition.

The resistance of his sisters and nieces—the latter soon to marry husbands with an inevitable interest in the matter: Henry of Bavaria and Frederic-Augustus of Saxony & Poland, whose lands bordered on Habsburg domains—overcome, he mounted an intense diplomatic effort to obtain advance agreement to his daughter's eventual succession from other European powers: should they on his death deem the ruling house extinct, Habsburg possessions would offer rich pickings, from the Habsburg Netherlands (today's Belgium) through chunks in Germany to Bohemia (including Moravia, and Silesia), and even the Austrian provinces themselves.

And then there was also the problem of the Kingdom of Hungary. There was, indeed, one precedent for female succession: Mary Anjou, daughter of King Louis *the Great*, had followed her father on the throne in 1382. However, even then there had been considerable resistance to female succession, to the point of some years of civil wars, nor had Parliament yet learnt to flex its muscle at that time. But on the next occasion, when King Sigismund died in 1437 leaving no son, it was not the coronation of his daughter Elizabeth but that of her husband, Albert Habsburg, that Parliament had approved. In the next ninety years thereafter Parliament had, in the absence of male heirs, invited outsiders to the throne on four more occasions: Ferdinand I Habsburg in 1526 had been the last of these.[15] There was thus an established tradition of the throne reverting to the nation and Parliament picking its next occupant whenever there was no male heir of the ruling house to succeed to it. A tradition whose implications were particularly vivid in Hungarian minds in the wake of numerous anti-Habsburg risings during the previous century, and the recently terminated civil war led by Rákóczi.

Leopold I would have attempted to impose succession in the female line on Hungary by strong-arm methods. But his sons, Joseph I and Charles III, no longer of the seventeenth century's rigidly conservative counter-reformation spirit, were more open, flexible, and willing—indeed: keen—to achieve their ends with their subjects' co-operation. Joseph I, impatient of his father's antiquated policies, had, as we have seen, appointed John Pálffy to terminate the Rákóczi civil war by negotiation, and had supported him against die-hard elements at court: the resulting settlement had laid the foundations for a reconciliation between nation and dynasty that would have been unthinkable in the days of Leopold I. Charles III, more of a pragmatist than a man of abstract ideas, had then approved the peace terms of Szatmár when he suddenly came to the throne: now he set about securing his daughter's succession to the throne of Hungary by constitutional, Parliamentary, means.

In the same spirit he also filled all Hungarian senior offices of state—the first Habsburg king in a long time to do so regularly—and, moreover, sought and heeded their advice. He also called several Parliaments (if not every three years as legislation prescribed), which passed much useful and progressive legislation, includ-

---

[15] The previous three had been Ulászló (Władysław) I Jagiello in 1440, Matthias I Hunyadi in 1458, and Ulászló (Władysław) II Jagiello in 1490.

ing, in particular, that setting up the Lieutenancy Council under the Palatine to govern Hungary on his behalf, and legislation to rein in the *Neoacquistica Commissio*. True, like all his family he remained (despite many mistresses) a fervent Catholic, but never considered the open persecution of Protestants in his father's style, although pressure was brought to bear on them by subtler means.

⚜

In the task of extending the Pragmatic Sanction to Hungary by constitutional means Charles III was much aided and assisted by Nicholas, now Palatine, and then John Pálffy. It is on record that as early as 1713 Nicholas was invited to the series of confidential—"secret", the sources say—discussions at court at which the Pragmatic Sanction was elaborated into a final document: it is reasonable to assume (if minutes were kept, which is doubtful, none survive) that the principal contribution of Nicholas—just then appointed Justice of the Realm—would have been to clarify the specifically Hungarian constitutional, legal and political implications of the policy being embodied in that document.

At that time, as already noted, the Pragmatic Sanction, made public the same year, was merely a contingency plan for an eventuality that might not arise; by the end of the decade this had changed. By the terms of the Pragmatic Sanction—so far binding only on members of the House of Habsburg (and hence *ipso facto* in the Hereditary Lands, treated like private estates)—the heir apparent was now the baby Maria Theresia, and the time had come to take formal steps to ensure her succession in Hungary too. John, recently retired from military service, swung into action in Croatia, whose viceroy he still was, and persuaded the regional assembly of that province[16] to endorse Maria Theresia's succession. He then joined his brother Nicholas in Hungary to work on preparing the ground for a Parliament that would formally enact her succession in Hungary as a whole. This meant lobbying on the spot to get proudly independent elected county assemblies to pass resolutions in favour of Maria Theresia's succession: each county sent two members to Parliament, who would not there vote otherwise than in accord with what the assembly of their county had already approved. Nicholas and John also worked on, though here less effort was required, hereditary members of the Upper Chamber.[17]

Owing in large measure to their preliminary efforts, and continued work on members once Parliament had met, in 1723 Parliament incorporated the dispositions of the Pragmatic Sanction that ensured the succession of Charles III's

---

[16] Croatia, its crown long joined to Hungary's, had recently been granted a regional assembly.

[17] Alexander Károlyi of the Szatmár peace negotiations, by now raised from baron to count, proved a fervent supporter.

[18] Without making of this a general principle: its right to decide how the throne was to be filled in the future, should the same situation arise again in a later generation, it retained.

Nicholas Pálffy who as Palatine piloted the Pragmatic Sanction through Parliament
and laid the foundations of the National Archives

daughter[18] into Hungarian law by Act I of that year; Acts II and III furthermore
"perennially and indissolubly" linked the Kingdom of Hungary with the Hereditary Lands through their common monarch, henceforth to be one and the same
person at all times, and declared that Hungary and the Hereditary Lands were

---

[18] Without making of this a general principle: its right to decide how the throne was to be filled in the
future, should the same situation arise again in a later generation, it retained.

bound to give each other mutual military support.[19] Other significant legislation of that Parliament included the creation of the Lieutenancy Council *(consilium locumtenentiale)*, chaired by the Palatine or in his absence the Justice of the Realm, to govern Hungary on the king's behalf.

Charles III was delighted that his daughter's succession in Hungary had been assured, and rewards were soon forthcoming: having thanked Nicholas in a letter in his own hand—wherein he addressed him as *My dear old & crooked* (a reference to his limp, not corruption) *Palatine*, and as *Mein Nickerl*, a very Viennese diminutive of Nicholas—within the decade both he and John received further extensive estates,[20] the last time the family increased its wealth by royal munificence for services rendered.

However, Nicholas achieved more as Palatine than just ensuring female succession for the House of Habsburg in Hungary. He had piloted an act through the Parliament of 1715 that gave him powers to start sorting out the mess created by the *Neoacquistica Commissio* set up by Leopold I, and to clamp down on this most unpopular body.[21] And—exasperated, as far as one can tell, by the difficulties of locating earlier relevant state papers and documents during the Parliament of 1722–1723 that was debating female succession—he encouraged the passing of, and then vigorously followed up, an Act that laid the foundations for the National Archives, seeing to it that the archives of cathedral and monastic chapters, county administrations, government offices, even major private collections, were searched for documents of lasting value and interest relating to matters of state and other issues of national importance, to be removed from there and brought together in a single central depository at Pressburg (where Parliament met); by an act of Parliament of 1765 this depository became the Hungarian National Archive.[22] And he was, of course, the first to preside over, and thus set the pattern for the structure and working methods of, the new Lieutenancy Council set up in 1723.

By the time Nicholas died in 1732, aged seventy-five and plagued by the gout, he could look back on an outstandingly successful public career, both as a soldier and in politics. As a private individual he had been a patron of the arts and sciences (he appears to have become seriously interested in these during the years of his enforced retirement after being seriously wounded at Belgrade), smoothing

---

[19] This last would have been most welcome two centuries, even one, earlier; now, Hungary facing no external threat since the Turks had withdrawn, it worked to the advantage of the Habsburgs in their European wars.

[20] Szentgyörgy and Bazin, which two—adjacent, and situated halfway between Pressburg and Vöröskő—the family had long, since the "great" Nicholas' day, coveted to round off its possessions in that region.

[21] Further acts of 1723 then made it subject to the King's Bench Court, and reinstated previous owners in their property; it was finally abolished by Maria Theresia's Coronation Parliament of 1741.

[22] Since the late nineteenth century housed in a gaunt redbrick building, which pretends to Romanesque features, at the northern end of the Castle Hill in Budapest; by a miracle building and contents survived bombing, shellfire, as well as the depredations of retreating German and advancing Russian troops, during the siege of Budapest in winter 1944/45.

the path and supporting practitioners of these, Matthias Bél—a Lutheran pastor (Nicholas, though a good Catholic, was no bigot), who wrote prodigiously on the history and geography of Hungary, founded one of the first periodicals of the country, and revolutionarised secondary education—in particular. His married life had been happy too, but blighted by the fate of many of their eleven children: of seven boys three had died in early infancy, of the four who survived into adulthood all but one predeceased him, and only one, the eldest, gave him grandsons to carry on the line (all four girls grew up, to be married off well).

⚜

Following that Parliament of 1722–1723, whose enactments were to attach Hungary to the reigning dynasty and Austria for the next two centuries (almost), John's career was less spectacular for a decade or so. In 1724 he was appointed a member of the Lieutenancy Council and in 1731, when that office fell vacant, he was named Justice of the Realm. When yet another war with the Turks broke out in 1736 he expected—although by then seventy-three—to receive command of the forces sent against them and was bitterly disappointed to be passed over in favour of Francis of Lorraine, since the preceding year husband of the heiress Maria Theresia. The campaign proved a military disaster: by the peace that concluded it in 1739 the Turks regained territory south of the river Száva that had already been re-taken from them. John quite likely muttered "I told you so..." to anyone at court who would listen and, to placate him it would seem, Charles III bestowed the Golden Fleece on him.

Not long after, in late 1740, Charles III died, somewhat unexpectedly, and Maria Theresia succeeded to the Habsburg inheritance. Despite all diplomatic preparations for this eventuality during the preceding decades, some powers, notably Frederick of Prussia, were having second thoughts, started making territorial demands and preparing for war. John was in his element, personally calling all Hungarians to arms and promising to lead them himself in defence of the young queen's inheritance. In practice she first had to be crowned, and before that a Parliament called to approve the coronation: meeting in May 1741, one of its first actions was to elect John to the then vacant office of Palatine (quite properly from among four candidates put forward by the crown).[23]

---

[23] With this office went, by then, the office of Judge of the Yazigs & Cumans (*Iudex Yazigium & Cumanorum*), two peoples who had in the thirteenth century fled the Mongols to Hungary and been settled between the Danube and Tisza, where they (although linguistically long absorbed by Hungary) constituted an administratively distinct Yazig-Cuman District until the 1870s: as a special personal favour Maria-Theresia authorised him to *charge* that district's coat of arms (place in its centre) with his; to this day those enhanced arms can be seen above the main gate of the building that used to be the District's administrative headquarters in Jászberény (today it is the Town Hall of what, for above fifty years, was my maternal grandfather's, Albert Apponyi's, constituency).

Maria Theresia was duly and with much pomp crowned queen regnant of Hungary[24] at Pressburg, John as Palatine sharing with the Archbishop of Esztergom the task of placing the Holy Crown on her head, as was by then traditional. Not long after she summoned Parliament into her presence and, clutching her recently born son (the future Joseph II), appealed to it for help against her enemies. At twenty-four she was a young—and pretty in her blonde and plumpish way—mother looking to the gallant Hungarians to defend her from wicked enemies: by acclamation Parliament voted her all the troops and money she asked for. So in 1742 John finally had the satisfaction of being named commander-in-chief of the army raised in Hungary, whose actions contributed in no small measure to the frustration of Frederick *the Great's* initial attack[25] (but to what extent owing to John being in nominal overall command is a moot point).

The remaining years of his life—he lived, in full possession of his faculties, to be eighty-eight—encompassed the first quarter of Maria Theresia's reign: John continued as her paternal[26] friend, confidant, and gentle adviser, helping to ease her into the role of reigning monarch, she reciprocating with a stream of personal gifts. Queen and nation mourned him alike when he finally passed away: the last of the generation that had fought the Turks under Vienna, to retake Buda, and then to evict them from all of Hungary and, moreover, the architect of reconciliation between Hungary and the reigning dynasty by his insistence, to the point of exceeding his authority, on generous peace terms at Szatmár.[27]

---

[24] The chanceries of foreign powers, their diplomats, and other contemporaries, usually referred to her as *the Queen of Hungary* rather than by any of her other titles, since this one outranked all others she bore in her own right—Empress she was later merely as the consort of Francis of Lorraine after he had been elected to that dignity, not in her own right (unlike, for instance, Catherine of Russia).

[25] Although he did in the end gain Silesia by it.

[26] In private letters—she was a dedicated writer of letters—she addressed him as *Mein Vater Pálffy!*

[27] He is represented by one of the statues surrounding Maria-Theresia's outside the Kunsthistorisches Museum in Vienna, but has no memorial in Hungary.

The last to hold major public office (18th century)

The preceding chapter concentrated on the careers of Nicholas and John Pálffy, who carried on the family from the mid-seventeenth well into the eighteenth century. Both long-lived, both fathers of sons born in the late seventeenth century—who, with one exception, predeceased their fathers—they were the originators of the family's two main lines, the senior descended from Nicholas, and the junior (or, from their favoured country seat: Királyfa) from John. So, to continue our story we have to go back to the end of the 1600s, starting with the senior line.

The four sons of Nicholas who grew up into adults became soldiers. Two of them fell victim to their profession, still unmarried: John, by then a colonel, was killed in 1716 at Pétervárad fighting the Turks, Charles died in 1720 from wounds and injuries sustained during the 1717 siege of Belgrade, where his uncle John had also been present. Francis, the only one to outlive his father, survived a number of battles and rose to major-general, but having early in his life taken the vows of a professed—as opposed to just honorary—Knight of Malta, which precluded marriage, had no offspring.

Thus of four adult sons only one, Leopold the eldest, was to became the father of several children and carry on the line, despite having been being seriously crippled—as his father had been some twenty years earlier under Belgrade—in 1704 at the Battle of Höchstadt: leading his regiment in a cavalry charge against the French he was knocked off his injured mount but his troopers, following too close behind and moving too fast to rein-in, continued galloping to the charge, their horses trampling over him.

Five of his children died in infancy—infant mortality seems to have been especially high during the eighteenth and early nineteenth century—but of the four survivors, all born after he was crippled, three were boys who became the originators of three branches of the family, each known by the name of its main country seats: Nicholas of the *Detrekő* or *Malaczka* branch (later to be more commonly referred to as the "princely branch"), Leopold of the *Stomfa* or *Borostyánkő* branch (later to be more usually known as Pálffy-Daun)—both of which died out

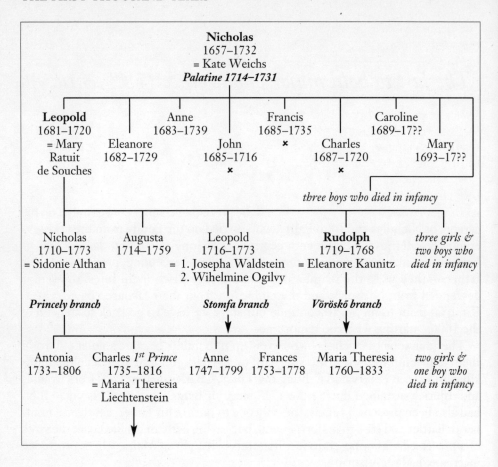

Nicholas
1657–1732
= Kate Weichs
Palatine 1714–1731

Leopold 1681–1720 = Mary Ratuit de Souches	Eleanore 1682–1729	Anne 1683–1739 John 1685–1716 ✕	Francis 1685–1735 ✕	Caroline 1689–17?? Charles 1687–1720 ✕	Mary 1693–17??

three boys who died in infancy

Nicholas 1710–1773 = Sidonie Althan	Augusta 1714–1759	Leopold 1716–1773 = 1. Josepha Waldstein 2. Wihelmine Ogilvy	**Rudolph** 1719–1768 = Eleanore Kaunitz	*three girls & two boys who died in infancy*

Princely branch   *Stomfa branch*   *Vöröskő branch*

Antonia 1733–1806	Charles *1st Prince* 1735–1816 = Maria Theresia Liechtenstein	Anne 1747–1799	Frances 1753–1778	Maria Theresia 1760–1833	*two girls & one boy who died in infancy*

comparatively recently, after the Second World War—and Rudolph the youngest of the still thriving *Vöröskő* branch.[1]

Their active lives spanned the reigns of Charles III and Maria-Theresia, those of their sons extended beyond hers into (and even somewhat beyond) that of Joseph II, reigns during which both Hungary and its rulers were in many ways different from what they had been during the sixteenth and seventeenth centuries.

---

[1] On inheriting and sharing out all family estates Nicholas and John, the later Palatines, had agreed to hold Vöröskő, the main family seat, *jointly* in the proportions 5/8–3/8; that Rudolph the *youngest* son then inherited his father's 5/8 portion probably reflects the old Hungarian custom of dividing estates equally between sons but leaving the family homestead to the youngest, least likely to have a family of his own yet and, therefore, best able to look after their widowed mother.

During those earlier centuries war with the Turks, who held large swathes of the country occupied, had overshadowed and formed the background to all events in Hungary; following their expulsion this incessant warfare came to an end (occasional campaigns in the south were now largely on or beyond the borders of Hungary). Of the past, also, were armed rebellions and civil wars against the Habsburgs, which had culminated in that led by Francis II Rákóczi, terminated in 1711 by the Peace of Szatmár negotiated by John Pálffy, which peace treaty had finally made it possible for nation and dynasty to seek and find a new rapprochement. So during the eighteenth century the country was gradually recovering.[2]

But that peace settlement would not have been possible, in that form, had not the attitudes of the country's reigning monarchs changed too. The new approach to ruling, and to Hungary, adopted by Joseph I and after him Charles III, so different from that of their father Leopold I, has been briefly sketched in the preceding chapter. The daughter of Charles III, Maria Theresia, would also seem to have absorbed much of then fashionable Enlightenment thinking, becoming keen to put those aspects of it that she approved of into practice. In her dealings with Hungary she was, during the first ten years of her reign, gently guided by the old Palatine John—*Mein Vater Pálffy* as she addressed him—and also influenced by Hungary's splendid response when she had been hard pressed by Frederick of Prussia. But later, John dead and the emotional impact of that response fading as her throne became secure, she began to feel increasingly impatient with her Hungarian subjects: she wanted to change, alter, modernise, certain that what she wished to do was both right and well-intentioned, yet they kept resisting change, remaining reluctant to accept that "mother always knows best."[3] Reason was, to an extent, on her side; but the Hungarians were not totally unreasonable either.

Habsburg rulers had, from the day they had acquired its throne, sought to impose direct rule by royal decree, as exercised in their Hereditary Lands, on Hungary too. Hungary had, however, already evolved constitutional practiccs of government by the time they had become its kings, the cornerstone of these the principle that the ruler cannot promulgate valid laws on his own, but only with the nation's consent as expressed through Parliament.[4] Fearing that if they agreed to *any* modification of *any* aspect of their constitutional practices this might open

---

[2] *Very* gradually, to begin with: in describing her journey from Vienna to Belgrade in 1717, by way of Győr, Komárom, Buda, Mohács and Eszék, Lady Mary Wortley-Montagu writes (letter dated 30 January): *"We continued [...] through the finest plains in the world [...] extremely fruitful; but for the most part deserted and uncultivated, laid waste by the long war between the Turk and the Emperor, and the more cruel civil war occasioned by the barbarous persecution of the Protestant religion by the Emperor Leopold."*

[3] Until her death each of the eleven children of hers who survived infancy (she had had sixteen in all) received a weekly letter of maternal guidance, in her own hand, telling them what to do in politics as in private life—even when already fully adult and ruling a territory (e.g. Leopold in Tuscany) or married to a foreign sovereign (e.g. Marie-Antoinette, Queen of France).

[4] As the summary of Hungarian laws completed in 1514 and known as the *Tripartitum* puts it (Pt II. Ch. 3, §3): *"The ruler on his own and absolutely [...] cannot make laws, except by calling together and asking the people whether such laws are agreeable to them or not? if they reply in the affirmative, such decrees shall thereafter be observed as laws."*

the way for erosion of that key principle, Hungarians clung to the immutability of all and every feature of these.

Thus Hungarian constitutional practices were in the eighteenth century still largely frozen in their early sixteenth century condition (Latin, for instance, remained the language of parliamentary debates and of legislation, for fear that if Latin were abandoned then German would be foisted on them), yet much was by now in desperate need of being overhauled and brought up to date. The notion, in particular, that only those who could claim noble status, approximately one man in twenty, were fully-fledged citizens was out of date by then: most of these were far from wealthy (or, indeed, much educated), but they all enjoyed considerable ancient privileges—of which the exclusive right to own land (most had some, though often not more than they could farm themselves) and exemption from all direct taxes were the most important, setting them apart from and above the rest of the population, especially the tied peasants who worked their land and paid all taxes—to which they clung tenaciously. By the eighteenth century this legally sanctioned mediæval stratification (which actually lasted until 1848, if with gradual ameliorations during the first half of the nineteenth century) was patently out of date; but since only nobles were enfranchised, no measure that threatened any aspect of their privileged position was likely to pass Parliament.[5]

Motivated by humanitarian as well as economic considerations, Maria Theresia was determined to improve the tied peasants' lot (which had deteriorated since the end of the Turkish wars), if without ruining the land-owning nobles. To this end she called a Parliament in 1764, the third and last of her reign, which, however, proved resolutely unwilling to cede an inch of "ancient privileges". No Parliament was to be called for the next twenty-five years, and in 1766 Maria Theresia simply issued a royal decree to regulate the *urbarium*,[6] the rights and duties of peasants, in Hungary: this did not do away with the system as such, but by codifying less onerous standards of service for the peasants, and by setting up mechanisms to police the implementation of these (such as village by village registers, visiting commissions), it went some way to eliminate the worst abuses inherent in widespread reliance on "customary law".

Her adored (despite his many infidelities) husband Francis of Lorraine died in 1765; their eldest son Joseph II—the baby in her arms at the 1741 coronation Parliament—was, after a brief Bavarian Wittelsbach interlude, duly elected Emperor, and Maria Theresia recognised him as co-ruler, although technically this did not extend to Hungary. For the next fifteen years they were at loggerheads: both

---

[5] Such reluctance was, in point of fact, a serious brake on their own economic advance too: farming by age-old methods only adequate to meet the landowner's and peasants' own needs, they were perennially short of money; but modernisation to produce for the market—even if wished for—would have required investment, which they could not afford because, owing to their entrenched sole right to own land, they could not raise mortgage loans on it. Only large estates of enlightened magnates, with capital to spare, were operated to produce for the market.

[6] Apparently *socage* or *soccage* (the SOED accepts both) in English.

keen on enlightened reform from above, she was reluctant to let him interfere with her maternal approach, he fretted at being denied real power to set about introducing changes in his more radical way.

On Maria Theresia's death Joseph II became king of Hungary too, and prompt-ly upset the nation by refusing to be crowned[7]—he neither wished to call a Parlia-ment to approve his coronation, nor did he want to tie his hands with the solemn undertakings of a coronation oath—and then caused further offence by removing the Holy Crown and regalia, *mere trinkets from a superstitious past*, from Hungary to the court museum in Vienna. He spent the next ten years imposing innovations, rooted in his personal interpretation of Enlightenment rationalism, in all his realms, Hungary included, extending to everything from administrative structures and bureaucratic procedures to education and prison administration,[8] from citizen's rights to religious toleration, often damaging the plaster too while sweeping away cobwebs. Old conservatives were horrified (and, indeed, got him to retract most of his innovations on his death-bed), but many, including numerous Hungarians, gave him their unstinting support: his intentions were on the whole laudable, but viti-ated by the arrogant high-handedness with which he set about implementing them.

Of Leopold's three sons Nicholas the eldest, and after him his son Charles, were virtually the last of the family to play a serious positive political role in Hungary. Nicholas began his career at court, being made a chamberlain at the age of twen-ty-two and Marshall of the Royal Hungarian Court (roughly comparable to the ceremonial duties of England's Lord Chamberlain) two years later, which gave him regular access to the sovereign, then still Charles III. Five years on, in 1739 and still only twenty-nine, Charles III appointed him a councillor at the Hungar-ian Chancellery, and he served in this capacity for the next six years: tensions must, however, have arisen between him and Maria Theresia, on the throne from 1740, since in 1746 he abruptly resigned—although she conferred the honorific digni-ties of imperial, and then also Hungarian, privy councillor on him—and retired to private life for the next twelve years.

He did, however, keep very much in touch with official circles, notably with his great-uncle John's successor (from 1751) as Palatine, Count Louis Batthyány;[9]

---

[7] To this day Hungarian popular historiography tends to refer to him, since he ever only wore a hat but never a crown on his head, not as a "crowned" but as the "hatted king" *(kalapos király)*.

[8] The man-of-letters Ferenc Kazinczy, actively involved in the implementation of Josephine reforms in Hungary but, two reigns on, sentenced to a long term in prison for "sedition", complains in his prison diary *(Fogságom naplója)* that, since Joseph had set a low upper limit, arrived at "rationally" of course, on how much could be spent on a prisoner's daily food-ration, but those running prisons continued to steal as much of this as before, the food was hardly adequate to survive on.

[9] Whose son, also Louis, some twenty years later married Nicholas' daughter Frances.

politically they saw eye to eye on the need to keep Maria Theresia's relations with her Kingdom of Hungary on the course set under the influence of the late Palatine John Pálffy. In 1758, conceivably on Batthyány's advice, Maria Theresia invited Nicholas to accept the post of Hungarian Chancellor. The invitation could not have come as a complete surprise, since on accepting it he handed her a lengthy memorandum, doubtless prepared some time in advance, detailing his advice on how she should rule Hungary.

It opened by pointing out the importance of not hurting national sentiment, not even prejudice; it went on to elaborate this principle by stressing the need to pay attention to the country's constitutional rights and existing laws in all dealings with it, and warned against any actions by the Crown or its agents that might contradict these principles and thereby undermine the Crown's standing in Hungarian eyes. Legislation, it continued, should be introduced only through Parliament, in accordance with established ancient constitutional practices, which it should, however, be sought to improve and render more fit for the age. Next it suggested the need for a thorough overhaul of property law, especially in relation to land ownership, and went on to recommend cautious revision of taxation; as a first step to these it proposed the creation of a land registry based upon a new survey of all land, and the concurrent compilation of new tax registers, these tasks to be entrusted to reliable Hungarians (i.e. not German bureaucrats), adding the tentative idea that the Church might be taxed too, subject to agreement with Rome. Other denominations, Protestant and Orthodox, should be treated, it concluded, on the same footing as the Catholic.

This government programme, for that is what it in effect was, which successfully balanced and blended Hungarian national aspirations with progress in the spirit of the Enlightenment, initially met with Maria Theresia's approval. For the next few years Nicholas, soon awarded the Golden Fleece, and Batthyány the Palatine had her ear concerning all matters Hungarian. Under their influence she set up the Hungarian Noble Guard in order to bring the main county families—often wealthy but untitled nobles, the bedrock of Hungarian anti-Habsburg attitudes—closer to herself in sentiment:[10] consisting of young men nominated by their counties (which, of course, chose the "presentable" sons of the locally most influential families), who spent five years each at court next her person, it was hoped they would absorb loyalty to the Habsburg monarchy and then take this attitude back to their home county (the unintended longer-term result was, however, that while in Vienna many of them discovered French Enlightenment literature, and returned home converted to political ideas that went far beyond what she approved of).

---

[10] The magnates—tempted to court, if Catholic or willing to become so, with honorifics and a cascade of hereditary titles (whose number more than doubled at the time), and once there encouraged to intermarry with their Austrian, Bohemian, or Moravian counterparts (but of Nicholas' four daughters three married Hungarians, as did one of his two sons)—were to a large extent already so.

Excell ac Illustr Dñus   Dñus Leopoldus e
Comitibus Palffy   ab Erdöd S.C.R
et A. M. Consiliari   us actual. intim
Generalis rei Tor   ment. Praefectus
Vñ Leg. pedestr.   Hung. ord Colonel
lus; nec non S.   Regni Hung
Coronae   Conservator.

Sc. Zeller St. Posony.

Leopold Pálffy who in 1760 became the first Captain of the Hungarian Noble Guard

In 1760 Nicholas had the satisfaction of swearing in the first contingent, his brother Leopold its first captain.

But by 1762 there was a swing at court against undue leniency to the Hungarians, Maria Theresia no longer favoured Nicholas' approach, and he was peremptorily dismissed (the Palatine could not be dismissed, but also out of favour he was effectively locked out of her councils). The upshot was predictable. In 1764 Maria Theresia called what she intended to be a reforming Parliament, its task to begin sweeping away the remnants of mediæval practices in Hungary. But the ground had not been tactfully prepared in advance, in the spirit of Nicholas' memorandum, nor was Parliament carefully managed and massaged when it met (as had been the Parliament of 1723 by his grandfather and great-uncle). In vain did the queen, perhaps hoping for a repeat of the success of her personal appearance in 1741, attend in person to inform Parliament of her proposals for reforming measures: unprepared for most of these, not swayed by the sight of the portly matron she now was as they had been by the pleading young mother twenty-five years earlier, Parliament—its members in the main deeply conservative backwoodsmen—bristled, dug in its toes, and refused to budge on any of the matters, often sensible reforms, dear to Maria Theresia's heart, perceiving these to be merely yet another Habsburg attack on Hungary's "ancient liberties", which many members readily equated with their own privileges. Dissolved the following year, Parliament left most of what the queen had wished to achieve unfinished.

Frustrated, Maria Theresia came to appreciate that if she was to make headway in Hungary she needed the services of such as Nicholas Pálffy and, hardly had Parliament dispersed, she appointed him Justice of the Realm. The Palatine dying the same year, and not replaced because to do so a new Parliament would have had to be called, Nicholas now became *ex officio* acting president of the Lieutenancy Council; as such he was again much consulted by the queen, especially in connection with implementation of her decree concerning the rights and duties of the peasantry in Hungary, the *Urbarium* of 1767, a matter which, as is clear from that earlier memorandum of his, was close to his heart too. Awarded the Grand Cross (limited to twenty persons) of the Order of St Stephen founded a short time earlier, a few years later and barely into his sixties he died in harness, having served both his country and his monarch well—often not easy to combine during the centuries of Habsburg rule in Hungary.

⚜

Nicholas' only son Charles (a second had died in his swaddling clothes) began his official career in the administration of Lower Austria,[11] whence he was soon transferred to the Imperial Treasury, by 1774 rising to become its deputy pres-

---

[11] Since his family owned estates there and had some generations earlier acquired local *indigenatus*, a form of naturalisation, there was no technical bar to his doing so.

ident. Why he should have followed this initial path rather than seeking office in Hungary is not clear: perhaps he wanted to keep out of the shadow of his father. However, in 1777, a few years after his father's death, Maria Theresia appointed him deputy Hungarian Chancellor and thereafter all his official activity related to Hungary.

His real break came, one gets the impression, in 1778 when he was sent to join Joseph II at military headquarters in Bavaria, where a desultory war of succession was in progress.[12] Joseph II was never a stickler for protocol,[13] but in the atmosphere of a military camp he was even more relaxed than at the Hofburg in Vienna: this gave Charles an excellent opportunity to get close to his future king. They doubtless had much in common: Joseph II, whether or not a Freemason (as his father had been), was dedicated to the ideas of Enlightenment rationalism; Charles most certainly was a Freemason (eventually Grand Master of all Hungarian lodges) and this, in the context of that age, implied a very similar outlook. Whatever private conversations they had there at the time, from then on Joseph II trusted and relied upon Charles Pálffy, who eventually gained considerable influence with him.

Two years on Joseph II (r. 1780–1790) came to the throne of Hungary too —although, as already noted, he refused to be crowned—and set about imposing reforms on his realms with more zeal than consideration for his subjects' sensitivities. Few of his subjects were more sensitive than the Hungarians: decrees imposing religious toleration they welcomed, on extending this to schools they were in two minds,[14] but their hackles rose at the abolition of age-old counties, and thus local self-government, in favour of "rational" administrative districts run by bureaucrats, at the imposition of German as the only official language, and —worst of all— at his known intention to introduce uniform taxation in all his realms, the tax-burden to be equitably shared by all subjects regardless of ancient privileges (the list is far from complete, but gives the flavour).

There were, however, forward-looking and enlightened Hungarians who actively supported many of Joseph II's reforming measures, including Charles,[15] who

---

[12] The Bavarian Wittelsbach line had died out and the Rhine-Palatinate line now claimed Bavaria; disputing that claim Maria Theresia staked her own, Frederick of Prussia intervened, armies marched and counter-marched but fought no battles; in the end the Rhine-Palatinate Wittelsbachs got Bavaria, and Austria a slice of land east of the Inn (including Braunau, where Adolf Hitler was to be born).

[13] In a letter to his father Mozart describes how Joseph II let himself be jostled by the crowd of onlookers, commoners watching their betters dance, at a court ball at Schönbrunn.

[14] Hitherto all schools had been in effect denominational; Joseph II sensibly declared that, while it made sense for religious instruction to be given by a minister of the pupils' own denomination, he could see no reason why a Protestant master should not teach Catholic pupils mathematics or a Catholic one Protestant pupils geography.

[15] Count Charles Zichy, Justice of the Realm following Nicholas Pálffy's death, was closely associated in this with Charles; other persons still well known who worked for Joseph's reforms included Count Francis Széchényi, founder of Hungary's National Museum and Library, and Ferenc Kazinczy, man of letters and rejuvenator of Hungarian literary language.

Charles Pálffy confidant of Joseph II, Grand Master of all Hungarian Freemasons, Hungarian Chancellor under three monarchs, and finally created Prince

was in 1785 advanced from deputy to Chancellor (also of Transylvania: the two hitherto separate chancelleries had been merged). However, knowing Hungary, Charles—in the spirit of his father, grandfather, and great-uncle—kept working on the king to persuade him of the advantages of associating Parliament with the introduction of, certainly necessary, changes and innovations: just moving the seat of the Lieutenancy Council from Pressburg to Buda, the country's ancient capital, was insufficient to smooth ruffled feathers. For a while Joseph II appeared minded to heed such advice: in 1783 he commissioned the architect Hillebrandt to create a meeting-place for Parliament at Buda, setting him a deadline of two years; and, indeed, by 1785 work on it was completed.[16] But, despite Charles's increasingly persistent pleas and urgings, Joseph II then seemed unable to bring himself to actually call a Parliament. He did, however, show his appreciation of Charles himself by investing him with the Golden Fleece (in 1782) and then the Grand Cross of the Order of St Stephen (in 1787).

However, by the time Joseph II lay dying in the Hofburg early in 1790 France was rapidly moving towards bloody revolution, his sister Marie-Antoinette and her husband Louis XVI virtually under house arrest. These deplorable developments were perceived to be rooted in Enlightenment tenets, which now appeared less attractive: even Joseph II could be persuaded to retract the most radical of his reforms on his death-bed.[17] The Holy Crown, in particular, was now removed from Vienna and taken to Buda (Pressburg castle had burnt down some years earlier), with much pomp and rejoicing, each county—these too had just been restored—contributing a mounted guard of honour to accompany it part of the way.

By the time it arrived there Joseph II was dead and his brother Leopold II (r. 1790–1792)—until then ruler of Tuscany inherited from his father,[18] which he had ruled well and in a liberal spirit—had succeeded to the throne. Despite death-bed retractions and the Holy Crown's return, much of Hungary was still seething at earlier Josephine reforms, while it was also enthused by the French Constituent Assembly's achievements. This was a dangerous mix: a similar one had a short time earlier led the Austrian Netherlands (which forty years on became Belgium) to declare their independence from the House of Habsburg. In consequence Leopold II, who retained Charles as Hungarian Chancellor, listened to advice his predecessor had disregarded and immediately called a pre-coronation Parliament, to meet at Buda (the first to do so since the early sixteenth century).

Meeting again after a gap of twenty-five years, Parliament proved stroppy: it started off its work by drafting a coronation oath that—inspired by France, and intended to forestall any repeat of Josephine absolutism—included constitutional concessions that went far beyond anything any king had ever sworn to, or

---

[16] The building converted for this purpose was the huge convent of the Poor Claires—whom, along with all other religious orders that did not either nurse or teach, Joseph II had dissolved—on the Castle Hill, which accounts for there still being a Parliament-house Street (Országház utca) up there.

[17] He insisted, however, on retention of those relating to religious toleration and to the easing of the peasantry's condition.

[18] When Louis XV of France had married the Polish Maria Lesczinska, he gave Lorraine to her father to rule; the Duke of Lorraine was compensated with territories in northern Italy.

Leopold II would accept. For the next several months Charles was busy soothing, cajoling, and negotiating with Parliament so the coronation could go ahead; he finally succeeded in persuading it to accept a coronation oath identical to that which had been sworn by Maria Theresia.

That issue resolved, by mid-autumn Parliament moved to Pressburg, approved Leopold II's coronation, and set about filling the vacant (since 1765) office of Palatine, who had a key role to play at the coronation. By then somebody—who?—had had a brilliant idea: why not a Habsburg archduke as Palatine? and Leopold II suggested his son Alexander-Leopold. The Crown, however, had to propose not one but four names, two Catholics and two Protestants, for Parliament to choose and elect one of them: in the event, in no small measure owing to Charles' efforts, Parliament agreed to abstain from formally opening the sealed list of four names received from the Crown, electing Alexander-Leopold—known to be one of the candidates—by acclamation.

Since revolutionary ideas seeping out of France seemed the most serious threat,[19] Parliament was thereafter given a reasonably free hand to pass legislation that rectified national grievances at disregard of ancient privileges, provided none of it was tainted by "Jacobine" tendencies; Parliament was also prevailed upon to enact Maria Theresia's *Urbarium* decree that regulated and eased the condition of the peasantry. Throughout Charles—the Chancellor's role was becoming increasingly similar to that of a prime minister, if not yet dependent upon majority support in Parliament—managed to steer a course equally acceptable to and appreciated by the king and by Parliament: before it rose in 1791 the latter even ordered his final winding-up speech to be printed and published at public expense.[20]

By the time Leopold II died, two years into his reign, and his son Francis I (r. 1792–1835)—a shy young man not yet twenty, initially rather unsure of himself[21]—came to the throne, war with revolutionary France had broken out. For Hungary Francis I retained the services of Charles, the Chancellor who had already served his uncle and father well, called a Parliament, at Buda, and was there crowned.[22] Charles thereafter continued to serve him as chancellor for

---

[19] To hinder their spread Leopold II instituted strict censorship in all his realms; in Hungary Parliamentary legislation was bypassed by the fiction that licensing publications was, and had always been, a royal prerogative.

[20] Parliamentary proceedings, and notably individual speeches, were not at that time reported in detail (there was no equivalent of *Hansard*), only the resulting Acts were published following royal assent.

[21] Sent, still a teenager, to the court of his childless uncle—who referred to him, heir presumptive after his father, as *a monarch apprentice*—they did not get on: the ever active Joseph II kept sarcastically berating him for physical and mental indolence while he, in turn, felt crushed and developed a deep aversion to all the ideas and works promoted by his uncle.

[22] In the Church of Mary-Magdalene on the Castle Hill: much damaged during the Siege of Budapest in winter 1944/45, the post-war Communist régime had it pulled down to its foundations, except for the tower, which has been restored.

another fifteen years, a period dominated by the international upheavals resulting from the French Revolution and Napoleon's ambitions. In Hungary, as elsewhere in Francis' realms, anything that smacked of Jacobine tendencies was
severely repressed, especially in the 1790s,[23] but otherwise matters continued
on an even keel, not least because Parliaments were needed to raise taxes for
military expenditure—in this Parliament even went to the length of imposing
an exceptional tax on otherwise tax-exempt nobles[24]—and army recruits for
those wars (as also to elect Archduke Joseph, another brother of Francis I, Palatine in place of Alexander-Leopold who had blown himself up while preparing
fireworks).

In 1807, by now seventy-two years old, Charles finally resigned from the office
he had so successfully held for twenty-two years under three kings. Francis I
rewarded him for this long service by raising him, and his male successors by primogeniture, to the rank of Prince *(Fürst)*; not of Hungary, where there was no
precedent for this title, nor of the Holy Roman Empire, which had a year before
been formally abolished, but of the newfangled Austrian Empire, invented but
three years earlier to match Napoleon; the title was subsequently granted official
recognition in Hungary too. His descendants, the family's princely branch, are
discussed in the next chapter.

The *Stomfa* (sometimes also referred to as the *Borostyánkő*) branch originated
from Leopold's second son, also Leopold. Charles III had appointed him colonel
of a newly formed regiment of foot when still only eighteen and he remained a
soldier all his life. Shortly after coming to the throne Maria Theresia promoted
him to major-general, and ten years latter to full general. As such he became, as
already mentioned, the first captain of the Hungarian Noble Guard, was soon
promoted to field marshal, and then appointed commander-in-chief in Hungary,
also receiving the Grand Cross of the Order of St Stephen. Not yet sixty when he
died he had never, as far as one can tell, seen serious action.

The line was carried on by his eldest son, yet again a Leopold. For ten years
he served at the Hungarian Chancellery as a councillor, after which he was
appointed Lord Lieutenant of County Csongrád and at the same time Marshal

---

[23] In Hungary this culminated with the "discovery" in 1794/95 of an alleged Jacobine conspiracy—known
by the name of its chief instigator the Abbé Martinovich, who may have been an *agent provocateur* but
was executed nevertheless—most of whose leading members, in the main Freemasons, were sentenced
to death and several of them executed (on the field, now a park, below Buda's Castle Hill known since
as the Bloodfield *[Vérmező]*), the sentences of the remainder (including Ferenc Kazinczy) were commut-
ed to incarceration at the king's pleasure.

[24] There had, in fact, been a couple of seventeenth century precedents for this, to pay for defence against
the Turks.

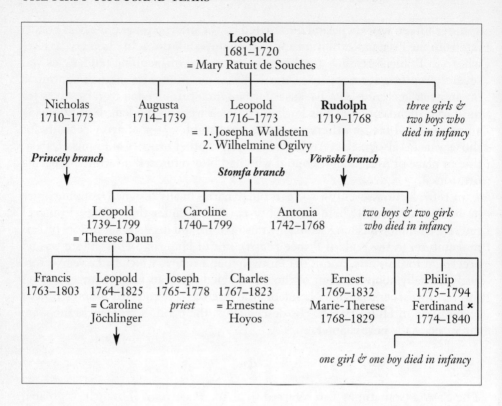

Leopold
1681–1720
= Mary Ratuit de Souches

| Nicholas 1710–1773 | Augusta 1714–1739 | Leopold 1716–1773 = 1. Josepha Waldstein 2. Wilhelmine Ogilvy | **Rudolph** 1719–1768 | *three girls & two boys who died in infancy* |

Princely branch

Stomfa branch

Vöröskő branch

| Leopold 1739–1799 = Therese Daun | Caroline 1740–1799 | Antonia 1742–1768 | *two boys & two girls who died in infancy* |

| Francis 1763–1803 | Leopold 1764–1825 = Caroline Jöchlinger | Joseph 1765–1778 *priest* | Charles 1767–1823 = Ernestine Hoyos | Ernest 1769–1832 Marie-Therese 1768–1829 | Philip 1775–1794 Ferdinand ✗ 1774–1840 |

one girl & one boy died in infancy

of the (Hungarian) Court; since the court was permanently at Vienna, run by the Imperial Marshal of the Court, the latter appointment was purely honorific. Five years on, on the death of Maria Theresia, he resigned all his offices and retired to private life, perhaps not seeing eye to eye with the reforms of Joseph II. He re-emerged on the public scene briefly in 1790, returning to County Csongrád to soothe tempers there in the wake of Josephine reforms and in preparation for that year's Parliament. From his wife Therese Daun he had nine children of whom seven sons attained adulthood. But only two married and only one of these had children: this Leopold, the fourth in succession, joined the regular army after a brief stint with the Hungarian Noble Guard, fought in several campaigns against the French, and retired with the rank of brigadier-general in 1810; his successors are briefly discussed in the next chapter.

Of his brothers Francis became a councillor with the North Italian provincial government at Gorizia; Joseph took holy orders; Charles retired from military life as a lieutenant-colonel; Ernest became a professed Knight of Malta and a soldier, but never rose beyond captain; Ferdinand, after a brief stint as a diplomat, retired to devote his life to the arts (the theatre in particular), social life, and the creation of a splendid park filled with exotic plants (all of this in Vienna and its environs); finally, Philip the youngest also joined the army, only to be killed in action, still only a captain, fighting the French at Landrecies—near the present Franco-Belgian border—in 1794 (where his brothers Leopold, Charles and Ernest were present too).

This leaves trampled-by-his-troopers'-horses Leopold's youngest son Rudolph: a soldier like his father before him, Rudolph fought in the Seven Years War against Frederick of Prussia, was soon colonel-in-chief of a regiment of hussars, and finally major-general. Inheriting his father's 5/8th share of Vöröskő—once again the youngest son did—he made it his main residence when not on active service; as a cavalryman he improved its facilities with new stabling for twenty-four horses, which had running water from a nearby spring, and a covered riding-school (both by now, alas, destroyed). In accordance with the taste of the age he also built up a collection of antiquities, ancient vessels, coins, and the like.

Of his two surviving sons John, the elder, became a gunner who retired with the rank of major before the French Revolutionary Wars started; his son Charles

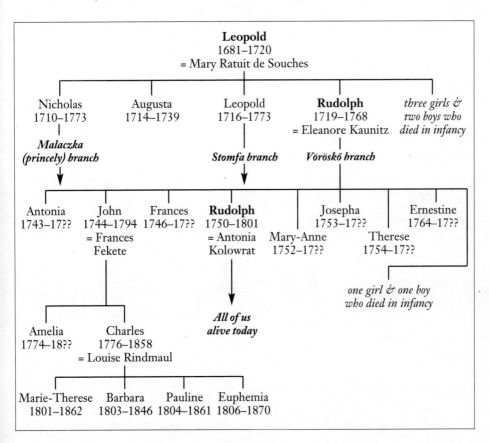

served in them briefly as a dragoon subaltern, fathered four daughters, and lived in uneventful country retirement to the ripe age of eighty-two.

The second son of Rudolph, also Rudolph, is the ancestor of all of us alive today. Soldiering for a while as a cavalry captain, he retired from the army with the rank of major, to die in 1801 aged but fifty. By then his wife had given birth to no less than fourteen children, nine of whom were still alive, and was expecting her fifteenth. The sub-branches of the family descended from four boys of this numerous progeny are the subject of the next chapters.

Finally, it is time to turn to the Junior Line, the descendants of the Palatine John:

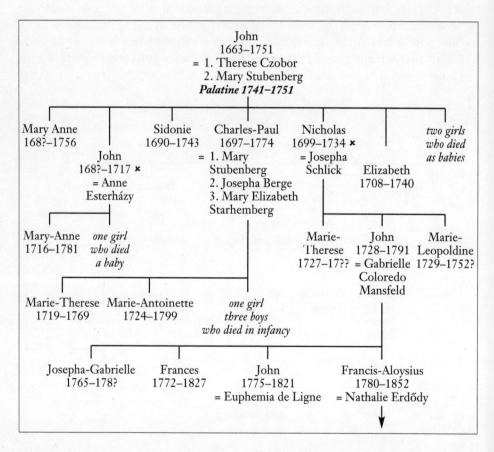

Of the Palatine John's three sons John the eldest died, by then a lieutenant-colonel, from wounds received in 1717 under Belgrade, leaving only a baby girl; his second son Charles-Paul rose to field marshal and died in his bed, but of his children only two daughters reached adulthood. The line—also known as the *Királyfa* line, from their preferred country seat—was carried on by his youngest son Nicholas, who also fell, colonel of a regiment of cuirassiers, fighting the French at Parma in 1734.

This Nicholas' only son John made it to lieutenant-general without getting killed fighting. The elder of his two sons, John again, married a daughter of the renown Prince de Ligne—wit, gossip, diplomat and memorialist, friend of Marie-Antoinette, Catherine the Great and Potemkin—but they had no children.

Thus the line was carried on, if but for two more generations, by the lieutenant-general's younger son Francis-Aloysius, who does not seem to have done anything noteworthy at all, apparently content to lead the idle life of a well-heeled landowner. But he did father the last member of this line, a John yet again, who is discussed in the next chapter.

Comparative decline (19th century to First World War)

*A*t the time the seventeenth century had turned into the eighteenth the family had numbered seven adult men, but five of these—four of them killed in action—left no sons. The descendants of the two survivors, the brothers Nicholas, in particular, and John (discussed in Chapters IV and V), had, however, repopulated the family thoroughly: by the dawn of the nineteenth century it consisted of twelve adult men and seven boys under twenty (one of whom died a few years later), divided into two main lines and one of these into three branches.

Many of these men and boys proved long-lived and sons were born to quite a few. However, this numerical burgeoning was not, sad to say, matched by a

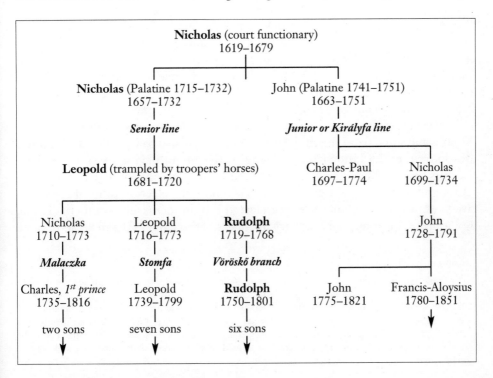

role in Hungary's public affairs—whether in military, political or administrative fields—comparable to that played by their forebears during the three preceding centuries.

⚜

True, the post-Napoleonic age was different: inherited wealth, title, and connections were still an advantage, but no longer assured a head-start quite as pronounced as in earlier times—although it had always taken more than just that head-start to rise to the top and make a serious impact.

Military careers were no longer as tempting, nor as rewarding, as they had been. Austria and Hungary—bound to joint defence by the 1723 legislation consequent upon the Pragmatic Sanction—had absorbed the lessons of defeats at the hands of Frederick the Great of Prussia and later Napoleon: the age demanded disciplined professional armies. Thus, by the nineteenth century the officer corps of the Imperial-Royal army (as it was then known) consisted to a large extent of men who had attended military cadet schools followed by officer training establishments; promotion was strictly by seniority and slow;[1] the Napoleonic wars over soldiering was, moreover, reduced to uneventful garrison duty in boring provincial towns.

Politics were, at least at the formal level, for a while static: Metternich, in charge in Austria, aimed only to freeze the *status quo*. For Hungary this meant unquestioning acceptance of the link with Austria, as formalised by the Pragmatic Sanction legislation of 1723; subordination of the Hungarian Chancellery's—the nearest thing to a ministry, if appointed by the monarch and located in Vienna—policy-making role to the views and influence of Metternich; and local administration of the country's day-by-day affairs by the Lieutenancy Council headed by the Archduke-Palatine Joseph,[2] brother of Francis I.

However, despite an attempt to do without them following termination of the Napoleonic wars, from the mid-1820s Parliaments had to be called again, if not all too frequently: Hungarians became restive about paying taxes and raising recruits unless these had been approved by parliamentary legislation. And, although the government did its best to promote the election of loyal conservatives, reform-minded members got elected too, in increasing numbers. These, and some of the younger hereditary members of the Upper Chamber, soon came

---

[1] The English practice of purchasing commissions, including promotions, was totally unknown; only archdukes were promoted rapidly, but rarely entrusted with actual commands.

[2] Resident at Buda, much to Vienna's distress he rapidly "went native" and endeavoured to champion Hungarian interests (indeed, at one point wrote a formal memorandum suggesting that Austria might benefit from adopting the "Hungarian model" i.e. Parliamentary legislation); since he was the monarch's brother Metternich could not stop him communicating directly with the Emperor-king, but he could "advise" on how to respond.

118

to be grouped round and inspired by the ideas of Count Stephen Széchenyi,[3] who stressed the need for Hungary's economic advance without questioning the constitutional link with Austria. The focus of Hungarian politics was now here, at Pest and Buda (still two separate towns) when Parliament was not in session, at Pressburg when it was, not at court in Vienna where, in any case, respectful but easy direct relations with the monarch—such as earlier Pálffys had had, notably Nicholas with Charles III, John with Maria Theresia, and Charles with Joseph II—were no longer in fashion: Metternich alone was to have direct influence with the monarch (who kept everybody at arms length: he was *Your Majesty* even to his own brothers).

Finally, although the most senior administrative dignities—Hungarian Chancellor, Justice of the Realm—still went to titled magnates, their deputies and subordinates, the councillors and secretaries of the Hungarian Chancellery and the Lieutenancy Council who did most of the work, were by now largely hardworking and loyal professionals from more modest backgrounds: such posts were no longer, as they had been, primarily training ground and stepping stones towards top positions for young magnates. Much the same applied to the diplomatic service: only senior ambassadorial posts went to wealthy magnates as a matter of course, since representing the Emperor-King at a foreign court in appropriate style was an expensive business; but there were few of these (London, Paris, Berlin, Saint Petersburg, the Holy See) and ambassadors often stayed *en poste* for decades. Independent thought and initiative were, moreover, discouraged in members of the home administration as much as in the diplomatic service.

⚜

To begin with the eldest, the princely, branch of the senior line, down to its extinction:

Joseph-Francis, the elder son of Charles the first prince, who eventually inherited the new title, did for a while serve as secretary, and later councillor, at the Hungarian Chancellery, but retired from these offices at much the same time as his father did from that of Chancellor, his public activity thereafter limited to county honorifics (hereditary Lord Lieutenant of County Pressburg). Charles' younger son Nicholas became a professed Knight of Malta, joined the army where he rose to major-general, and was in 1800 killed in action—the last of the fami-

---

[3] A dashing cavalry subaltern during the Napoleonic wars, his father Count Francis Széchényi (they spelt their surname differently) was a knight of the Golden Fleece, had been Maria Theresia's ambassador to several foreign courts, then a supporter of Joseph II's reforms: thus Stephen was well connected—even Metternich, and his wife Melanie in particular, were personal friends if political opponents—and also widely travelled, in the East as well as in western Europe, a member of the Reform Club in London, on close terms with England's Whig grandees (indeed, his brother Paul had married from there, a Lady Caroline Meade).

119

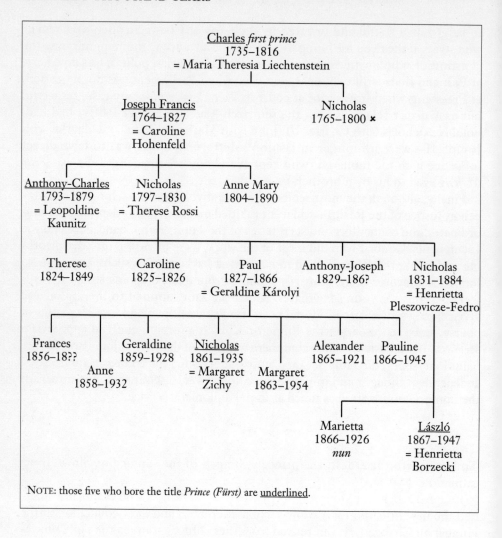

Charles *first prince*
1735–1816
= Maria Theresia Liechtenstein

Joseph Francis
1764–1827
= Caroline
Hohenfeld

Nicholas
1765–1800 ✗

Anthony-Charles
1793–1879
= Leopoldine
Kaunitz

Nicholas
1797–1830
= Therese Rossi

Anne Mary
1804–1890

Therese
1824–1849

Caroline
1825–1826

Paul
1827–1866
= Geraldine Károlyi

Anthony-Joseph
1829–186?

Nicholas
1831–1884
= Henrietta
Pleszovicze-Fedro

Frances
1856–18??

Anne
1858–1932

Geraldine
1859–1928

Nicholas
1861–1935
= Margaret
Zichy

Margaret
1863–1954

Alexander
1865–1921

Pauline
1866–1945

Marietta
1866–1926
nun

László
1867–1947
= Henrietta
Borzecki

NOTE: those five who bore the title *Prince (Fürst)* are underlined.

ly to so die—fighting the forces of the later *maréchal* Masséna in the Aosta Valley in Italy.

Anthony-Charles, the elder son of Joseph-Francis (why this sudden plethora of double names?), joined the foreign service, serving as minister extraordinary and plenipotentiary at the court of Saxony for a number of years in the 1820s; however, although invested with the Golden Fleece (as also the Russian Wladimir, Belgian Leopold and Bavarian Royal Crown orders), he never advanced to a serious ambassadorial post and left the service soon after he inherited the title in 1827; married but childless he lived to the ripe old age of eighty-six, with the result that the title was to jump one generation. His younger brother Nicholas —having served in campaigns in Italy, and been of the retinue that accompanied

Archduchess Leopoldine to Brazil for her marriage to its Emperor—in 1830 retired from active service still only a captain; it must, however, have been his destiny to die from a bullet, for he was inadvertently killed during a shoot, aged but thirty-three.

He had, however, by then fathered five children, including three boys. Paul the eldest retired from the army as a captain, conceivably (but this is not clear) because of the events of 1848-49 (*see* below); his brothers Anthony-Joseph, who remained a bachelor, and Nicholas, born posthumously, were also soldiers who never rose above major.

Paul carried on the line with two boys. The younger, Alexander, remained a bachelor, joined the diplomatic service, but never made it beyond councillor. His elder brother Nicholas—always talked about as Uncle *Nicolas*, the French version of his name, by my parents, both of whom were very fond of him (he died two years after I was born, so he may have known me, but I have no recollection of him)—inherited the title of Prince, to say nothing of sizeable estates, from his great-uncle when still a teenager. Apart from brief, by that time compulsory, military service, which gained him a reserve subaltern's commission, he led an entirely private life, except that up to the First World War he attended the Upper Chamber of Parliament regularly and participated in the work of some of its committees. However, although happily married, he had no children.

Of the many stories my parents told me about him I remember, alas, only very few. One of these, recounted by my mother, told of the occasion when she and my father were staying with him as a recently married young couple: Uncle Nicolas invited some boring country neighbours with several marriageable daughters to dinner, had my mother—who at the time had a slim boyish figure and short cropped hair—put on a dinner jacket for the evening, and introduced her and my father but vaguely as "my young cousins"; one daughter spent the evening flirting with my father, the other with my mother, and Uncle Nicolas enjoyed himself hugely.

On his death the title, as well as still substantial estates (many in Lower Austria on the border with Moravia, including a couple of splendid country houses), and the town house in Vienna on the Josefsplatz by the Hofburg, passed to his first cousin László, by then nearly seventy and, although he had been married, also childless. Thus, when the Second World War ended he alone of the family was still well off: in Austria, unlike Hungary and Czechoslovakia (whence most members of the family had fled from the Soviet advance in winter 1944–1945, to reach regions that would be occupied by the Western Allies), estates were not expropriated after the war. But by then he was a widower in his dotage: under the influence of a self-claimed lady-friend from his remote youth, who suddenly (re?)emerged with the alleged fruit of their past dalliances, a daughter, in tow, just days before he died he signed—by then he was in no condition to draw up—a new will, from which all members of the family were excluded (family entails had ceased to be recognised in Austrian property law after 1918, but Uncle Nicolas had dis-

121

posed of his estate as though such were still in force); this was exceptionally hard on his penniless refugee cousins, especially the elderly among them. With him the princely branch of the family died out.[4]

⚜

Had it died out before 1919, when there still was a reigning monarch, the title would doubtless have been transferred to the next-most-senior, the *Stomfa*, branch, descended from the second son of the "trampled-by-his-troopers-horses" Leopold. By now also extinct, it is summarised to the end, 1963, below.

The fourth Leopold had—as told in the previous chapter—joined the army fighting revolutionary France and then Napoleon, to retire from the army a brigadier general in 1810. The only one of seven brothers to have children, his son, the fifth Leopold in succession, appears to have done little of note during his long life (he was ninety-three by the time he died in 1900). Little, that is, beyond extending his surname to Pálffy-Daun and becoming *Duke of Theano* (all of which went with appropriate extensions and modifications to his and his descendants' coat-of-arms): the third Leopold had, about a century earlier, married a Countess Therese Daun, whose soldier father, having won battles in Italy, had been rewarded with that Italian title (much of northern Italy was at the time ruled by Habsburgs). When the Daun family died out in the 1850s the fifth Leopold sought and obtained imperial-royal permission to add his grandmother's surname to his own, and a few years later also to use the Italian title that had been granted to her father.

Of the first Pálffy-Daun's four sons the eldest—the sixth and last Leopold—soldiered a bit, in the Imperial-Royal and later the Papal Armies (this was just before the new Kingdom of Italy swallowed the Papal State), developed an interest in art and history, and died childless at the age of fifty. He, however, appears to have been the first to suggest at a family reunion—such seem to have been held regularly in those days—that a family history, a *Pálffy Codex*, be compiled (some of the sources referred to in the *Bibliography* claim to be in part based upon material gathered for that purpose; where is it now?): the present volume might be considered its belated implementation. The third son, George, also took service in the Papal Army that was attempting to fend off Victor Emanuel, only to be shot dead, in his early twenties, in a duel fought, it is not known over what, with a (not further specified) Prince Odescalchi at Viterbo; the fourth and youngest son, Charles, took holy orders.

Only the second son, the first of this branch to be called William, outlived his father by a few years, having soldiered in the Imperial-Royal Army before transferring, after the Compromise of 1867 (*see* below), to the newly created distinct

---

[4] Even as this was being written the lady-friend's heirs and successors auctioned off, at Vienna in November 2005, all remaining family portraits, as well as many other objects (china, furniture, etc.), once the possession of the princely branch, in a sale they had the *chutzpah* to advertise as "From the Estate of Prince Pálffy".

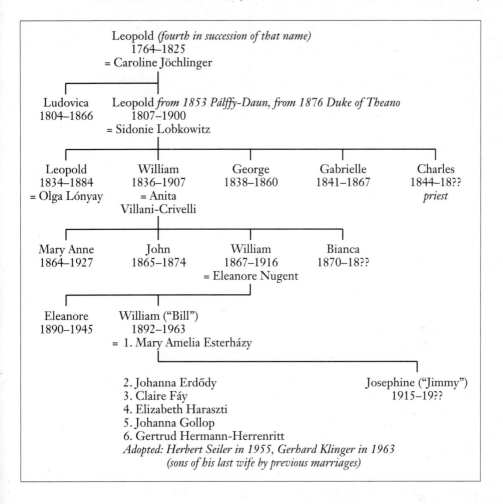

Hungarian Army *(honvédség)*, from which he retired as a major-general. His son, the second William (an elder son, John, had died as a child) was liberal member of Parliament for a few years, then appointed Lord Lieutenant of the County of Mosony; he died, not yet fifty, during the First World War. Finally, his son, the third and last William, universally known as Bill, married repeatedly but had only one daughter—Josephine, generally known as Jimmy[5]—and lived until 1963, the last decades of his life in emigration in South America.

---

[5] It was she who gave us two pairs of horses and two carts in late autumn 1944, should we wish to flee west from Budapest before the Soviet Army got there, with the words *rather you than either the Germans or the Russians*; horses, carts and a stable-boy made it to Budapest from eastern Hungary, got stuck with us during the siege, and the poor horses perished when the house next door where they were stabled took a hit and collapsed.

Which finally brings us to the *Vöröskő* branch of the family, carried on by the descendants of the younger Rudolph, ancestor of all Pálffys alive today.

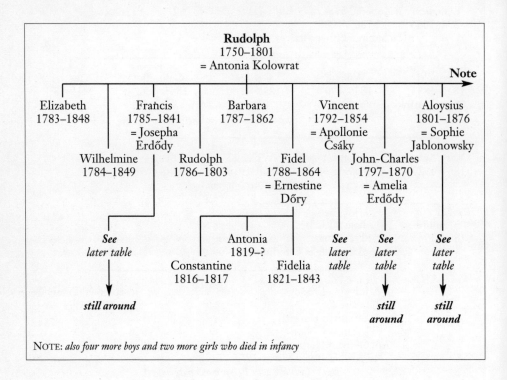

When he died in spring 1801 he left, it will be recalled from the preceding chapter, a pregnant widow: nine of the fourteen children she had already borne by then were alive and well, five of them boys, as was to be the child she was bearing at the time.[6] One of these boys, yet another Rudolph, died as a teenager, but the other five grew up to marry, four of them becoming the originators of as many sub-branches, three of which are still very much around.

The only one of Rudolph's sons to rise to national prominence—if not approbation—was Fidel, who failed to initiate a sub-branch. Initially employed at the Lieutenancy Council, where he soon became councillor, he moved on to the Hungarian Chancellery and rapidly rose to head a department. Following a brief stint as Lord Lieutenant of County Árva he returned to the centre of affairs, appointed

---

[6] Maria Theresia had given birth to sixteen, and her son Leopold II had had fifteen children: these royal examples seem to have encouraged many of their subjects to have large families too.

principal treasurer *(főtárnokmester)* and then a member of the *Tabula Septemviralis*, Hungary's highest court of law at the time. Still only thirty-two, he was next also appointed acting Lord Lieutenant of County Pressburg; ten years later he became Master of the Treasury, the nearest thing to a Hungarian minister of finance at the time; finally, in 1835, he was promoted to the office of Hungarian Chancellor, which had been held by his father's first cousin Charles (raised to Prince on his retirement) for twenty-two years.

Kinship apart they had nothing in common. Charles, a Freemason (indeed, Grand Master of all Hungarian lodges) and adherent of Enlightenment progress, never ceased to be a Hungarian, mindful of the needs and aspirations of his country and countrymen, to promote which he used his office even while he loyally served three Habsburg monarchs in succession. Fidel, in contrast, was a dyed-in-the-wool conservative, an unquestioning adherent of Metternich and his system, an obedient bureaucrat loyal the Habsburg Crown only, equally impatient of progressive notions and Hungarian constitutional "pretensions".[7]

Which was, of course, exactly why he was appointed Hungarian Chancellor at that juncture: the Parliament called in 1832 was still in session, and many of its members, who had by then organised themselves into a coherent group, were voicing reformist views and national demands that ran counter to and threatened to undermine the post-Napoleonic *status quo* imposed by Metternich (who was even more completely in control from 1835, following the death of Francis I and the accession of his somewhat simple-minded, epileptic, son Ferdinand V[8]). Fidel, bearer of an historic Hungarian name but otherwise entirely Austrian in outlook, was seen as the perfect person to handle this situation. He did not, in fact, handle it very effectively, merely became extremely unpopular in Hungary. He became even more so once Parliament had been dissolved, when he had members of the reform-minded Conversation Society arrested for "sedition", and then Louis Kossuth and Baron Nicholas Wesselényi (the most outspokenly radical among younger hereditary members of the Upper Chamber), both to be charged with and sentenced for "treason".[9]

---

[7] In mitigation one should perhaps add that, only twelve when his father died, he grew up entirely under the influence of his mother: not only did she come from a family, Kolowrat, that had long been firmly attached to the ruling dynasty and suspicious of Hungary, but—a young widow with ten children to look after—she would also have felt it necessary to imbue her children with loyalty to the dynasty in order to promote their careers.

[8] Ferdinand I in Austria, where they had restarted numbering following dissolution of the Holy Roman Empire.

[9] Kossuth spent three years in the comfort that was in those days afforded political prisoners learning English and studying the latest West European political and economic literature; the sanguine Wesselényi— a hero even to those not much interested in politics: when devastating floods hit Pest in winter 1838, destroying over half its houses, he personally rescued hundreds from the flooded ruins while others were still talking of relief committees—on the other hand went blind, and eventually lost the balance of his mind, during his incarceration.

Erdödi Gróf

PÁLFFY FIDELIS,

Vöröskő Vár' Örököse,

Magyar Ország Királyi Fő Tárnok Mestere

s a't.

Fidel Pálffy a most unpopular Hungarian Chancellor
in the 1830s since utterly devoted to Metternich's system

So unpopular was Fidel's Chancellorship in Hungary that Metternich judged it prudent to have him dropped—to be replaced by the more moderate Count Anthony Mailáth—before elections to the next Parliament, due to meet in 1839, were called: it was becoming apparent that his continued presence as Hungarian

Chancellor would merely boost the election prospects of reformist parliamentary candidates opposed to the unpopular ultra-conservative policies with which his period of office was associated. As a sop he was invested with the Golden Fleece before retiring from public life for good.

⚜

The Parliaments of the 1830s and 1840s were harbingers of events about to overtake the country; a brief account of these is here necessary, to provide context for the next part of our story.

Although the government employed every dirty trick at its disposal—intimidation and bribery in the counties, "forgetting" to invite reform-minded hereditaries to take their seats in the Upper Chamber, and the like—progressives calling for reforms steadily gained ground in Parliament. In the course of the 1840s, moreover, ever more radical views and voices, which went far beyond the reasonable demands of the reformists, began to be heard too (so much so that in 1847 Count Stephen Széchenyi, desperately worried by this development, stood for and was elected to a seat in the Lower Chamber[10] in order to be able to debate against Kossuth—proponent of the radical trend and also elected that year—face to face on the floor of the House). In retrospect it is clear that these developments could have been contained and channelled into positive advances had Metternich been willing to abandon rigid adherence to the system imposed after the Napoleonic Wars, and had he let the monarch—who merely did as Metternich advised—make concessions to Hungarian aspirations (as also to the increasingly restive peoples of Austria). But age was making him less, not more, flexible, while court circles, remembering how events had unfolded in France after 1789, feared that *any* concession and reform would inevitably result in bloody developments similar to those that had led Marie-Antoinette to the guillotine.[11]

In February 1848 revolution broke out in Paris, deposing the mild and liberal-minded "citizen-king" Louis-Philippe. News of these events spread rapidly across Europe, and in its wake revolutionary stirrings: by mid-March Vienna was affected too, and soon Metternich considered it safest to resign and flee abroad.[12] This encouraged the Hungarian Parliament, in session at Pressburg, to pass radically

---

[10] Hereditary members of the Upper Chamber could always opt to stand for and be elected to the Lower, merely waiving their right to sit in the Upper for the duration of that Parliament.

[11] It is easy to forget how vividly people still remembered, a mere fifty years on, the Paris terror of 1793: my maternal grandfather (born 1846) well remembered stories of its horror told him as a boy by his grandmother, a teenager at the time of the French Revolution, who had heard of them from French émigrés.

[12] To settle, like Louis-Philippe (who had already lived there earlier too), in the vicinity of Twickenham.

reformist—for the time and place—legislation which, in the absence of Metter-nich, received the royal assent of Ferdinand V in April, whence this raft of legis-lation has become known as "the April Laws".[13]

In essence these laws represented a belated leap from the sixteenth into the nineteenth century: all special privileges attaching to noble status were abolished (although the Upper Chamber of Parliament including titled hereditary mem-bers was retained) as was the institution of tied peasantry, all citizens thus becom-ing legally equal in all respects, except that the franchise—as was general across Europe in those days—was tied to property, income or educational qualifications;[14] Transylvania was to be re-united with the Kingdom of Hungary once its own Parliament approved (which soon happened); the Hungarian Chan-cellery was abolished,[15] its place to be taken by a responsible ministry answer-able to Parliament (both to have their seat at Buda) not the king: henceforth no royal decree, enactment or appointment was to be valid unless countersigned by the appropriate minister. This is just the gist, but it gives the flavour—yet court circles wedded to *ancien régime* attitudes perceived these measures to be verging on revolutionary Jacobinism.

A ministry of all talents was formed—and elections held on the new franchise, which confirmed it in office—with Count Louis Batthyány as prime minister: a man of integrity and high moral principles, he unfortunately lacked the experi-ence and force of personality needed to impose his will and forge a coherent team out of the disparate personalities and political views present in his Cabi-net. Unable to resolve increasingly acrimonious tensions between court and nation, nor to control the ever more radical tendencies of Kossuth and the Par-liamentary group led by Madarász (who and which were to a large extent respon-sible for those tensions), by autumn the Batthyány Ministry resigned and the running of affairs was taken over by a Defence Committee headed by Kossuth. By now Austria, having successfully "pacified" northern Italy, was in a position to use armed force against Hungary—which had already had to deal with upris-ings by Serbs in the south, numerous Vlachs in and near Transylvania, and a formal armed attack from Croatia, all fomented by Vienna—so that for almost a year, until the following August when the Hungarian army surrendered to the commander of the Russian troops the czar had sent to Austria's aid, Austria and Hungary were fighting a full-scale war.

---

[13] The events of 15 March 1848 at Pest and Buda, much celebrated, and elevated into chief national holi-day in the twentieth century, were a splendid operetta-revolution, copiously written about afterwards since many of its principal participants were young writers and poets, but at the time their impact upon developments was negligible.

[14] But with the necessary twist that the poorest petty nobles, who had hitherto had the vote but would now have failed to qualify, were exempted from these qualifications: to disenfranchise them now was unthinkable.

[15] The very last Hungarian Chancellor was my great-grandfather, Count George Apponyi.

Hungarian attitudes to all of this were not uniform, but ranged from enthusiastic support through cautious approval, disquiet, and serious misgivings, to out and out rejection, even within the same family (including ours[16]); as time went by attitudes shifted, moreover, in the light of developments. By autumn 1848 Széchenyi, a member of the Batthyány cabinet, had had a complete nervous breakdown and had to be institutionalised; many more began to worry about the increasingly intransigent line taken by the Defence Committee headed by Kossuth, and by that winter a "peace party" had emerged, which put out feelers to Vienna that were, however, rejected. For things had moved on in Austria too: in October his immediate family had coerced Ferdinand V into resigning in favour of his nephew, the then eighteen year old Francis Joseph who—completely under the influence of his mother the Archduchess Sophie[17] and her arch-conservative circle—promptly declared, in an amazingly novel constitutional twist, that he did not consider his predecessor's royal assent to the April Laws binding on himself.

By winter the Hungarian government and Parliament had moved to Debrecen in the east of the country; quite a few of the more moderate members, who could no longer stomach the Defence Committee's handling of affairs, quietly failed to follow. At that point Francis Joseph "abolished" Hungary as a distinct kingdom by decree, reducing it to the status of a province of the Austrian Empire; Kossuth responded by stampeding what remained of Parliament into deposing the House of Habsburg and appointing him acting head of state, Governor, pending the election of a new king. This frightened off even more Hungarians: fighting to force the monarch to adhere to valid laws was one thing, with numerous precedents (rooted in the Golden Bull's ancient *ius resitendi* clause, even if this clause had by then long been formally abrogated)—but declaring the ruling house deposed was unprecedented, and abhorrent to many.

By August 1849 it was all over, an outcome that became inevitable once the Czar—incensed to see Poles who had played prominent roles in the 1830 anti-Russian uprising now fighting with the Hungarians—had agreed to send an army to support Austria. The Austrian commander Field Marshal Haynau, already known from his earlier actions to "pacify" northern Italy as *The Hyena of Brescia*, promptly instituted a reign of terror. Kossuth and some of his immediate circle had fled to Turkey; Prince Pashkievich the Russian commander insisted that General Görgey, the last Hungarian commander-in-chief who had signed the surren-

---

[16] If not to the extent of some others: in the character sketches he wrote in the early 1850s (*Magyarországi és erdélyi urak*, 'Gentlemen of Hungary and Transylvania') János Pálffy—of the Transylvanian family of the same name, not a relative—mentions the story of two brothers called Bujanovich, who served as officers in the opposing, Hungarian and Austrian, armies. At one point they found themselves fighting in the same battle; they never came face to face during it, but years later asked each other what they would have done had this happened. *"Fight on to kill"* was the response of both *"but then commit suicide rather than live with the memory of fratricide."*

[17] For years she insisted, for instance, on checking *and approving* his official appointments diary every day.

der, be spared;[18] but within months Haynau had thirteen Hungarian generals executed at Arad, as also Batthyány at Pest. Military tribunals sentenced many more, including civilians, to death—some *in absentia:* they were hanged symbolically by having their name nailed to the gallows—and large numbers to long prison terms; Hungarian officers were reduced to the ranks and sent to serve as privates in Austrian regiments in northern Italy and elsewhere.

By the following year Vienna put a stop to executions, which were harming Austria's image abroad, but the crack-down continued: all those who had played any part in Hungary's government, administration or army during 1848-49, or had just indicated undue sympathy with that cause, continued to be hunted down and imprisoned.[19] Direct rule from Vienna was administered on the spot by bureaucrats sent to Hungary from elsewhere in the Austrian Empire, and German was made the only official language of administration, law courts, and all education above primary level: from the name of Austria's then chief minister the whole period is known as the Bach Era. The bulk of those not in prison or emigration (the latter including not a few who, although they had not participated in the events of 1848-49 directly, chose to escape abroad from the oppressive atmosphere in Hungary[20]) adopted sullen passivity; a few, a reviled few, co-operated and accepted office to become known, from the fancy uniform invented for them, as "Bach-hussars".

It took above a decade and a succession of military defeats—beginning in northern Italy at the hands of Napoleon III and culminating at Königgrätz (Sadowa) at the hands of Prussia—for Francis Joseph to begin to seek a way out of this situation. Neither an all-Austrian constitution imposed from above, which still treated Hungary as just another Austrian province, nor an attempt to return to something resembling the *status quo ante 1848* proved acceptable. Finally in 1867 an agreement, based on a scheme put forward by Francis Deák—minister of justice in the Batthyány government of 1848—and on the April Laws of 1848, was hammered out: in general parlance known as the **Compromise** *(kiegyezés, Ausgleich)* it was enacted by the Parliament called (on the 1848 franchise) to do so as Act XII of 1867, opening the way for Francis Joseph to be crowned King of Hungary,[21] which was henceforth to be an equal partner in the Austro-Hungarian Dual Monarchy.

---

[18] Görgey, who had begun his military career in the Hungarian Noble Guard, lived to the eve of the First World War (initially under house arrest in Austria) much reviled—unjustly—for having surrendered and survived.

[19] The case of the author Imre Madách is typical: learning that he was about to be arrested for having briefly harboured Kossuth's secretary in autumn 1849, he hid on a country neighbour's estate disguised as a coachman; unfortunately, driving his "employer" and an Austrian official somewhere he thoughtlessly turned round to correct a classical reference one of them had got wrong. His cover blown he was arrested and imprisoned.

[20] My great-grandfather, Count George Apponyi the last Hungarian Chancellor, was one of these.

[21] Whose prime minister was now Count Julius Andrássy, sentenced to death and "executed" *in absentia* in 1849: a handsome man, in his Paris exile he was known as *le beau pendu.*

For the next half-century (almost), to the First Word War, this framework—albeit on occasion, especially towards the end, creaking—worked.

Returning to the decades before 1848-49, the story of the three sons of Rudolph, who originated the three sub-branches of the Vöröskő branch, and of their nineteenth century descendants can be resumed (Fidel, the son who did not originate a sub-branch, has already been discussed). Best taken in turn, we shall start with the sub-branch that descends from Francis the eldest (for clarity's sake his sisters, and the brother who died as a teenager, are left off the tables that follow).

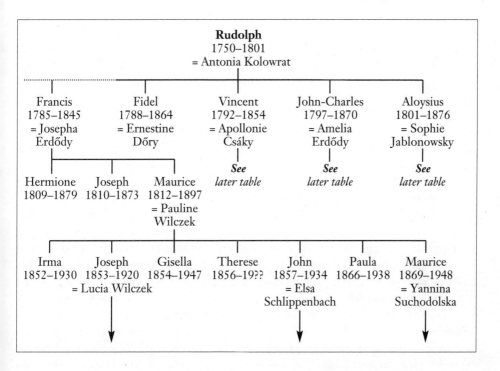

Francis himself does not seem to have done much beyond managing his estates; having married Countess Josepha Erdődy—a miniature of whom is in my possession—in his early twenties, he found himself a widower with three young children before he was thirty, and this may have discouraged him from seeking a public career. At the time of their mother's death in 1813 their daughter Hermione was but four, their elder son Joseph three, and Maurice the youngest not even a year old. Whether owing to losing their mother when still so young—who and how brought them up, looked after them, gave them affection?—it is impossible to tell, but perhaps owing to sibling-rivalry the two boys developed into very different personalities.

Joseph threw himself into county, and then national, politics as soon as he was of an age to do so. Ensured of a seat in the Upper Chamber of the Parliament of 1839–1840 on coming of age,[22] he there firmly allied himself with the reformist-progressive minority among the hereditaries, soon becoming well-known (or notorious, depending on point if view) for his speeches attacking the government's ultra-conservative policies, and by the next Parliament of 1843–1844 emerged as one of the leading figures of the progressive party. In 1848 a supporter of the April Laws and the new constitutional Batthyány government he had, however, no stomach for the radical trends that became prevalent when Kossuth took over, nor for open warfare with Austria, and by that autumn retired to his estates. Only in the run-up to the *Compromise* did he become active in politics again: by 1865 a Parliament had met as part of Francis Joseph's the attempt to restore the *status quo ante 1848*, and Joseph was of the delegation that delivered its formal rejection of that initiative to the monarch. Once the *Compromise* of 1867 had been achieved, and Francis Joseph crowned, he seems to have withdrawn from active politics, to die, still a bachelor, a few years later.

The outlook and career of his younger brother Maurice, my great-grandfather, was very different. Having joined the army when still virtually a boy, by the time he was twenty he was already captain in a regiment of cuirassiers; not, however, promoted further during the next fifteen years, in 1847 he resigned his commission and accepted the post of governor of County Pressburg.[23] This position he left on formation of the constitutional Batthyány government in 1848, a development to which he, unlike his brother, was deeply opposed. In September of that year, as the crisis between Hungary and Austria was getting ever more bitter, a mob encouraged by extreme radicals murdered General Count Lamberg, sent to Pest by the Court to attempt to negotiate an accommodation, as his coach was crossing the pontoon bridge that linked Buda and Pest (the first permanent bridge was not yet quite completed). This uncalled-for bloody event shook many: Maurice it sent scurrying to Vienna to offer his services.

Instantly promoted major—court circles must have been delighted to find the bearer of such a prominent Hungarian name openly declare against those "rebels"—he was attached to the Austrian army commanded by Prince Windisch-graetz; when this took Győr in December he was entrusted with the honour of

---

[22] In Hungary, until after the Second World War, the age of majority was 24, so he missed the previous Parliament of 1832 by a whisker.

[23] Ahead of elections to the Parliament of 1847 the government took to appointing governors to head counties—in place of lords lieutenant who, it feared, might be too amenable to local pressures—in order to better 'influence' the elections in favour of pro-government candidates.

delivering the town's keys to the new ruler, Francis Joseph, at Olmütz where the Court, scared of Vienna, was still cowering. Completely dedicated to the Austrian side against his compatriots, in spring he added his signature to a manifesto issued by a handful of like-minded aristocrats that urged the people of Hungary to lay down their arms, and then he became active in trying to raise, with little success, Hungarian volunteers to fight the "rebels".

At about this time he was promoted at first lieutenant-colonel in the gendarmerie, then colonel of hussars. Hungary by now crushed and subject to Vienna's direct rule, in 1852 he accepted the Order of St Stephen (albeit, since the Court appears to have been grudging with rewards, merely the lowest of its three grades). By 1855 he had been promoted major-general in command of a cavalry division, by 1859 lieutenant general commanding an army corps. Finally, in 1861, he was also named colonel-in-chief—a purely honorific appointment—of the 15ᵗʰ Hussars. Loyalty to court against nation had clearly not harmed the military career of the erstwhile captain not judged deserving of promotion for fifteen long years.

In 1861 he was also appointed military governor of Hungary, Vienna's all-powerful representative in the country. In this capacity he carried out all of Vienna's instructions with unstinting devotion, indeed zeal beyond the call of duty, seeing to it that any slightest manifestation of "rebellious" attitudes by public or press was promptly repressed and that counties, for long the seats of national consciousness, were firmly controlled,[24] so much so that from time to time he even found himself involved in argumentative disputes with the King's Bench Court, which was trying to maintain a degree of judicial impartiality and adherence to legal forms. True, he resigned—but was rapidly prevailed upon to withdraw his resignation—when the then Austrian chief minister Schmerling wished to modify the franchise in Hungary so as to favour the country's ethnic minorities at the expense of Hungarians (this was just before the Parliament of 1865, already mentioned in connection with his brother Joseph, was to be called).

Soon after he was, however, dismissed from the post of military governor and returned to active service in the army, in time to fight against the *Rissorgimento* in Italy (where he received a sabre-wound at the Battle of Custozza, a risk to which few lieutenant generals expose themselves these days). In 1867, the *Compromise* now in place, he retired from the army (and was some years later invested with the Golden Fleece, as well as being promoted field marshal). For the rest of his years (he lived to be eighty-five) he frequented the Upper Chamber of Parliament, often speaking—predictably: against—reform of that chamber

---

[24] A family anecdote illustrative of this spirit, handed down by my father, tells of the occasion when he arrived on an inspection tour in a county town and found only the Hungarian red-white-and-green tricolour, but not the Austrian Imperial black-and-yellow colours, flying on the county hall: looking at the reception committee of local notables there awaiting him, he ordered the parish priest stripped of his black soutane, the mayor of his yellowish summer suit, and had these clothes run up the flag-pole in place of the Hungarian tricolour.

(finally carried in 1885) and diminution of the role and standing of the Catholic Church.[25]

Having in 1850 married Marie-Pauline Wilczek—sister of Count Hans Wilczek, well known for his dedication to restoring mediæval castles, the most famous of them Kreuzenstein near Vienna[26]—the first five of their seven children, three girls and two boys, were born at few-year intervals; then, after a gap of near on a decade, another girl and finally my grandfather, also baptised Maurice. If family legend is to be believed, great-grandfather Maurice was a typically remote and domineering Victorian father: that my grandfather, away at boarding school most of the year, never had a room of his own in the family home at Szomolány has already been mentioned; his sisters were dumped in convent schools, and the good nuns paid extra to keep them during the holidays too: then, when of marriageable age, they were retrieved from the convent, equipped with ball-gowns, and launched into society to find a husband—amazingly, all but one did (she, Aunt Irma, later found her vocation looking after her nephew, my Uncle Pali mentioned in the *Prologue*).

His eldest son Joseph, having taken a Law degree as was usual in those days (it was virtually a requirement for government and administrative posts) then, unusually for the times, went on to study natural sciences at the Vienna Polytechnic, followed by a stint at an agricultural college. Next he set out on travels, initially a grand tour of Europe, then to Arabia and the Sudan, and up several tributaries of the Blue Nile into Abyssinia. Having, perhaps, had enough of hot climates, in the 1880s he joined an Austro-Hungarian arctic expedition, sponsored by his uncle (and father-in-law: he had married a first cousin) Hans Wilczek, whose main purpose was to explore, and set up meteorological observation posts on, Jan Mayen Island; since the island was previously unmapped he gave his name to one of its extinct volcanoes: the large Times Atlas of the World still shows the Pálffy Crater on the map of Jan Mayen Island and lists it in its index.[27]

---

[25] The Upper Chamber contained far too many ex officio members, too many pennyless hereditaries, but of the country's Churches only the Catholic bishops had seats; this was modified in 1885. The main Church-related issues were divorce, possible for Protestants but not Catholics, and mixed—Catholic-Protestant—marriages and the religion of children born of these: as the law, of which the Church disapproved, then stood sons were to be baptised into their father's and daughters into their mother's religion. Eventually, and against the resistance of the Catholic hierarchy, state registration of all births, marriages (and hencee state divorce), and deaths was introduced, while church weddings and baptisms were relegated to the private sphere.

[26] He was given to idiosyncrasy in other matters too. When Napoleon III and Eugénie came to Vienna on a state visit he was detailed to accompany the empress on a tour of the major construction works then in progress as the old city walls were being replaced by the Ringstrasse; on her expressing polite interest in a viaduct being built, he simply he picked her up bodily (he was a big, strong man) and carried her across the unfinished structure that was yet narrow and without banisters; Court and Ministry of Foreign Affairs were not amused.

[27] His grandson, my cousin Martin, visited the place, travelling there under sail, shortly after the original expedition's centenary: he reports that the crater, to whose rim he climbed, is apparently still in good condition.

Eventually he took over the running of the extensive family estates, much of them forest, centred on Szomolány. Being dedicated to stalking and shooting, during the autumn all forestry work, whose noise might disturb the rutting red deer, was suspended for several months. Being a fair sportsman, he was also very strict with shooting guests: those who missed were given a single second chance that season, but those who merely wounded an animal without killing it were never invited again. He died with the old world shortly after the First World War came to an end; his attempts to re-build Szomolány Castle, and his three sons my uncles Józsi, Peter and Carl, are mentioned in the *Prologue.*

His brother John, generally known as Hans, received enough of their father's estates, centred on Pudmericz not far from Szomolány, to lead the comfortable life of a country gentleman (and to commission a Viennese architect to raise the mock-Loire-château mentioned in the *Prologue*), sporadically attending the Upper Chamber of Parliament at Budapest, where he was for a time a member of the Committee that occupied itself with the joint Austro-Hungarian national debt. A bachelor into his forties, he then married Countess Elizabeth Schlippenbach; within a year they had a son who, although actually baptised Francis of Paula,[28] was known to everybody as Pali, the Hungarian diminutive of Pál i.e. Paul (under which name he later even published books): for some reason it was the qualifier that stuck. Not many years later she bolted with an Italian naval officer, her husband divorced her, and their child—my Uncle Pali, already mentioned in the *Prologue*—was brought up by his unmarried aunt Irma.

The third son, and youngest child, of old Maurice was my grandfather, also Maurice but generally known as Morkó. Educated in the Jesuit boarding school at Kalksburg in Austria,[29] he then obtained a Law degree and joined the Austro-Hungarian diplomatic service; he and his life are written about in the *Prologue.*

The sub-branch descended from Rudolph's son Vincent appeared numerous: seven children and nine grandchildren who survived into adulthood.

Vincent himself had served as a cavalry officer during the final years of the Napoleonic Wars, but had retired from the army still only captain soon after they were over, and thereafter led the peaceful life of an unambitious country gentleman for almost four decades, fathering ten children, seven of whom attained adulthood. The two boys among these had, between them, ten children (one of whom died in infancy). Nevertheless, in 1924 that sub-branch died out in Vincent's grand-

---

[28] There being at least five Saints Francis—in the sequence of their birth: of Assisi, of Paula, Xavier, Borgia, and of Sales—it is quite common to indicate which of these is the infant's patron saint; my father's was Xavier.

[29] Where my maternal grandfather Albert Apponyi had also been a pupil, if some decades earlier.

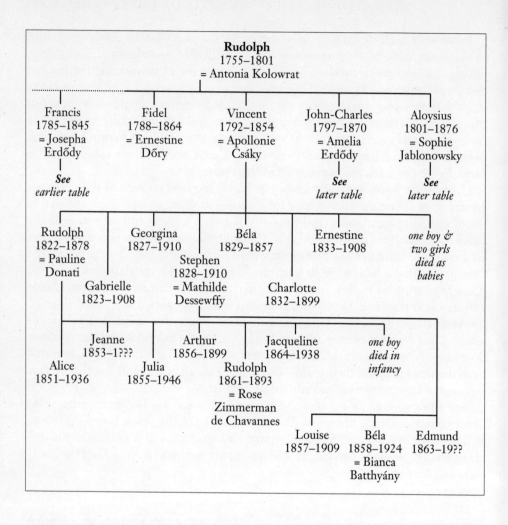

son Béla. However, owing to the numerous daughters born into this sub-branch we have lots of, if somewhat remote, relatives by marriage, such as current-day members of the Schell and Bolza families (through Vincent's daughter Ernestine and granddaughter Alice, respectively).

Vincent's eldest son Rudolph appears to have led an entirely private life; of his three sons one died in infancy, one unmarried in his thirties, while the third, also Rudolph, at Lausanne married a lady of uncertain social standing but considerable means, with whom he settled in the United States; not many years later he died and was buried there, hardly into his thirties.[30]

---

[30] She outlived him by more than four decades, and in the 1930s willed her dollars to several (all?) Pálffy men of my father's generation, in equal dollops to each.

Only the middle son, Stephen, was active on the public scene, in a pattern that reflects the shifting politics of the period. In 1848, shortly after he had taken a Law degree, he joined the then newly created Hungarian Ministry of the Interior as a civil servant, in the lowly grade of *fogalmazó*.[31] However, unable—like many others—to accept the ever more intransigently radical policies pursued by Kossuth and the National Defence Committee that had replaced the Batthyány government, by the end of that year, as Parliament and government moved from Pest to Debrecen, he quietly retired to private life. But at his father's insistence—in those days adult sons still did as their fathers wished—he soon accepted an appointment in the "Hungarian section" of the supreme court at Vienna, whence he was in 1857 transferred to the (briefly resuscitated) Lieutenancy Council. His father by now dead, in 1859 he finally abandoned government service for good, devoting himself for the rest of his life—apart from a brief stint as an elected member of the abortive Parliament of 1865—to running the family estates and promoting agricultural improvements in his home County of Pressburg. His elder son Béla, married but childless (and the penultimate of the family to own and inhabit Vöröskő[32]), led the peaceful life of a country gentleman—only interrupted by attendance in the Upper Chamber of Parliament, until this body was dissolved at the end of the First World War—to his death in 1924. Edmund the younger son, a cavalry officer, remained a bachelor.

Vincent's unmarried youngest son Béla died when not yet thirty, captain in a regiment of hussars. What is perhaps interesting about him is that he appears to have been the first Pálffy to receive an out-and-out Hungarian name in baptism:[33] all earlier, and most later, men of the family had solidly international saints' names (John, Nicholas, Charles, Francis, Stephen the most popular, in that order) unless—initially usually because a monarch stood godfather—names common in the House of Habsburg (Ferdinand, Leopold, Rudolph). Vincent's eldest son was named Rudolph, conceivably for his grandfather, and the second Stephen: why the choice of Béla for the youngest remains unknown, but a first cousin of his born five years later (*see* below) was given the even more Hungarian name Géza.[34] The upsurge of interest in the mediæval period characteristic of the 1820s–1830s might be the reason.

John-Charles, Rudolph's third son to originate a sub-branch, joined the army as an ensign at seventeen.

---

[31] This roughly corresponds to what was the starting grade in the Administrative Class of England's civil service.

[32] By his death situated in the new Czechoslovakia, whose law no longer recognised entails, he willed it to the youngest son of his second cousin once removed Joseph, my Uncle Carl.

[33] The name of four of Hungary's mediæval Árpád kings—two of them, III and IV, outstanding—Béla is on occasion translated (especially in older Austro-German sources) as Adalbert but, one suspects, only in order to associate it with a recognised saint.

[34] Duke Géza (r. 972–997) was the father of king Saint Stephen, and there were also several Árpád kings of that name.

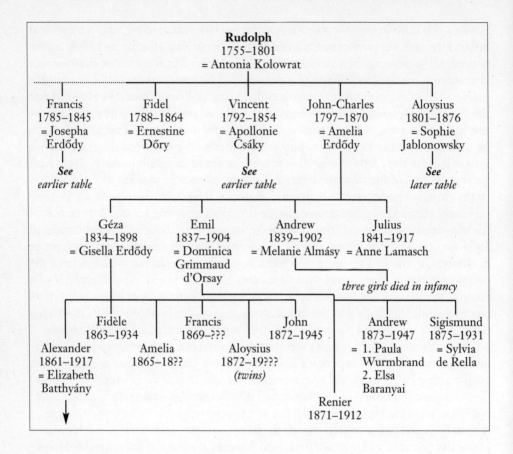

Rudolph
1755–1801
= Antonia Kolowrat

Francis
1785–1845
= Josepha
Erdődy

See
earlier table

Fidel
1788–1864
= Ernestine
Dőry

Vincent
1792–1854
= Apollonie
Csáky

See
earlier table

John-Charles
1797–1870
= Amelia
Erdődy

Aloysius
1801–1876
= Sophie
Jablonowsky

See
later table

Géza
1834–1898
= Gisella Erdődy

Emil
1837–1904
= Dominica
Grimmaud
d'Orsay

Andrew
1839–1902
= Melanie Almásy

Julius
1841–1917
= Anne Lamasch

three girls died in infancy

Fidèle
1863–1934

Alexander
1861–1917
= Elizabeth
Batthyány

Francis
1869–???

Amelia
1865–18??

John
1872–1945

Aloysius
1872–19???
(twins)

Andrew
1873–1947
= 1. Paula
Wurmbrand
2. Elsa
Baranyai

Sigismund
1875–1931
= Sylvia
de Rella

Renier
1871–1912

Still only a captain after sixteen years of service he resigned his commission, but under pressure from his mother soon returned to active service again. Having then eventually, if rather gradually, risen to lieutenant-general, he finally resigned from the army for good in his early fifties. John-Charles had four sons, three of whom lived into the twentieth century, and seven grandsons whose lives straddled the nineteenth and twentieth, so around 1900 this sub-branch was by far the most populous. The sons of John-Charles all followed their father into the army. Géza the eldest was for years the colonel commanding the state stud that bred horses for the army.[35] Emil the second son was picked from a regiment of hussars, when still but a lieutenant, to serve as ADC to Archduke Renier—who evidently stood god-father to his son, baptised Renier—and then transferred to the Royal Hungarian

---

[35] An adequate supply of good horses was essential for nineteenth century armies, both for the cavalry, still a key component of armed forces, and for the horse-drawn field artillery and supply trains; Hungarian army stud-farms had at the time developed a breed of horses called Nonius—tough, sturdy, equally good under saddle or in harness—that was the envy of armies across Europe.

Guards.[36] Andrew the third son saw action in Northern Italy as a cavalry officer before he was attached to the military household of Archduke Rudolph, the heir apparent, whose Master of the Horse he eventually became, and then Principal Chamberlain of the heir's wife Archduchess Stephanie;[37] from here he went on to become, successively, lieutenant general, commandant of the Royal Hungarian Guard, and finally full general and colonel-in-chief of the 8th Hussars. Only Julius the youngest son resigned his commission while still a subaltern, to retire to private life.

Two of Géza's sons, Alexander the eldest and John the youngest, became professional soldiers in cavalry regiments, as did two of Emil's three sons; those decades being a happy period of international peace they largely spent their military lives in stultifying garrison duty. But Géza's eldest daughter Fidèle should be mentioned: she married Baron Gabriel Apor, their son William took holy orders, was for years a notably dedicated parish priest, and by the time the of Second World War Bishop of Győr. Having in this capacity preached and worked against the Nazis during the war, in spring 1945 he was killed by Soviet soldiery—shot in the stomach, he took some days to die—from whose gang-raping intentions he was trying to protect townswomen who had sought refuge in his residence: formally recognised a martyr by the Church, he has of late been beatified, the initial step towards inclusion in the Calendar of Saints.[38]

Alexander's four sons, the only men to carry on this, at one time so populous, sub-branch into (and beyond) the twentieth century, are discussed in the final chapter.

Rudolph's posthumous youngest son Aloysius, originator of the fourth sub-branch, did not follow his father and two elder brothers into the army, but chose, or was pushed into, a bureaucratic career, initially in the administration of his home county Pressburg.

However, he soon gained employment in the Hungarian Chancellery—brother Fidel, some thirteen years his elder and already there, might have arranged this—from where he was transferred to the administration of the Veneto, at the time a Habsburg possession, rapidly rising to become the region's Governor before he was forty, a post he held until just before the outbreak of revolutions, there as elsewhere, in 1848. By then his wife, Princess Sophie Jablonowsky, was seriously ill; a few months later she died, and he retired to the Bohemian estates inherited through her, where their descendants lived until the end of the Second World War (earning them the family sobriquet "the Czech Pálffys").[39]

---

[36] Not to be confused with the Hungarian Noble Guard created under Maria Theresia, which was dissolved after 1848.

[37] The Aunt Stephanie mentioned in the *Prologue.*

[38] Budapest now has a square named for him, on which his statue stands.

[39] The town house in Prague still known as the *Palais Pálffy,* nowadays an upmarket restaurant with that name, had been in their possession for a few decades during the second half of the nineteenth century.

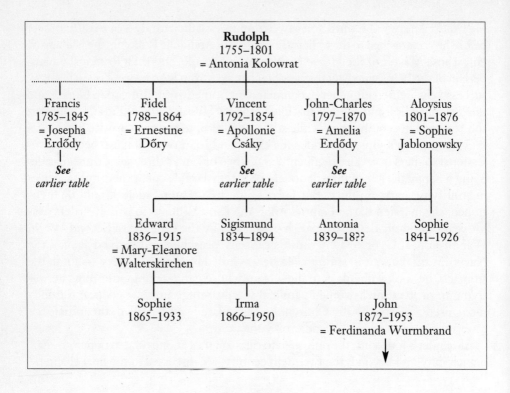

Of his two sons Sigismund, the younger, soldiered all his life, retired from military service a colonel, and never married. Edward, the elder, having spent a few years in administrative appointments—first at Brünn then Buda—soon retired to the Bohemian estates the family had inherited, much enhanced when a great-uncle on his mother's side made him the sole heir of extensive estates in Bohemia and Styria. His son John, in turn, continued running those estates until he became a refugee after the Second World War. His descendants belong to the final chapter.

Finally, the junior or Királyfa line, descended from John the Palatine. Of its two members who lived into the nineteenth century (*see* table at the beginning of this chapter) only the younger, Francis-Aloysius, had a son, when he was almost fifty: a John again and the last of the line (1829–1908). Never married, and apparently keeping aloof from the rest of the family, this John was the possessor of considerable wealth: around 1700 the brothers Nicholas and John had divided all Pálffy estates between themselves, but whereas the former had numerous descendants, between whom his inheritance was fragmented, the John Pálffy here discussed inherited, when only twenty-three, all estates that came down from John the Palatine. He spent the first few decades of his adult life travelling between the capitals of Europe—to an extent perhaps to avoid getting embroiled in the events, and aftermath, of 1848-49, since later in life he gave evidence of a strong patriotic streak—and at one point maintained an *hôtel particulier* in Paris.[40]

At some stage during his travels he began collecting fine paintings and furniture. Of the former he eventually bequeathed a hundred-and-twenty Old Masters to the nation: these can now be seen in the Budapest Museum of Fine Arts (labelled as such again: during recent Communist decades their provenance was left unmentioned). With the furniture he furnished his two country houses, Bajmóc—originally a foursquare mediæval hilltop fortress that he reshaped into a mock-Renaissance château in the spirit of Viollet-le-Duc—and Királyfa, as well as his town house at Pressburg, each in a different style: Bajmóc Italian Renaissance, Királyfa French Empire (which matched the building's classicising style), and the town house Baroque-Rococo. These also he left to the nation on his death in 1908, to be maintained and shown to the public as museums; however, in the 1920s the "progressive and democratic" government of the new Czechoslovakia, within whose borders all of these properties now lay, auctioned off their carefully assembled and matching contents to raise foreign currency, rather than keeping them as museums for the edification of the people: some pieces are now in the Getty Museum, the rest scattered beyond recall.[41]

In addition to the foregoing public-spirited legacies, in his lifetime he made generous donations to numerous charitable causes, ranging from relief following natural disasters to supporting new or improved educational establishments, the latter culminating in an educational foundation: to this he transferred an estate of some nine thousand acres, its income to be disbursed as scholarships for secondary school and university pupils of promise from impoverished backgrounds. To the annoyance of the rest of the family he also directed that his 3/8th portion of Vöröskő be made available for teachers, and deserving recipients of those scholarships, as a holiday home; since there was no way his 3/8th of the castle could be physically separated from the rest, the owner of the other portion eventually negotiated a deal by which other property, elsewhere, was made available for this purpose instead.

His will also caused further serious ructions, which lasted three decades. The complex entails it set up—a proto-seniorate, its income to be enjoyed by the second-eldest man of the family, and trust-endowments to support young Pálffys

---

[40] An anecdote handed down in the family tells of a Parisian society hostess adding *en grande tenue hongroise, s'il vous plait* to a dinner invitation; the company eventually sat down to dinner without him, at which point his valet entered bearing his Hungarian gala-uniform on a hanger and announced: *Voici la grande tenue hongroise: en l'opinion de mon maître c'est la seule chose qui vous interesse en lui.*

[41] The contents were, however, not only catalogued but also *photographed in situ* at the time these buildings became the property of the Hungarian state: catalogue and photographs are preserved in the Museum of Industrial Art *(Iparművészeti Múzeeum)* in Budapest, where an exhibition of these—interspersed with illustrated pages of the Czechoslovak auction catalogue—was mounted a few years ago.

short of funds during their studies, as also impecunious Pálffy widows, and girls who had remained unmarried—raised questions and was disputed straight away: his sister Gabrielle, by then long Countess Emanuel Andrássy, claimed prior inheritance rights as his nearest living relative; Pálffy cousins, more distantly related but bearing the same name, held that to keep his estates—some 200-300 thousand acres of land and forests, as well as numerous apartment buildings in Vienna and Budapest (where his annual tax-bill was among the highest)—most of which had been acquired by Pálffy ancestors in the family, the bulk of these ought to be distributed among them.[42]

Litigation—initially between his executors, his sister, and comparatively remote cousins—was, to the legal profession's greater delight, inevitable; his sister died in 1914, but after 1918 a new dimension was introduced: the new Czechoslovak state's law no longer recognised entails, nor the type of endowments the will had set up, so now it became necessary to determine who of the many fifth or sixth cousins, once or twice removed, was to inherit what. Argument and litigation between members of the family were eventually resolved by mutual agreement, everybody getting something, but only some twenty years on—and thirty after John had died—on the eve of the Second World War, after which the matter became academic.

---

[42] Stephen the then *Senior* of the family called and chaired a number of meetings of all adult Pálffy men to discuss and consider what steps could and should be taken to this end.

Survival (20ᵗʰ century)

*T*he twentieth century was dominated by two World Wars—and the aftermath of these, which affected the family, and the fate of its members, more than those wars themselves did.

In the decades leading up to the First World War—the worst catastrophe caused by human stupidity to befall Europe (and, arguably, the world as a whole), from which all subsequent horrors of the twentieth century followed—the Pálffy family, numerous as it was, was hardly prominent in public life. Comfortably off, some positively wealthy, indubitably of the *erste Gesellschaft*, the top layer of the Austro-Hungarian Dual Monarchy's aristocratic society, imperial & royal chamberlains[1] as a matter of course, theirs was a comfortable and seemingly unshakeably secure life, grounded in the past achievements of their forebears.

But perhaps the atmosphere of the Dual Monarchy's final decades encouraged such lassitude: it, too, survived on its past, owing to which it was still classed among the Great Powers of Europe (and thus, at that time, of the world), a status manifested in sending and receiving ambassadors (not just ministers plenipotentiary) to and from other Great Powers, in the erection of huge pompous buildings and memorials in Vienna as Budapest, in rich colourful uniforms, in complex court ceremonial, in annual military manoeuvres attended by the Emperor-King (at which "our side" always won). Since the north Italian débâcles followed by defeat at the hands of Prussia in the 1860s the Dual Monarchy had been at peace (a couple of minor, and largely bloodless, incursions in Bosnia-Herzegovina apart); the price of basic commodities, as also the value of salaries and pensions, had not changed in decades; Johann Strauss, and latterly Ferenc Lehár, composed delectable valses, polkas and operettas. The surface seemed serene and set to continue for ever.[2]

Beneath it tensions were, however, mounting. The Austrian half of the Dual Monarchy may have been German in principle, but the bulk of its population were Slavs

---

[1] By then the only condition of becoming one was an adequate number of quarterings; once appointed they were entitled to wear a small gold key attached to their evening attire on full-dress formal occasions (on less formal ones only the slip to which to attach the key was worn).

[2] The three-volume novel *Transylvanian trilogy* by Count Miklós Bánffy is by far the best literary treatment of the society, and political, scene in Hungary and Transylvania during these decades.

—Bohemians, Moravians, Poles, Galicians, Slovenes—and its Parliament was increasingly the scene of slangig matches between German and Slav deputies. The Compromise of 1867 with Hungary had been just that, the best accommodation that could be achieved at that time, but was by now creaking: its maintenance without change the cornerstone of successive Hungarian governments' policy, the view that it had best be replaced by a mere personal union—the person of the monarch the only link between Hungary and Austria (much as had been the relation between England and Scotland before the Act of Union of 1707)—was neverteless gaining serious adherents.

In addition there was the heir to the throne, Archduke Francis-Ferdinand. Impatient of "the Old Man"—as he habitually referred to his great-uncle Francis Joseph, who just would not die, although in his eighties and on the throne for above sixty years already[3]—he was commonly known to have gathered an influential circle of political and military advisers about him, a sort of government-in-waiting, ready to take over and radically reshape the structure of the Dual Monarchy just as soon as he came to the throne: the Compromise with Hungary, which country he hated,[4] and its special standing would be abrogated, the Slav people of the Monarchy given an equal say with its Germans and Hungarians in some form of Trialist or federal structure. Assassinated, with his wife, at Sarajevo in June 1914 he never got a chance to put his ideas into practice, but brought down the Austro-Hungarian Dual Monarchy for good by providing the spark that ignited the First World War, a war that had been waiting to happen for some years by then.

By the late autumn of 1918 it was all over: the remnants of the Austro-Hungarian army, the apple of Francis Joseph's eye, resplendent on parade but abysmally led and prone to defeat in real war, were retreating home and breaking up as they went. Charles IV (I in Austria) who had succeeded Francis-Joseph in 1916—and who, horrified by the carnage of the war, had twice attempted to make peace: in 1917,[5] but had then let himself be browbeaten into carrying on by William II of Germany, and again in summer 1918, when the Allies refused to negotiate—now announced that he would abstain from interference in government: in Austria he was soon thereafter forced to formally abdicate and sent into exile in Switzerland.

In Hungary the last prime minister he had appointed, Count Michael Károlyi, declared a Republic, whose president he soon became; this was rapidly replaced by a Soviet Republic, led by one Béla Kun, that instituted a reign of Leninist red

---

[3] All else apart Francis-Ferdinand also much resented that Francis Joseph had tried to stop him marrying the lady of his choice, Countess Sophie Choteck, since she was not of royal birth, and eventually only agreed to the marriage on condition that she would *not* become Archduchess, would *not* be styled Imperial & Royal Highness, would *not* mount the throne alongside him, and that any children they had would be debarred from inheriting it.

[4] So much so that if compelled to travel across Hungarian territory he would draw the curtains of his railway carriage rather than set eyes on that hated land.

[5] Great-uncle Albert Mensdorff-Pouilly, my maternal grandmother's brother and to 1914 ambassador at the Court of St James, had been the emissary sent to Bern in 1917 to negotiate a settlement with General Smuts, the Allied representative.

terror and lasted until August 1919.[6] Meanwhile Romania—which had declared war late in 1916, had been overrun and concluded a separate peace, but had declared war again a few days before the armistice was signed in 1918—moved its essentially intact army into Transylvania, and then further into Hungary all the way to Budapest; the new Czech Republic rapidly created an army of deserters from Czech units of the Austro-Hungarian army, and moved it into Hungary's Highlands, now re-christened Slovakia and claimed as a component of a new Czechoslovakia; Serbia declared its union with Croatia-Slavonia (as also Slovenia), and thence moved troops into a broad swathe of southern Hungary.

The Peacemakers—to employ the term Margaret MacMillan used as the title of her excellent book on the subject—had by then long been in session in Paris, imposing the victors' version of a "lasting and just peace"[7] on war ravaged Europe: this largely meant punishing Germany (to an extent that filled Maynard Keynes, among others, with forebodings) and honouring secret promises made to Italy, Romania, Serbia, and the self-appointed Czech government-in-exile during the war. But Hungary, since it was judged to have no acceptably stable government during most of 1919, was not even invited to send a peace delegation to Paris until the end of that year: by the time it arrived there in January 1920, headed by my maternal grandfather Count Albert Apponyi, all decisions had been taken. By May my grandfather resigned rather than sign the terms imposed,[8] and a political nonentity was eventually found to sign them —at Trianon, from which the treaty is since known—in June that year.

The terms were onerous in the extreme: Hungary was reduced to a mere 28 per cent of the area it had consisted of—losing the Highlands to Czechoslovakia, Transylvania and a large swathe of territory around it to Romania (which *gained* more territory at Hungary's expense than what was left of Hungary), Croatia-Slavonia and a large southern chunk of the central plains to Serbia, and even a slice in the west to Austria (where this is now called Burgenland)—and its population to about one third of what it had been. Roughly 30 per cent of the population of the regions thus detached from Hungary was, moreover, ethnically not Slovak, Romanian, or Serb, but Hungarian: strategic and commercial considerations, such as where major railway lines and roads ran, had influenced those drawing lines on maps far more than the officially mouthed principles of "ethnic self-determination".

⚜

During the war Pálffy men of a suitable age joined up, to be commissioned subalterns and fight, largely in trenches even if cavalry officers, on the Eastern and Italian fronts. Uncle Pali was wounded, and saw out the last years of the war as

---

[6] Kun then fled to the Soviet Union, where Stalin had him purged in the 1930s.
[7] Of which Misha Glenny writes in his book **The Balkans:** *"Paris was the Looking-Glass Peace Conference. To succeed, a proposition there had to be either unjust, absurd, plain unworkable or better still all three."*
[8] See the *Prologue.*

military attaché at Bern, where my grandfather was head of mission. My father and Uncle Józsi both sought to join the 8th Hussars—with whom the family had links going back to the regiment's foundation by Charles Pálffy in the late seventeenth century, although by this time, Emperor William II of Germany its colonel-in-chief, the regiment had been renamed William Hussars—as soon as they had left school aged eighteen: the colonel of the regiment balked at two young Pálffys joining simultaneously, accepting only Uncle Józsi, the elder by a few months, so my father had to start his military career as a gunner (but managed to transfer to the hussars later). Others served too. But none of them ever talked much of their wartime experiences.

The war over the family was hit by the dismemberment of Hungary. The bulk of Pálffy estates lay, as will be recalled, in the north-western counties of Pressburg and Nyitra. This had been an advantage at the time of the Turkish wars, since those parts were never occupied, and only rarely attacked, by the Ottomans; but now all of this region became part of the new Czechoslovakia, cutting them off from their natural homeland, Hungary. To preserve their estates—trimmed by the new state, but still adequate—they had to become Czechoslovak citizens, which *a fortiori* excluded them from any public role in truncated remnant Hungary (to seek such roles in upstart Czechoslovakia never occurred to any of them, even had that fiercely anti-Hungarian state countenanced it). So they entrenched themselves in private lives on their country estates, went shooting and stalked deer, and once travel and currency restrictions between Czechoslovakia and Hungary had eased, from the 1920s, visited Budapest regularly, if but for social purposes; of my visits to those parts and the various uncles I there knew I have already written in the *Prologue*.

⚜

The exception, firmly in Hungary, were the younger generation of the sub-branch descended from John-Charles and more immediately from Géza, commander of the military stud, and his son Alexander, who died in 1917 still only in his fifties.

None of Alexander's four sons got on with their domineering mother née Countess Elizabeth Batthyány, a prolific if somewhat turgid[9] writer on religious and devotional subjects, whose wards they were until they had attained their majority (at age 24 as Hungarian law then stood) and who controlled the purse-strings. Alexander, the second son, died not long after his father, leaving a young widow and a baby son, László (the current *Senior* of the family): they moved to her Szirmay parents' country estate in eastern Hungary, on the edge of the Great Plain and virtually within sight of wine-growing Tokaj; the other three sons also removed them-

---

[9] To judge by her book on Saint Francis of Padua, which I found by chance in a second-hand bookshop.

selves from their mother's tutelage to Hungary as soon as they could, initially to attend universities, and then remained there to keep away from her meddling.

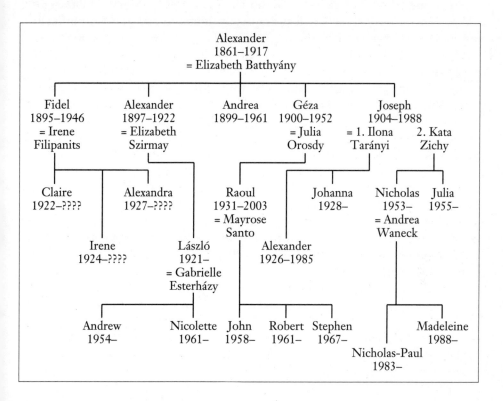

Here Fidel the eldest gradually came to admire what and how Hitler promised to do[10]—for long Hitler's principal public message was that the unfair peace-terms imposed at Versailles had to be annulled, an idea that found obvious echoes in truncated Hungary—and this led him to become a founder and leading figure of the Hungarian clone of the German National Socialist (Nazi) Party; this clone initially also adopted the swastika as its symbol, but when the use of this as a party-symbol in Hungary was officially prohibited in the 1930s it was changed to a cross ending in arrows: from this the party that had by then split off from Fidel's became known as the Arrow Cross (*nyilaskeresztes*, or just *nyilas* for short) Party, the name by which it later became infamous. Advocating, besides revision of the Trianon peace terms, a muddled mixed bag of social reform, restructuring of the state on Nazi lines, and "Turanian" racial superiority, it gained sufficient electoral support, principally in working class districts, to constitute a middling but vociferous

---

[10] Much as Sir Oswald Mosley did somewhat later in England.

opposition group in Parliament, in favour of course of ever closer ties with Nazi Germany.

Following Hitler's attack on the Soviet Union in 1941 Hungary, until then neutral but surrounded by the Reich and countries under its occupation or influence, was reluctantly dragged into the war by German pressure. The government that came into office a short time later (headed by Miklós Kállay) had three main preoccupations: to limit Hungarian participation in fighting, to avoid Hungary's occupation by Germany, to which end it was willing to make many apparent concessions, and to find a way out of the war. Unfortunately it ultimately failed in all three of these: the Hungarian Second Army was destroyed on the Don,[11] and on 19 March 1944, aware of the Hungarian government's secret negotiations with the Western Allies—only, since Hungary (rightly) feared the Soviets as much as the Nazis—Germany *did* occupy the country. However, Admiral Nicholas Horthy the Regent[12] was left in place as head of state (which at least enabled him to put a stop to the deportation of Jews that Eichman and his cohorts had set in motion: it was too late for most Jews in the provinces, but those of Budapest largely survived), although forced to appoint a pro-German government. Then on 15 October he broadcast an announcement instructing Hungarian military units to cease fighting; unfortunately, fearing that his intention would leak out to the Germans, no military commander had been warned of this in advance. By the time they sought confirmation Horthy and those loyal to him had been removed by SS stormtroopers, while new men dedicated to the German cause had taken over all key posts and issued orders to continue fighting. The next day Ferenc Szálasi, the most prominent among the extreme Arrow-Cross[13] leaders (who had in the late 1930s served a couple of prison terms for propagating extreme measures to overthrow the legal government), was sworn in as head of state—Leader of the Nation (*nemzetvezető*), mimicking Hitler's Führer title—and government.

Fidel now, perhaps stupidly, agreed to set aside differences and serve as minister of agriculture in this new government. Most of Hungary was by then occupied by the advancing Soviet Red Army, leaving his ministry little scope for activity. About the only official measure he instituted was to have the brood-mares and stallions of the State Stud at Bábolna moved westwards: as a result this valuable

---

[11] With total losses, killed, wounded, and captured (many of who then died in Soviet POW camps), of between 150 and 200 thousand men.

[12] Admiral Nicholas Horthy—the last commander-in-chief of the Austro-Hungarian navy, bottled up in the Adriatic during the First Word War, and before that ADC to Francis-Joseph—had in 1919 been given command, as the most senior officer to hand at the time, of a counter-revolutionary army; in 1920 he was then elected acting head of state, Regent, by Parliament pending resolution of how the throne was to be filled. The latter issue was never resolved, so Hungary continued as "a kingdom without a king, headed by an admiral without a sea".

[13] The original Arrow Cross Party had fragmented into three some years before; besides Szálasi's—which even the Germans viewed with suspicion—there was by then one of a roughly similar outlook lead by Béla Imrédy and the Hungarian National Socialist Party set up and led by Fidel Pálffy.

equine breeding stock ended the war in the USA occupation zone of Germany, from where the horses were eventually returned to Hungary; had they been left *in situ* they would have been taken to the Soviet Union and Hungary would never have seen them again. Nevertheless, having been handed over to Hungary after the fall of Germany (to where the entire Szálasi government had fled in winter 1944–1945) he was promptly tried—along with all other members of that government—as a "war criminal", sentenced to death, and hanged.

The next brother, Géza, owed his death to the Soviets too, if for different reasons. A dedicated anti-Nazi—like most of Hungary's upper classes (Fidel was a rare exception)—he denounced them in speeches in the (re-constituted) Upper Chamber of Parliament, of which he had become a member,[14] and elsewhere, as well as articles in the press. In March 1944, rightly assuming that he would be on the Nazi's black-list, he went underground before the Gestapo got him and joined the resistance movement: soon after the war was over he was officially decorated for this.

But he was appalled, like many, by the rapacious behaviour of the Soviet forces who invaded Hungary—not only had the Red Army's soldiery looted and raped its way across the country, also carting off tens of thousands of civilians as "prisoners of war" to make up the inflated numbers of opposing forces front commanders had reported to Moscow, but teams of Soviet experts following in their wake had also methodically removed everything, from works of art to factory equipment, not taken or destroyed by the retreating Germans, to the Soviet Union as "reparations"[15]—and by the rapid growth in the power of the Communist Party, a minority group in Parliament (in 1945 it had gained just above 17 per cent of the popular vote) which, however, had the fullest backing of those same occupying forces and increasingly exercised its power through the political police, modelled on and advised by the Soviet NKVD, that was under its direct control.

Most of this was not known in the West, where the Soviet Union was still largely thought of as the valiant war-time ally who had helped defeat Nazi Germany to make the world safe for democracy. Thus, when he met a journalist from the USA who had come to Budapest on a fact-finding tour in 1946, Géza told him in detail how matters really stood. His words and the facts he recounted made their impact: on returning to the USA the journalist published articles detailing the iniquities of Soviet occupation in Hungary. Unfortunately he repeatedly referred to *my informant Count G. P.* as one of his sources, assuming, in a typical instance of western naiveté, that this concealed Géza's identity adequately. Predictably,

---

[14] The rules governing membership were complex, but allowed for a certain number elected to it from among themselves by those who would have been entitled to sit as hereditaries in the pre-War Upper Chamber (somewhat like the remnant hereditaries at Westminster today).

[15] Officially all of this was known as "liberation", in Hungarian *felszabadulás;* in an untranslatable pun in private this came to be pronounced *felszabadúlás*—with that long *ú* it evokes the word *dúlás*, 'devastation', long applied to what the Mongols and the Turks had done to Hungary.

however, it did not take the NKVD's Budapest station long to identify who *Count G. P* must be: not even bothering to inform Hungarian authorities, let alone involve them in the action, officers of the NKVD promptly arrested him in his flat, and took him to the Soviet Union in the short-sleeved summer shirt and cotton slacks he happened to be wearing. There he vanished in the Gulag, where he died in, it is believed, 1952.

The youngest of these three Pálffy brothers, Joseph—known to all and sundry by the diminutive form Józsi (indeed, often as *minus* Józsi, to distinguish him from his elder, by six years, cousin, my Uncle Józsi)—had, having finished university, initially sought independence from maternal apron-strings as a journalist, then accepted an administrative appointment. But, increasingly interested in politics and concerned about the agricultural situation in Hungary (which became desperate after the crash of 1929 and during the Depression that followed), he soon entered Parliament as a Christian Liberal, while also playing an active role in the creation of Producers' Associations that enabled farmers to pool their produce for sale to obtain better prices.

Throughout this he had watched the steady growth of the Third Reich's influence in Hungary, in the economic as the political field, with increasing concern, making no secret of his views on this matter in or out of Parliament. Thus, following the German occupation of Hungary in March 1944 he promptly joined those politicians and others of influence, notably trade union leaders, who—putting aside whatever political differences had separated them up to then—rapidly formed a clandestine anti-Nazi group, designated the *Hungarian Front*, to resist the Germans.[16] Not well versed in underground conspiracy, most of them were soon arrested, Józsi too (while on his way from Buda to Pest, a proclamation by the trade union leader Szakasits, which called for a general strike against the German occupation, in his pocket).

However, after a while in a Gestapo prison but still in Budapest he managed to get away following the Arrow Cross take-over of 15 October 1944. In a futile attempt to legitimise his new standing as *Leader of the Nation*, the Arrow-Cross leader Szálasi wished to be seen to have obtained parliamentary approval of this status, but had a problem: arrests of many of its members, and the disappearance underground of many more, since the country's German occupation had reduced that body to a rump that was questionably quorate. So, to boost the number of members present, those of them held in Gestapo and other prisons were taken to the Parliament building, under suitable guard of course; however, since *appearances* were the point of the exercise, their armed guards remained in the lobby as members under arrest entered the chamber. Here Józsi reported to the Chair that

---

[16] They included MPs of the Smallholders (notably Endre Bajcsy-Zsilinszky, who was later to be executed), National Peasant, and Social Democratic parties, all of them up to then of the parliamentary opposition, and representatives of the officially illegal Communist Party.

he had been held under duress in disregard of his parliamentary immunity, then quietly slipped out of the chamber, and thereafter the building, by side-doors known to him from his years as an MP.

For the next few months he lived in hiding—with false identity papers, and a real moustache grown to change his appearance—at first briefly in the Jesuit House at Pest, then on the Castle Hill in the house of Count Stephen Zichy, one street away from where we lived. He may have been in hiding, but his presence there was certainly no secret to us (nor, I suspect, to many others): that was when I first met him,[17] delivering one of the several braces of pheasants we had received from friends in the country. Indeed, we saw quite a lot of him then, and during the siege of Budapest (from December to mid-February), nipping across in intervals of shelling from our cellar to theirs or vice-versa.

His resistance credentials enabled him to re-enter Parliament in 1945, as leader of the party he had founded, the Democratic Peoples' Party *(Demokrata Néppárt)*; I remember cadging a lapel-badge of this party off him (it certainly included the Hungarian red-white-and-green tricolour, but I forget what else) and for a while proudly wearing it, and also obtaining his promise that I would be admitted to its Youth Section once I was of suitable age. But of course, none of that came to anything. With the support of Soviet pressure the Communist Party forced a grand coalition government of all major parties on the country even though the Small-holders Party had, with 57 per cent of the popular vote, an absolute majority of seats.[18] Gradually the Communists, who had from the start insisted upon one of their own serving as Minister of the Interior, in control of the police (ordinary and political), wore down and eliminated—crudely, by arrests or fake accidents, or else softly, by threats and intimidation—those opposed to them; Józsi saw the writing on the wall, and in 1947 or thereabouts managed to cross the border, illegally of course, into Austria.

With Fidel hanged, Géza dragged off to the Gulag, and Józsi forced to emigrate, in Hungary the family was reduced to but two members: their nephew László and myself (what befell me there is recounted in a separate section).

Called up, and commissioned an ensign near the end of the war, László's major military deed was to disobey orders. Left in command of Győr—despite his lowly rank, but things really were falling apart by then—with a squadron of dismounted cavalrymen and orders to defend the town against the advancing Russians to the last bullet, he—as he recounts it—mounted the tower of the cathedral, looked

---

[17] He was apparently slightly put out, if also amused, when I straight away addressed him just as "Józsi", rather than as "Uncle Józsi".

[18] The election was held on the basis of "party lists", so seats gained were proportional to votes cast.

east, saw and heard guns firing, re-descended, had his squadron line up, and issued the order: *"Boys: acquire civilian clothes and vanish. Dismiss!"*

After the war he resumed his interrupted studies in Budapest, but seeing how matters were developing attempted to cross the border into Austria illegally;[19] caught while trying to do so, he and his wife Gabrielle—*née* Esterházy, a family and name the Communists hated with exceptional fervour—then spent years in prison, some of the time in the notorious ÁVO headquarters at 60 Andrássy Boulevard (in 1944 the headquarters of the Arrow Cross thugs, many of whom simply changed uniforms and continued to serve there after 1945), now the House of Terror museum. Eventually released they, and their then baby son András—the last Pálffy to have been born in Hungary—fled to Austria in 1956.

⚜

As to the others: the end of the war changed their lives—up to then reasonably comfortable[20]—too. In the winter months of 1944–1945 most (some stayed put, to die in poverty a few years later or, in one case, as the Siege of Budapest came to an end) fled westwards ahead of the Red Army's arrival, driven by fear of the Bolsheviks and a preference for liberation by the Western Allies. Many still had vehicles, at the very least horse-drawn carts, in which belongings accompanied them on their flight; retrospectively viewed—none are alive any more to be asked—it seems that the more optimistic saw this as a temporary move, intending to return home once the Red Army had withdrawn to the Soviet Union following the war's end. Having made it to the western half of Austria (where quite a few, including my father and grandparents, as well as Aunt Therese and Uncle István Mailáth, were taken in for the time being by relatives who had sizeable country houses in those parts) they did indeed finish up in what became British or US occupation zones. But they soon had to realise that Soviet occupation, and with it the expropriation of landed estates and unremitting "class war" against the upper classes, was set to be permanent in all of East-Central Europe. So they became stateless émigrés, forced to find ways of making a living as best they could.

How each and every one of them—in their forties and fifties, some considerably older—set about and managed to start a new life from scratch I do not know in any detail. Uncle Józsi's (of Szomolány) wife came into a small property near Salzburg, with a charming little baroque château atop a low hillock: they added more bathrooms and took in paying guests, mainly people come from other countries, often the USA, to attend the Salzburg Music Festival; the more snobbish among these got an extra kick out of staying with "a real count and countess".

---

[19] It was by then no longer possible to obtain a passport and exit permit.

[20] A highly entertaining picture of the inter-war period, if somewhat in the nature of a sarcastic caricature (but all names are disguised), is presented in László Pálffy's book **Narren im Paradies** (*Fools in Paradise*), published in Vienna in 1981 but now regrettably long out of print.

His brothers Uncles Peter and Carl for a number of years ran a much lauded, but financially not totally successful, restaurant and pension in Kitzbühel in the Tyrol.

My father, who had been passionately addicted to stalking stags in the Carpathians (and elsewhere) all his life,[21] and consequently knew all there was to know about managing game, was eventually offered a job as a special gamekeeper by a remote relative, Count George Thurn: his extensive forestry estate in Carinthia, on the border with Slovenia, had for long had hardly any red deer in it but, owing to the war and partisan activity in Yugoslavia, herds of these had migrated across the Karavanken mountain range into his forests. A lifelong sportsman keen on shooting and stalking, Georg Thurn was delighted, and wished to make sure they remained, but none of the local gamekeepers knew anything about managing red deer: my father was taken on to fill this gap.

Others would have had similar experiences, some even straying to distant continents for a while, with variations. In any case, by the time I set foot in Austria some twelve years after that initial exodus they all seemed to have settled there— Austria was, after all, familiar and almost home—into some modest but acceptable lifestyle.

There are still quite a few of us but, apart from myself who have moved back, all living away from Hungary, mainly in neighbouring Austria. The *Epilogue* contains a very brief survey of what members of the family are up to now, as this is being written.

---

[21] As a child, my father told me, he had been convinced that families had the largest animal they had ever shot in their coat-of-arms: our stag was fine, but he rather looked down on those with but a mountain goat (the Wilczeks, his grandmother's family) or a mere bird. I wonder what he made of the Apponyis' blackamoor-head?

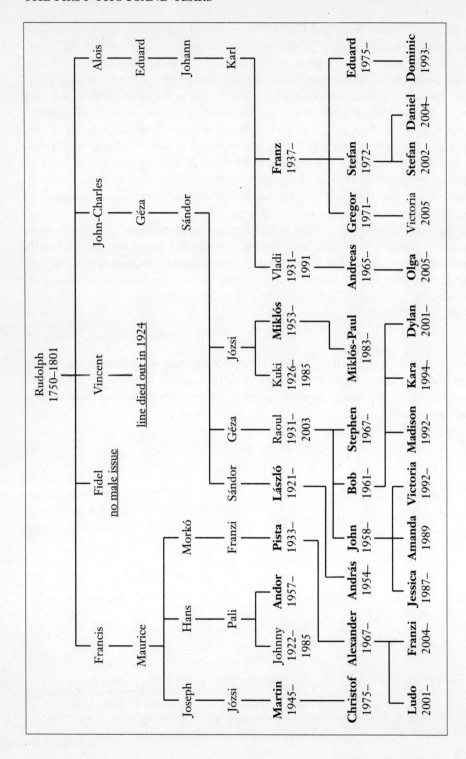

Epilogue—into the 21st century …and beyond?

*B*y the time of writing the generation of post-war forced émigrés, my father's generation, has died off. So it might be appropriate to round off this story with a rapid, and doubtless incomplete (since it is based merely on what I happen to know), review of what has become of the family in my generation and in the next (the generation beyond, the very youngest, are still small children). It might be best to take the sub-branches and sub-sub branches descending from our common ancestor Rudolph in turn, as shown in the much simplified table across (in which: of earlier generations only those are shown through whom we descend from Rudolph; those still alive are in **bold**; names are in the form that was/is in most general use; dates are only given for my generation and younger ones; and, regrettably, girls have been left out for lack of space except in the very youngest generation).

Martin now lives in Vienna: qualified as a lawyer—*Dr iuris*—and tax accountant he is also involved in various business ventures, whose details I have never quite fathomed. His two younger sisters, Kathrein and Sabine, are married, the former in Salzburg the latter, restorer of church paintings, in Bavaria. Martin's son Christoph, possessor of an international MBA, works for a bank and married recently; his elder sister Anne has been married for some years—and is the mother of four boys—and works for the Dorotheum fine art auction house in Vienna; his younger sister Charlotte also married recently, has a son, and works in Vienna too.

Uncle Pali's elder son Johnny, whose mother was from the USA, made a career in the financial world of New York after the war: determined to accumulate enough wealth by the time he was in his fifties to retire to a life of leisure, he succeed in this, but was then carried off by a heart attack in his early sixties; his only daughter Gina is married to a Swiss banker of Hungarian extraction and has two children, his sister Caja (pronounce Caya) lives in Mexico. Uncle Pali's second son Andor, from his eighth and last wife and thirty-five years Johnny's junior (indeed, at just fifty the youngest of my generation), lives in Berlin where he is, by his own account, a big shot in an insurance company, controlling a budget of hundreds of millions as well as hundreds of staff; divorced and recently remarried, he has no children.

I myself (since the family tree says it is my turn) was released from prison during the Revolution of 1956 and then left Hungary. Fortunate to be taken in by Trinity Hall, Cambridge, I then lived and worked (mainly as a "systems consultant") in England until the 1990s, when I returned to live out my days in Hungary. My son Alexander, possessed of a BA in English and qualified as a cabinet maker, has settled in the northwest corner of New Zealand's South Island, where he follows the injunction at the end of Voltaire's *Candide: il faut cultiver nos jardins*; he has two sturdy and stomping sons, Ludo(vic) and Franzi (whom he named after his two grandfathers). My daughter Georgina, with a Cambridge First and a Diploma in Journalism under her belt, is far too nice a person to have made it in the nasty world of journalism, drifting into publishing as an editor instead; fortuitously she also fetched up in New Zealand, the country of her husband, if on the east coast of the North Island, but has now returned to England with their delightful son and daughter. These four grandchildren are the principal addressees of the present volume.

László, at well past eighty the eldest of my generation, established a successful practice as an interior architect in Vienna after he escaped from Hungary in 1956, in his spare time producing weird cartoons (and the book mentioned in a footnote in the previous chapter); a nasty fall a few years back brought him to the verge of death, but although largely tied to a wheelchair since, he is determined to keep going and very successful at doing so. His son András, the last Pálffy to be born in Hungary, is an internationally acclaimed, because very original, architect winning competitions and gaining commissions across Europe, from Newcastle-on-Tyne to Pressburg, and beside this also professor of architecture at Vienna University;[1] he married recently. His sister Nicolette, invariably known as Niki, qualified as a doctor, in the way of medical students married a doctor while still at university, had a son, but some time after divorced, re-trained as a dentist and now runs a successful dental practice in Vienna.

Géza's son Raoul I met, although we were near contemporaries, but once or twice, shortly before his death a few years ago; he spent most of his life, from about the time of the outbreak of the Second World War, in the USA (his mother was part-Jewish, a good enough reason to get away from Central Europe in those days), and I do not really know what he did there. His three sons, John, Robert, and Stephen, I have never met and know very little about: John worked for the Raegan Administration in the 1980s and has been investment banker, professor, and financial consultant since then, his wife Carla is also an academic and his three daughters are at various stages of their university careers; Robert, known as Bob, is Vice President of a finance company in Chicago, the father of two school-age daughters and a son.

---

[1] With vast and unjustified exaggeration he claims that my advice—when he visited us in England in his late teens—to follow his inclinations whatever else was being urged on him, finally swung him to take up architecture rather than some other "safer" but more boring career option.

Józsi *minus*, discussed in the previous chapter, fathered two broods (he was bare-ly in his twenties when he first married): Alexander, invariably known as Kuki, never quite found his feet in emigration—hardly twenty at the end of the war, he landed in post-war chaos and uncertainty in Austria not qualified for anything in particular—and rather drifted around Vienna in various unsatisfactory jobs until his early death two decades ago; his sister Hanna married a businessman from Switzerland immediately after the war, had a daughter, Gaby, divorced, and in the 1960s married my childhood friend Palkó Darányi, having Jeanne and Alex; now widowed she lives near Geneva. In the 1950s their father married again—Kata Zichy, in whose father's house he had been hidden in 1944, is much the same age as her step-daughter Hanna—and they had two children: Miklós, who is mak-ing a career in banking—for a while he worked for the Budapest branch of the Austrian bank that employs him, then in Belgrade, but is now back in Vienna—has a son, Miklós-Pál, currently at university, and a daughter, Madeleine, who has just started at university; his sister Julie, married and the mother of two, at the time of writing teen-age, daughters, Luca and Kata, has recently separated and, after a stint at the Hungarian Embassy at Vienna, now works for an internation-al organisation in Vienna.[2]

I am not sure whether I ever met Vladi—once in a café in Klagenfurt, many decades ago, he was paged, but to my disappointment nobody responded—who worked as the manager of a company in Salzburg. His younger son Lukas died in an ski-accident in his teens; the elder, Andreas, is at the time of writing, in his own words, *selling railway engines on behalf of Siemens* in or from Vienna, but has had some earlier connection with informatics, in which capacity he has registered **palffy.com** in his own name on the Internet; married a couple of years back he is the proud father of Olga. His elder sister Alexandra, married and the mother of two boys and a girl, trained as a medical technical assistant and currently lives near Barcelona; his younger sister Livia, just married and the mother of a daughter, is a qualified upholsterer living in Vienna.

Vladi's younger brother Franz makes furniture, or at least he used to. Their grandfather owned a small property, a few hundred acres of woodland with a mod-est shooting lodge, in Austria in the Lungau just south of the Tauern mountain range, acquired some generations back merely for the occasional shooting and stalking it afforded: when all their Bohemian estates were lost this remained as a family base. When of an age to start earning his living Franz, as I understand it, decided against trying for some boring office job: instead he started making wood-en furniture in the village; the enterprise thrived—at one point years back he told me that his order-book could justify doubling the number of his employees, but

---

[2] Miklós, Julie and András all attended the same secondary school, where it caused much perplexity that, although virtually the same age and school form, András kept insisting that the former two were his uncle and aunt.

he would not, since if he did he'd become a desk-bound administrator after all, so customers just had to wait for their orders—and in due course he was even elected mayor of the village for a few years. The works are now run, I believe, by his middle son Stefan, father of two boys; I am not sure what the other two sons, Gregor and Edward, do nor what and where his daughter Clara does.

So the family has survived the upheavals of the twentieth century and has, indeed, numerous growth points: already, as the twenty-first century gets into its stride, six Pálffy boys have been born to carry it on, and there is no reason to doubt that more might yet be born in the next decade or so.[3] Yet...

Will the family cohere as a family? To the mid-twentieth century we all lived in comparative proximity to one another, and had one common language, Hungarian, even if everybody was fluent in a few others besides; today we are scattered, geographically as linguistically. Before the First World War meetings attended by all or most Pálffys, at which the *Senior* presided, were held regularly to discuss matters affecting the whole family; some years ago Martin made one valiant effort to gather us all together for a family meeting lasting several days, and a jolly time was had by all who made it—but will this be repeated?

Will, moreover, any members of the next generations assert themselves and excel sufficiently, in whatever fields of activity they choose (not warfare, politics or national administration, to be sure), to rise to, and to ensure that their descendants remain, at a level of prominence that might encourage one of our descendants, some centuries—or even a millennium?—hence, to consider it worth his or her while to extend this brief family history with new chapters?

---

[3] As this book goes to press the wives of Christoph and of Andreas, Heidrun and Gabriela, are expecting babies.

Appendix

My life in Hungary in the 1950s

Preface

In November 1956 circumstances made it both possible and essential that I leave Hungary. By January 1957, owing to a series of fortunate coincidences (best recounted in the *Epilogue*), I found myself *in statu pupillari* at Trinity Hall, Cambridge, reading for the Moral Sciences Tripos.

I soon laid my hands on a typewriter* (borrowed, I suppose, but I can no longer remember) and promptly embarked upon drafting, straight into typescript, an account of my experiences during the preceding years, a task completed during that Lent Term. Of late—fittingly, in the course of shifting belongings from England to my newly acquired flat in Budapest—I rediscovered that, long mislaid, text; fortunately with a photocopy made at some later time, since the original had been typed on "flimsies", to enable me to generate several carbon copies in one go, whose paper has seriously deteriorated since.

The text that follows is an exact transcript of what I wrote then, only obvious typos, spelling mistakes, and some of the most questionable punctuation, have been corrected. The account had no title, nor section-headings, only "break markers" (three asterisks in a row), which I have retained. At the time I had, however, felt it necessary to fudge certain details, notably in instances where these might perhaps have identified, to their detriment, persons possibly still in Hungary, should the text fall into the hands of the Hungarian authorities. These fudges are no longer necessary, and footnotes that include the term **fudge** in the opening phrase enlarge and explain; further footnotes have been added to clarify other matters, often of terminology, where this now seems useful.

Fudges apart the account written in spring 1957 also skates over that fact that, being at the time of the events described in my late teens and early twenties, I was—in parallel and intertwined with those events—also trying to cope with all the usual problems and upheavals of "growing up", of accomplishing

---

* The original text is typed on different machines starting from the "break" on p. 182 and then again from the paragraph that begins "Várpalota was..." on p. 188.

the transition from teenage schoolboy to young adult. There would be little point in attempting to recollect and expand on any of that now, but the reader might wish to keep in mind that that, too, was a constant counterpoint to the events described.

Finally, in the early months of 1957 there was no need to set the scene, to explain what had happened in Hungary in the autumn of 1956. If today's reader no longer knows, (s)he might be better informed by the time (s)he has finished reading the account that follows.

S. P.
Budapest, May 2000

The account written in 1957

Somewhat more than a month has elapsed since I left Hungary. During this time I have been asked hundreds of questions about Hungary by people of many different nationalities, social standing, occupation, political, religious and economic creeds. And while answering those questions a general picture of what the West did know about Hungary and what it did not know was formed in my mind. I found: that while most people had a more or less accurate idea of what had actually happened in Hungary since 23 October 1956, few knew what life and the circumstances of living had been like during the past ten years, and consequently few understood what had led to the events of 23 October.

On the following pages I would like to give an account of my life in Hungary during the past few years, as in a way it may be regarded typical, and it will give me a chance I hope of explaining a lot of the true reasons for the October revolution.

* * *

Things in Hungary grew really bad in spring 1951. By that time all the industry had been nationalised, beginning with the banks and coal-mines in 1947, then the great-industry[1] in 1948, the small industries occupying above first 20, later 10, employees in 1949, and the remainder of private enterprise being choked gradually by the government's tax-policy and other methods typical of a police-state in 1950. By 1951 no one could make a living unless employed by some nationalised firm, which meant that everyone depended on the state for his bread. And this bread was small, black and difficult to earn. Wages were according to the amount produced, and always more-and-more had to be produced in the same given time to earn the same wage. There was a shortage of food and all products of direct

---

[1] Heavy industry is meant.

use to the population. By this time the ÁVH (Államvédelmi Hatóság = State Defence Force), the secret political police had been built up completely. Having been only a small department of the police-force at first, it was in 1951 the most powerful and feared institution in the country; standing under the orders of the Ministry of the Interior officially, it actually received its orders directly from the Executive of the Central Committee of the Party. It had its spies everywhere, not a home, not an office, not a workshop was without them. No one knew who was its informer, in consequence no one dared utter a word against the government, the Party, the Soviet Union, or the circumstances of life and work, for fear of being arrested, tortured, imprisoned for years, possibly without a trial, or in the "best case" loosing his job.

Things being as I described them, everybody thought that they were at their worst. But soon they had to find out that they were wrong, the government still had surprises in store for the population. Early in May that year rumours of people having been forced to leave their houses and belongings at 24 hours notice, and having been deported to out-of-the-way villages, spread in Budapest. Rumours at first, soon it became a certainty, as always more and more people received notice.[2] The notice to prepare for deportation was always handed over to the victims at night by policemen who would come in a Jeep at night. Next night a truck would stop at the door of the victims, they would pack what little of their belongings they were allowed to take with them onto it and be driven off to a railway station, there to be crowded into cattle-wagons and be carried off to hidden little villages on the Alföld, the great Hungarian plain.

It at first seemed that the campaign of deportations was directed against class-enemies only, former officers and civil servants, businessmen and leading officials of large firms, also what remained of the nobility[3] and aristocracy. But before long people of humbler social standing, factory workers, waiters, porters, small shop-keepers and the like were among the victims too. Perhaps they had once said something against the government or the Party, perhaps they had had a quarrel with their local Party Secretary, foreman in their factory or one of the ÁVH informers. Or perhaps it was only that they had a good flat and one of the ÁVH officers or informers had taken a liking to it. Nobody could tell. So as night came fear also came, people could not sleep expecting the ominous ring of the doorbell, which would announce the arrival of the policeman with a 24 hours notice to get ready for leaving the town.

There is no need to explain that we also feared being deported: having a title and my mother having a dress-maker's shop we were doubly class-enemies. I was doing my last year in gymnasium[4] at the time and it was just the period of the final

---

[2] *Notification* is meant.
[3] Something like the English *"landed gentry"* is meant.
[4] "Gimnázium", roughly the equivalent of a French *lycée*.

examinations. Yet we had no choice, we changed our quarters almost every week, and never spent a single night at our registered places of living.[5] Finally, by the end of June I had finished my examinations, and at once went off to the country to work at a place called Kazincbarcika[6] in the north-eastern part of Hungary, rather quitting Budapest on my own accord than being forced to do so. At the same time my mother went to a health-resort[7] on the excuse of being ill (which she actually was at the time) to avoid deportation.

Our plan for avoiding deportation only half succeeded. The police sought me with a notice of deportation at one of my registered quarters, but finding that I had already changed to another never followed up the line of my constantly changing addresses, and thenceforward left me in peace.[8] My mother, on the other hand, they tracked down, and on the evening of Christmas Day 1951 arrested her. I had only just arrived the evening before, to spend Christmas with her. Luckily she had still time enough to hand over her personal belongings, like her note-book, addresses and telephone numbers, to me before being carried off, the lack of which later much bewildered the ÁVH officer leading the enquiries against her. But of all of this I did not know anything at the time. All I knew was that she had been carried to the local police station, and after having been kept in custody there for a few days I was informed one morning that she had during the night been transferred to Budapest, probably to the Police HQ there. (I feel I must explain that the ÁVH was very seldom actually mentioned as having arrested somebody, in point of fact arrests were usually made by the Police and the arrested then handed over to the ÁVH. Also no one was ever officially detained at ÁVH HQ, they were said to be kept by the police.) I immediately travelled up to Budapest, but naturally could not find out anything about her whereabouts, not could the lawyer I hired. My leave expired in the meantime and I had to return to Kazincbarcika. It was here, some six weeks later, that I received the first news of my mother since her arrest,

---

[5] One's permanent address had to be registered with the police (as also any temporary address one stayed at for more than a certain—24 hours? 48 hours?—time).

[6] A "socialist construction site", where chemical works were to be built: few questions were asked of those who volunteered to work there. It was, however, essential to maintain a registered permanent address in Budapest since, once abandoned, permission to re-settle in Budapest was almost impossible to obtain.

[7] A partial **fudge**. She went to Hévíz, a spa of some renown near Lake Balaton, whose chief medical officer Dr Károly Moll, a family friend of many years' standing, provided medical "cover' for her.

[8] A **fudge**. At the time my registered permanent address in Budapest was the flat of one of the workers my mother had employed; to get into the building the police roused the concierge and asked him which flat I lived in. Owing to a clerical error the notification had my name as *Imre*, not *István*, and the concierge— bless him!—told them that no person of *that* name lived in the block. The police departed to check their records, but the flat's owner asked me to de-register. Following transitory registration at the address of a friend, an ideal solution then emerged: a couple living in a three-room flat feared that the authorities would impose a lodger on them, since it was larger than what they were "entitled" to. So they jumped at the idea of having me registered as the third "permanent resident" of their flat, on the understanding that I would never actually live there; if anybody queried my absence, the fact that I was "building socialism" at Kazincbarcika could be offered as an acceptable and adequate explanation.

in the form of a few lines scribbled in a hurry onto an odd piece of paper and smuggled out when she had been taken to be disinfected, because she had acquired lice in the cellars of the so-called "police" (actually: ÁVH) HQ.

My mother was later on transferred to one of the Budapest police-prisons[9] (actually run by the police in this instance) after the ÁVH proved incapable of producing even the shadow of evidence to built a charge of any sort upon against her. Hence she was transferred to a concentration-camp[10] some 80 kilometres to the south of Budapest, where she worked alternatively on cotton-fields and beside bricklayers until her release in February 1953.

Naturally any reader who has lived all his or her life in a democratically governed country would have difficulties in understanding both motives and methods of a police-state in a case like this one. I have tried to explain what the deportations were. It must not be forgotten, though, that a person deported lost not only all his political rights, but also a good many of his personal ones. Once having arrived at his destination, he no longer had the right of leaving it, not even to go to the neighbouring village. Did he do so, and was he caught at doing so, he could and would be interned in one of the many concentration camps for a term of at least six months. Had the six months expired, they could be renewed a further six months an indeterminate amount of times. But no more than leaving the village he was deported to had he the right to have a wireless set, to use the telephone or receive any visitors, to go to the local movie or to be anywhere else than at his registered lodgings between 10 p.m. and six a.m., to mention just a few of the restrictions. At the same time he had to in some way or another make a living, to feed and clothe his family, etc. As you see, restrictions were so many that sooner or later everybody offended against them, and if caught was sent to a concentration camp. Circumstances here were even worse. Crowded into barracks, cold in the winter hot in the summer, hardly ventilated, sleeping by twos on each bed, the beds being at least double-deckers and more often than not triple-deckers, with no accommodation for washing, no plumbing either of course, the prisoners thus kept were forced to work from early in the morning till late in the evening. My mother tells me that throughout the year she spent in a concentration camp she saw the sun rise and set every single day, as they were marched off to work eastwards every morning before dawn, and returned to their barracks westwards every evening after dusk. Once a month she was allowed to receive a visitor, unless she had offended against the rules of the camp, or one of the warders reported her to have done so. The visitor was also allowed to hand in a food-packet, but it was not allowed to contain any "luxuries". Biscuits, for instance, were regarded a luxury, and also all tinned food. Soap or a hair-brush only sometimes, if the warder in charge was good-natured, they were

---

[9] Probably better termed a *detention centre*, it was in the Mosonyi utca, near the Keleti pályaudvar.
[10] More accurately: a *forced labour camp*; it was at Mélykútpuszta, in County Fejér.

allowed in. And all this not for any particularly inhuman crime, not for murder, robbery, not even for picking pockets, only for offending against a restriction, an evidently unjust restriction, put upon a deportee, or for not occupying one's place of deportation.

In the meantime I was, as mentioned above, working at Kazincbarcika, having to keep the fact that my mother was under arrest and in a concentration camp a secret from everyone; for had it been found out, I would have been chucked out of my job. Not that it was a very grand job: I was officially an unskilled labourer, working for a railway and road construction firm. Actually the engineer who was in charge soon realised that I had finished gymnasium (a school-type more-or-less equivalent to a secondary school) and I was given the work of a technician to do—without the according pay of course.[11] Being a "class-enemy" I could never be anything than an unskilled labourer. The question may also have arisen in somebody: why did I not go to university? Well, there is a reply to it: I was a "class-enemy", dangerous to state and public alike. I was of course not the only one in such a situation, there were thousands of young people in Hungary who never got a chance to study, or earn more than the absolute minimum to keep body and soul together, merely because they were classified as class-enemies. It was enough to have a country doctor or a small clerk[12] in one of the ministries as father to be regarded a class-enemy.

In February 1953 my mother, as I mentioned, was released from the concentration camp. This does not mean that she was allowed to go where she liked or do what she wanted. On the contrary, a policeman accompanied her to a village[13] in the northern part of the country, where she had to remain same as the originally deported, under the same restrictions with a few added, like for instance having to report to the local police station every Sunday, not being allowed to write or receive any letters, and the like. She was given what was called the "summer kitchen" in the house of a so-called "kulak". A "kulak" according to the Communist phraseology is a land-owner owning more than 33–34 acres, or less than that if part of it is an orchard or vineyard (the acre of which counts as 3–4 acres of a field); but he will also be regarded a "kulak" in case he owns a threshing-machine, a tractor or any other sort of machinery. He is also to be regarded a kulak does he employ anyone through the whole year or even part of it. Communist ideology regarded the kulaks as the last remainder of the exploiting classes, and consequently Communist policy led a campaign to liquidate (also one of the favourite Communist expressions, curiously reminiscent of some of Hitler's) them. This

---

[11] Another **fudge**. The engineer in charge, Károly Pfundtner, was pretty well aware of who I was and why I had come to Kazincbarcika, but nevertheless risked employing me and making my working life as tolerable as possible, although he was a potentially 'suspect' person too: his wife was British (who could have left Hungary on her British passport, but chose to remain there with her husband).

[12] Something like *junior civil servant* is meant.

[13] Tarnaőrs, in County Heves.

was thought to be achieved primarily by a policy of impossibly high super-taxes, but also by means of force, such as taking the good fields away from a kulak and giving him bad ones instead, by taking away his machinery, by driving off his live-stock, by making him pay penalties for the most ridiculous reasons (like having straw littered over his yard, not having ploughed his fields by a certain date, or by pretending he had fed his animals grain), and if the kulak still was not liquidated after all that, a charge was brought against him that he had excited against the state, the Party or the local kolkhoz, and he would be sentenced to several years of prison. Of course, there were also numerous other reasons for imprisoning somebody, like: chopping out a tree in his own backyard without a permit, slaughtering his own pig or calf without a permit, buying an animal and reselling it at a higher price, etc. Any peasant stood in danger of being charged with any or all these capital crimes, but for a kulak the danger of it happening was tenfold. But had he paid all his taxes and super-taxes, his penalties, and had he not committed a single one of the abovementioned crimes, there still was the possibility of turning him out of his house and deporting him.

Giving the deportees from Budapest rooms and back-kitchens in the houses of kulaks was only one way of annoying the kulaks. For of course the deportees could not pay for their lodgings—nor were they expected to do so by the government.

In summer 1953, after general so-called "elections", the government was reshuffled, and Imre Nagy was appointed prime minister. It is really from this time that his immense popularity in Hungary dates. For though a Communist he was not a Muscovite,[14] and his first action on taking over the government was to abolish concentration camps, deportations, kulak-lists (the register at every village council of the kulaks), and to lay more stress on the production of consumer goods. Class distinction in the Communist sense grew laxer, even children of professionals were beginning to be allowed to study, etc. The forced grounding[15] of kolkhozes was put to a stop, and everyone forced into them previously was given a chance of leaving them if he chose to do so. Private enterprise was allowed again on a small scale, cobblers, tailors, grocers and other small shopkeepers, who had been forced to give up their businesses because of the impossible taxes and other official methods applied to strangle their business got back their licenses.[16]

Deportees from Budapest were not allowed to return to Budapest to settle down there again though, but they could settle down anywhere else in the country, in consequence of which all the villages and suburbs around Budapest were

---

[14] Actually, he had spent several decades in Moscow, only returning to Hungary in 1945; evidence now available suggests that the policies of the time associated with his name were largely inspired by Moscow which, following Stalin's death, was getting dissatisfied with the way arch-Stalinist Rákosi was running Hungary.

[15] *Founding* is meant.

[16] The exercise of any trade or craft was subject to an official permit.

practically flooded by former deportees. The rent of a room in these places was high above the rent of a room inside the town, although rents were high enough because the shortage of flats too. So my mother rented a room in Budakeszi, a village beside Budapest, like most people, and I began trying to get a job in Budapest too. But before I succeeded I was called up for my military service, which actually meant the beginning of a new chapter in my experiences of a Communist-ruled "peoples' democracy".

* * *

Up to 1949 Hungary had only a small volunteer army, but by then the Communists had taken over the government completely and started organising a relatively large regular army on the pattern of the Soviet Red Army. Since 1951 everybody was called up for military service in November of the year in which he reached the age of 20. The whole armed force was divided into three very distinct categories: the elite was the forces under the control of the Ministry of the Interior, namely the "belső karhatalom" (= Home[17] Force) known generally as "Kék Ávó" (Blue ÁVH, called so because of the dark blue ribbon they wore on their caps), which was supposed to cope with any troubles inside the country, like possible strikes, anti-government movements, etc. and they also had the duty of guarding the life and safety of high-standing Party and government officials, etc. They were practically[18] under the command of ÁVH HQ, providing the executive force for actions that needed a strong armed force. The other elite corps was the "ÁV Határőrség" (= ÁV Frontier Guard) known generally as the "Zöld Ávó" (= Green ÁVH, because they wore a pea-green ribbon on their caps), their duty being to guard the frontiers, not so much against smugglers or foreigners trying to come into the country, as rather against Hungarians trying to leave the country and flee to the West. They too stood under the ÁVH HQ's command. Only picked men served in these two elite corps, reliable from a political and class point of view, who could be expected to stand by the government in all circumstances.

The second category of the armed forces was the Air Force and Army, under command of the Ministry of Defence. Within this category the Air Force was regarded the elite, and the men picked accordingly.

The third category was the Labour Corps. It was supposed to be part of the Army, wore the same uniform, but had no arms save the spade and pickaxe. It consisted mostly of class-enemies and to a small part crooks.

Naturally treatment and living circumstances were different in each category. It is true that service was three years in the ÁVH's forces, but pay was something

---

[17] More correctly: *interior*
[18] *in practice* is meant.

like the double of that in the other armed forces, food was much better, living accommodation was better, and every possible favour was given. Service was three years in the Air Force, two in the Army, with better food in the Air Force and more possibilities of being promoted. In the Labour Corps service was two years, the food hardly edible, accommodation the worst, and of course absolutely no promotion, with almost inhuman treatment by superiors.

The armed forces being divided into three so distinct groups, it is but natural that everybody was very carefully screened several times before being called up. It began at the age of 19, a year before being actually called up, when one was the first time summoned to appear before the district's military commandature. Here, after having given all one's personal data, one found oneself confronted with a Board of Enquiry consisting of an officer of the Army, the Police, the ÁVH and an official of the District Council, who questioned one about one's job, family, friends, etc. One was screened in a similar fashion at least one time more a month or two before being called up, by a similar Board of Enquiry. One was also asked where one would like to serve, but I only know of very few cases in which anyone was actually called up to serve where he wanted to, and those may have been coincidences. Of course there was also a medical examination, but almost everyone was found suitable for service.

Things being as described above, I felt quite certain that I would have to go into the Labour Corps. My surprise can be imagined, when on being called up I suddenly found myself in the training battalion of the 37th Air-reconnaissance Regiment, then stationed some 40 kilometres to the south of Budapest. (It may sound funny, but it took me quite a time to find out where I was actually serving, for military units in Hungary, same as in Russia, handle their name and number as strict secrets, officially using their Post Box number instead. So for instance my regiment went under the name of "Unit PO Box 4747, Kiskunlacháza", the last word being the name of the place it was stationed in.) On arriving to my unit with some forty-fifty other young men of my age, under the command of two officers who had come to fetch us at the District Comandature, and who would not disclose where we were going until we actually arrived, the first thing that happened was that we were sheared bald—and this happened again every fortnight for almost a year. Then we had to lay off our civilian clothes, and after a bath and being powdered with DDT we received our uniforms.

Life was a tough affair in the training battalion, with a particularly hard winter and lots of snow, most of which the training battalion was expected to shovel off the concrete landing field of the airdrome. So it can be understood that when a sergeant of the regimental HQ appeared one evening and asked if anyone could type, I jumped at it and was the first to say I could. Two days later I was transferred to the general office and registry of regimental HQ. Had I known at the time what consequences this will have, I surely would not have done so.

By spring I knew the routine of my job fairly well, and when an order came from Air Force HQ to the regiment to send a man to a military registrar's course it was almost natural that I was sent. So I passed the course, and returning to my unit after it became the registrar of the regiment.[19] There had been one unpleasant moment during that course: when we were made to write a curriculum vitae and fill in forms for the purpose of receiving a permit to work with documents marked "secret" and "strictly secret", a permit issued by the 8th Independent Department of the Chief of Staff of the Hungarian Army. For the whole time I feared that one day they would find out that they had committed a fault[20] in calling me up to the Air Force instead of the Labour Corps, and would react nastily. But once being in it I hardly thought it possible that I should remind them of their fault. But nothing happened, after a few months I duly received my permit,[21] was promoted to lance-corporal, and life seemed to go on pleasantly.

Life in the Hungarian armed forces is naturally a thing quite different from that in a western country. Their regulations are copied from the Russian ones, which means they are rather strict. But even though they are strict, discipline, at least in the Air Force, is on a low level. Most of the officers have very little education, mostly less than the men in the ranks. The men say "why, he is no better than we are, knows less, so why obey him?" Another interesting feature is the bad morale (from the official government point of view) of the army. Though much stress is laid upon political teaching,[22] with 6–8 hours of political teaching per week, consisting mostly of the glorification of the Soviet Army, of trying to rub in the fact how much life has changed to the better since Russia "liberated" Hungary, and of trying to explain the government policy of the moment. This last is the most difficult part of it, partly because the soldiers see what is actually happening, and partly because the government policy changes constantly, which often makes it necessary to tell the soldiers that everything they had learnt concerning a certain question a month ago was completely false and wrong, and the truth is the contrary of it. I distinctly remember the difficulties our political lecturer had in explaining the friendly attitude towards Tito in spring–summer 1955, after having taught us to regard him as one of socialism's worst enemies till then. They also had much difficulty with the agrarian policy of the government, which usually changed up to three times within half a year.

Besides political lectures there were three institutions typical of Communist armies: political officers, the Party and the DISz. Political officers are officers specially trained to keep up the morale of the army, to supervise political lectures and

---

[19] *Regimental clerk* is meant. It was about this time that I discovered, now having access to the personnel data of the unit's national servicemen, that originally I had been earmarked for some other unit (although I never managed to discover what kind of unit: it was but a PO Box number), but had been shifted to where I was because I had turned up late at the recruiting centre, thus missing the group sent to that other unit.

[20] *Mistake* is meant.

[21] Security clearance is meant.

[22] *Instruction* is meant.

to keep an eye on the men. The commander of every unit has his so-called "political vice-commander", with whom he discusses every decision, etc. There was a time when any command issued by the commander was invalid unless it bore the signature of the political vice-commander. Political officers are subject to nobody and only receive orders from the Political Group of the Ministry of Defence, or the political officer of their higher unit—the political officer of a regiment from the political officer of his division, for instance.

The Party organisation and the DISz organisation (Communist youth organisation, Hungarian equivalent of the Russian "Komsomol") of each unit are also supposed to play a great part in keeping the morale of the armed forces on a high level. Of course, there are certain difficulties. In theory the Secretary of either organisation is freely elected from amongst the members thereof, and each member has the same right to any function. Yet it is difficult to imagine how an army would work, where a private is the party secretary of his superiors. So in fact the secretaries of either organisation are always officers, which makes it impossible to even pretend that they are democratic organisations. Their value is further reduced by the fact that membership of the DISz is in practice—though not in theory—almost compulsory. So no one cares much about the DISz, its meetings must usually be postponed for failure of members to appear at them, and if they are somehow herded together for a meeting, they do not show the slightest interest in what is going on, duly vote any motion put before them and are glad when it all has an end and they can go and have their suppers at last. The Party is taken a little bit more seriously, not because people are very much interested in it, but because they fear the consequences of not taking it seriously.

Then of course each unit has its intelligence officer as well. Intelligence officers have nothing but their uniform in common with their unit, for actually they are members of the ÁVH. As to their methods etc. I will still return to that in the course of my own experiences.

To return once more to the topic of regulations and discipline, I found that most breaches of regulations were committed by disobedience to orders, impertinence to superiors, and absence without leave. As to the reasons for the first two, I have tried to explain. Concerning the third, leave was difficult to obtain; according to regulations at least 70 per cent of the unit always had to be in its barracks, and of those on leave at least one third had to remain within the town or village where the unit was stationed. So 30 per cent was the maximum to be on leave, but usually the actual number to have obtained leave would be smaller. And if the commander felt like it, he could stop all leave for several weeks. Naturally soldiers disapproved of all this, which had as consequence that with 80–90 per cent of the ranks officially in, the dormitories were usually empty on Saturday nights.

Of course, volumes could be written on the Hungarian armed forces, their organisation and morale, but as it is not my intention to write a textbook on the question, I had better carry on with my story. Early in 1955 I had a quarrel with

171

some of my superiors,[23] in consequence of which I started pulling strings[24] to get transferred to another regiment. By the end I succeeded, and was transferred to the 23rd Fighter Regiment (PO Box number 4736) stationed at Tapolca, at the southwestern end of Lake Balaton, being one of the three regiments of the 28th Fighter Division (PO Box number 4707) at Székesfehérvár.

Two things of a certain interest and importance happened just before my transfer: I was promoted to corporal,[25] and received word in a roundabout way that the Intelligence Department was showing much interest in me[26], and had sent a report to Intelligence HQ stating that my father had been a count and that I had acquaintances and relatives living abroad, also in the USA. I do not know how they suddenly came to find all this out—not because it was so difficult to find out, but because they had not for more than a year.[27] Anyway, things being as they were I had no other choice than to carry on same as till then, and naturally make a secret of the fact that I knew anything about the Intelligence Department's activity.

On arriving to my new unit no sign of the Intelligence Department's activity concerning me was to be found, and I soon was on fairly good terms with all my superiors, particularly my direct superior, a certain Lieutenant István Mészáros, with whom I later in the course of events had a good deal of unpleasantness. But at the time all went well. Unluckily I was declined[28] all leave of absence for a whole month in consequence of some minor offence against regulations the end of July,

---

[23] In point of fact, the adjutant of the regiment (Captain Gecse, if memory serves), an NCO in the Air Force before 1945 who then turned Communist and thus earned promotion. On reflection it seems likely that the "quarrel" referred to, whose details I can no longer recall, had its roots in the matters presented in the next paragraph.

[24] As regimental clerk I was inevitably in frequent contact, by letter, telephone, and even in person, with several officers in various administrative sections of Air Force HQ; on some appropriate occasion I simply raised the question of a possible transfer in conversation with one of their number.

[25] Yet another **fudge.** My immediate superior was a barely literate middle aged captain (whose name I forget), who owed his rank to a solid background in pre-war clandestine Party activity; we got on well, and by tacit agreement I ran the registry, while he just signed where I told him to. During a surprise visit one night the divisional commander scrambled the unit, declared himself satisfied, and let it be known that he wished to promote some deserving men (promotion to lance-corporal and corporal was within his competence). I rapidly convinced my captain that he should recommend me as one of those men, and soon I had the satisfaction of typing up a Divisional Order of the Day that included my own promotion, of which the adjutant mentioned two footnotes earlier only learnt when I delivered a copy to his office.

[26] A further **fudge.** I was told all of this—very much in the vein of "how can they have such silly ideas?"— by a regular sergeant of the unit, with whom I was on friendly terms; although he never said so, he doubtless had it from his wife, who was employed at the air base as a typist, knew me, and occasionally typed documents for the Intelligence Section.

[27] They were, however, singularly incompetent. From the personnel records of national servicemen in the unit, which I maintained, I knew whom amongst our intake the regiment's Intelligence Section had initially considered in need of further investigation; living alongside them I also knew that not one of these was in any sense "dubious" from the régime's point of view. As against this, I had also identified those few among our intake whom a competent Communist Intelligence Section should have taken an interest in, but not one of these had aroused their interest.

[28] Refused, deprived of is meant.

so I could not go home to Budapest till the end of August.[29] This was unlucky, for owing to this I did not till the end of August learn of the enquiries at that time being carried out in Budapest against me.

On arriving to Budapest in the last days of August 1955, many of my friends told me that they had been summoned to appear at Military Intelligence HQ, or at ÁVH HQ, and had there been questioned about me, where they knew me from, since when they knew me, what they knew about my family circumstances, my relations to people living in the West, particularly in the USA, what they knew of my political views, other friends of mine, etc. A few of them had been summoned more than once and had been asked the same questions over again, to ascertain whether they were not telling lies and to see whether they did not get mixed up with their replies. Common in every instance was that they had, at the end of being questioned, to sign a statement that they would never mention or talk about their having been questioned to anyone, in some cases they had to write out the statement to that effect in their own handwriting. I also learnt that a captain of the Intelligence Department had been making enquiries about me at my registered lodgings. So I saw that something was up against me, without although being able to even guess what their ultimate aim or charge may be. I was positive that I had not committed anything criminal, not even according to the strict laws and military laws of Communist Hungary, so though slightly worried I dismissed any fear of real danger. Until, some time later, I suddenly realised how easy it would be for them to frame a charge of espionage against me, on the "convincing evidence" that I was in the Air Force and my mother had a dressmaker's shop[30] with a few customers who were members of western legations.

But whatever the situation may be, I could not do anything against it, I had no means of defending myself against any accusations that I was never openly charged with, and I regarded it the worst possible policy to alter any habit of mine or change anything at the moment, as this would only cause suspicion, and then it was not to be forgotten that officially I had, could have, no knowledge of the enquiries being carried on, as those who told me of their being questioned were risking their own safety and liberty, such as it was, in telling me all about it. So, on my leave expiring I returned to my unit, only to find that in my absence some people who were thought to know anything about me had been questioned concerning me, one of them being honest and loyal enough to tell me all about it, even though he too had to sign a statement that he would never mention it to anyone. I also found the attitude of my direct superior much changed towards me, he began being nasty in every possible manner an officer can be nasty to a corporal—and the possibilities are many.

---

[29] On reflection, this was probably due to the matters described in the next sentence and paragraph, the infraction of a regulation merely an excuse. As regimental clerk, sharing an office with the officer who could grant it, I had by then got quite used to being granted leave virtually every week-end, however stringent the restrictions on leave were in general (as discussed earlier).

[30] She had by then been permitted to re-start her business, on a very modest scale.

All through September and the first half of October we were playing hide-and-seek on the general idea[31] of "I know, but they do not know that I know, and I know that they do not know that I do know", until I was one day in private charged with espionage by Lieutenant Mészáros. It all happened because two orders from Divisional HQ concerning some details of the regiment's usual annual reorganisation, and naturally marked "strictly secret", had been mislaid. On not finding them where they ought to have been he charged me with having them, which I denied, as I actually had not seen them since three days. At this everyone was sent out of the room, and he told me that they knew perfectly well who I was, and found it a rather curious coincidence that papers of such importance should disappear after they had last been seen in my hands (which was a lie), and that I had better make a clean breast of it, etc. But as I continued denying any knowledge whatsoever concerning the whereabouts of the papers in question, and could not be bullied into admitting my guilt of anything I had not committed, he gave up for the time being, and shortly afterwards the papers were found in a dossier where they had nothing to do.

The situation changed slightly from then on, as it was clear to both parties that things could not remain as they were, or rather: I could not remain in my present place. Very optimistically I regarded demobilisation the only possible solution, as I had by then served almost two years, so that transfer to the Labour Corps, where service was only two years, was practically impossible. Nothing further was said about it though, till the end of November. Then one day Lieutenant Mészáros told me he had received orders from Air Force HQ to demobilise me.[32] I was to hand over my affairs to my successor and after I had done that travel to Budapest for my civilian clothes. On returning to the unit with them I would receive my papers of demobilisation.

At half past three on the afternoon of the 30th November 1955 I received my permit of leave to go to Budapest to collect my civilian clothes. I had on the previous day wired my mother that I was arriving either on the evening of the 30th or the morning of the 1st, and that she should expect me.[33] At 4.30 p.m. the train

---

[31] *Pattern* is meant.

[32] In point of fact the order clearly came from Intelligence/ÁVH, as is borne out by subsequent events. But also by the **fudged** fact that during these very months of tension my contacts at Air Force HQ were privately telling me—but not Lieutenant Mészáros nor anyone else at the unit—that they would soon need a new clerk in one of the HQ departments and that, since they considered me competent, they would arrange to have me transferred to work there (which suggests that Intelligence did not bother to inform Air Force HQ of their investigations). Naturally I was seriously worried by this, since as a clerk at Air Force HQ I would have been much more vulnerable to made-up charges of spying than as a mere regimental clerk, but I could do nothing to stop it without arousing suspicion: no national serviceman in his senses would turn down such an offer, which entailed promotion to sergeant and then working ordinary office hours, while living at home, in Budapest.

[33] She had by now, along with other ex-deportees, been allowed to move back to Budapest, where she rented a room as a lodger.

left Tapolca towards Budapest, with me on board travelling to Budapest for my civilian clothes to be demobilised…

* * *

A few minutes before a quarter to nine the train drew into the station of Székesfe-hérvár, some 80 kilometres from Budapest. I had put down the book I had been reading, and was staring out of the window, the way one does when a train arrives at some larger station. There was a general bustle inside the wagon, passengers were getting ready to get out, luggage was being hauled down from the nets over the seats, and some people were already moving towards the door to be first in getting out. It was then I first noticed ÁVH Second-lieutenant Gyula Szakály, intelligence officer of the regiment, standing at the far end of the wagon. I greeted him, which he returned with a smile, and then I focused my attention onto the platform, beside which we were just coming to a stop, again. There was nothing extraordinary in the intelligence officer travelling to Budapest, and it seemed no more than a coincidence that we were on board the same train. The refreshment car was next to ours, that would explain his sudden appearance.

The next thing I noticed was that he was standing beside my seat. "Put on your coat!" he ordered me. I stared, bewildered: "I, my coat? Why?" "Put on your coat, and be quick about it! Don't ask questions and don't call attention to us!" he ordered me a second time, and this time I understood… It was 8.45 p.m., 30 November 1955.

"You are being detained by the ÁVH! Do you understand? You aren't allowed to talk to anybody! Now follow me!" I was told a few minutes later, standing on an empty part of the platform.[34] We left the station building, and after a few minutes' wait a small military car appeared. Silently we took our seats in the back of it, and the driver, who evidently had his instructions already, drove off without a word being said. I could not at first guess where we were being driven to, but soon I recognised Division HQ, as our car came to a stop in front of the small building of the Divisional Intelligence department.

Silently we entered the building, silently I was ushered into a small office. It was clear that I was expected. A soldier with a tommy-gun came out of one of the rooms, saluted the officer bringing me and then took position behind me, the barrel of his gun pointed at me. Then 2nd Lt. Szakály passed into an adjoining room to report my arrest to his superior by telephone. Luckily he forgot to close the door, a padded one, properly, so I could overhear his conversation. One sentence

---

[34] Being arrested while *en route* between two places was routine: most commonly people would set out for work, or for home from their workplace, and never arrive at their destination. Not only did this avoid an awful lot of "emotional unpleasantness" with the victim's family or colleagues, it also resulted in uncertainty among them as to why, on what charge, the arrest had been made: *they* liked anything that increased the population's fear.

caught me attention: "…yes, he seems to be quite frightened already…" So the aim was to frighten me? Well, they would have a difficult job in doing so, especially now that I knew about it.

On having finished his report he returned to the room. Not a word had been said up to then since my arrest. Now the soldier guarding me was motioned to leave the room, and I was ordered to empty my pockets. While looking through their contents 2nd Lt. Szakály asked me what I thought the reason of my arrest was? I told him I could think of no other reason than my birth. He made a stupid face at this, and asked what was wrong with my birth? and seemed to dislike my telling him that I thought he knew as well as I did. "No—he said then—nobody is arrested in our free country for his birth, such things only happened during the 20 years of Horthy terror, and if you do not know the reason, you'll find out!" I did not know much more from this statement, so I could do nothing else than wait to see. The soldier was then called back, told to keep strict watch over me, and we were left alone. Knowing that I would need all my resources in the days to follow, I lay down on the floor, wrapped myself into my coat and soon was fast asleep—the last time for several days to come.

Next morning three more ÁVH officers went through the contents of my pockets,[35] the last of them, in civilian clothes, staying in the room after it. He was ÁVH Captain Sándor Házi, as I later learnt, and it was his job to question me. He sent out the soldier on guard, and after seating himself behind a writing-desk, placing a stout dossier with my name on it before himself, and beckoning me to sit down on a chair at the opposite end of the room, the interrogation began.

It would be tedious and not very interesting to go into the details of that interrogation, that lasted four days. It began with my being asked to give the story of my life, continued by my being told that I was telling lies, being made to tell it all again (to check, evidently); then I was asked to speak of my friends, photographs of each being produced and shown to me as their names were mentioned, to make sure we meant the same one, etc. Every now and then I was told that I was telling lies again, every now and then I had to repeat things said previously, and we would switch to unexpected topics at unexpected moments. When evening came a large heap of paper was placed on the table, and I was told to write down everything we had been "chatting about" during the night, and to be sure I did not omit anything. When not interrogated a guard with a tommy-gun sat beside me, and if I dozed off for a few minutes I would be awakened by the barrel of the gun being thrust into my ribs. After 48 hours I was so exhausted that I fell asleep the moment I was not questioned. Then they found out the method of making me stand fac-

---

[35] Curiously, none of those who did so spotted that I had (foolishly and carelessly) jotted some telephone numbers onto the back of a little Tapolca–Budapest railway timetable that I had typed up and carried: each in turn verified that it was indeed a timetable, as I said when asked, and put it down again without turning it over—yet every telephone number found on an arrested person was a potential "lead" in the investigation against him.

ing the wall, toes just touching it and my nose at about the distance of an inch from it. Did I alter my position I would get a poke of the gun or at least a shouted command not to fidget so much. All of this was within the bounds of law. It was prohibited to interrogate a prisoner for more than 8 hours a day. My interrogator took good care not to overwork himself by spending more time than that with questioning. But nothing prohibited a prisoner to write statements as many hours a day as he wished to so spend. Lunch time was one hour a day. My interrogator always took his time with meals. Only I was usually forgotten for that time, and so were my meals. I was allowed to sit while being questioned. That was eight hours. I had to stand the rest. That was sixteen hours. I was allowed to smoke—if my interrogator offered me a cigarette. And if one has not tried what it is like to stand hours on end motionless, face to the wall, never knowing what is going on behind one's back, then one cannot understand how exhausting it is both mentally and physically.[36]

I succeeded, though, in upsetting my interrogator once or twice, by asking him such questions at the end of the second day's interrogation for instance, as whose picture I was sitting beneath? (It was some Russian general, I forget his name.) I also found that he much disliked if I pointed out that he knew of something as well or better than I did.[37] But on the whole the situation was far from funny.

At the end of the fourth day I was called into another office, and a typed copy of my "statement" was placed before me to sign. I was allowed to read it carefully, then had to sign every page of it. The summary of the several pages it contained was that I had omitted at the time of my being called up to tell that I was a class-enemy, had in this way "smuggled myself" into the Air Force, and had by doing so endangered the integrity and striking power thereof, all of which was to be regarded as forgery, punishable according to paragraph 144 of the BHO (civilian law-book) and paragraph 97 of the Ktbtk. (military law-book) by imprisonment of 1–10 years. A nice, clean cut case, resting on undeniable evidence.

After I had signed my "statement" (as I saw no point in not doing so, for if they wanted to convict me, convicted I would be, statement or no statement, in the "worst case" they could detain me in prison for years without trial or conviction) the typist left the room, and Captain Házi began a nice little speech, telling me that I had committed a fault, but with regard to my young age there still was hope for me to repent of my fault and become a true son of my country, and they would give me a chance to prove my good intentions, and they are willing to drop the case against me, and all I had to do to regain my liberty and live a free citizen of socialist Hungary was to help the ÁVH by giving them a little information every

---

[36] It has the added advantage that it leaves no physical trace of maltreatment.

[37] And he never asked me any further questions about my uncle George Apponyi, then living in Brussels, after an exchange that went somewhat as follows: "Why did your uncle choose to go to the West?" "He did not 'choose to go', he was taken by the Gestapo, to Mauthausen." "What's this 'Mauthausen'?" "A concentration camp—the Nazis had them too." He did not like that final qualifier.

now and then about people with whom I could easily come into contact through my birth.[38] In case I would double-cross them, of course they always had my signed statement. After being very stupid and slow to grasp what he meant, so that he had to go into all the details and explain them to me for half an hour or so, I at last told him that I had not the slightest intention of turning informer, and never could he induce me to do such a dirty job. He seemed rather hurt at this, began shouting at me that now my true feelings had shown, and what else could one expect of such a dirty scoundrel of a class-enemy, etc. (all of which was rather a compliment to me), and that I would see the consequences and would have time during the years to follow to brood over my stupidity for not having accepted their "magnanimous" proposal in my prison cell, etc. In the end he gave me 24 hours "if I had anything further to tell him, or wanted to say something to him", which I did not.[39]

I was then taken out of the office where I had up to then dwelt and placed in a cell, to await transfer to the military prison in Budapest (well-known by the name "Fő utca", the name of the street it is situated in). It was early December, bitterly cold, the window of my concrete cell was broken, and my only companion was a little black spider, who marched round and round the cell all day long, same as I did. I called her Fidelio, how she called me I do not know. At least I had enough food here, because the common soldiers on sentry,[40] though it was strictly prohibited, would come to the door of my cell to ask what I needed, and though they could not provide me with blankets, they brought me more food than I could eat. In not a single one of them did I find any trace of class-hatred, nor any too great love of the government and ÁVH. Yet, oddly enough, "objective" Communist propaganda always wants to make us believe that it is the other way round. From this I draw the conclusion that one of us must be wrong.

After a few more days had elapsed I was transferred to the Fő utca,[41] to await my trial there. I must state that my first entry into a real large prison was a curi-

---

[38] *Background* is meant.

[39] It was perhaps fortunate for me that they were working to a time-limit: if I accepted their offer, the main point of the whole exercise, I had to return to my unit by the time my leave expired—any delay, especially if then overlooked, might have raised questions, might have suggested that I had been arrested, interrogated and then released, and might thus have marked me out as a possible informer.

[40] The cell was one of several in the ordinary guard-house of the air base, not part of the Divisional Intelligence Section's accommodation.

[41] A **fudge** lurks behind this sentence. I was taken from Székesfehérvár to Budapest by train, in uniform but without my belt, escorted by an armed national service corporal and private of the Air Force. Their attitude was much as described in general terms in the previous paragraph; I promised them that I would not attempt to escape, they bought me drinks and cigarettes. In the waiting room we happened to run into a soldier I had served with at Kiskunlacháza: they let me chat with him, we managed to stick to generalities, and he never realised I was under arrest. By the time we got to Budapest my escort and I were on sufficiently good terms for them to allow me to write a postcard to my mother, provided its text was innocuous, and agreed to post it on my behalf: I scribbled something on the lines of "I am well, but health concerns have interfered with my planned journey"; they did post it, and my mother understood: "health concerns" was a common enough code phrase.

ous sensation. A large red-brick building, with row on row of barred windows to the street (though these were only offices), the monotony of which was interrupted only by the heavy iron gates, ÁVH sentries with tommy-guns guarding each.[42] On entering through one of them and passing up a flight of stairs, a second iron gate, then a barred door was opened before me, only to bang back into its place with a loud clang after I had passed it. I found myself in a long, dimly lit, passage, with the guard-room at one end and doors leading to the guards' quarters and the prison offices all along it. Here I was told to stand facing the wall, in the way I was "used to" doing it during the days of my interrogation. After what seemed an endless space of time I was at last summoned to one of the offices, where at least a dozen forms were filled in by a uniformed official, containing all the details of my personal data, from my name to the education my father had had (!); why they needed this I do not know.[43]

Next followed a long wait facing the wall again, then I was summoned into another room, had to lay off all my clothes, then had to pass to the other end of it and there put on my striped prison attire. I was allowed to keep one handkerchief and my comb only. I tried to smuggle in a little stub of a pencil I had in one of my pockets, but being a beginner at the job was naturally caught at it. Then I was handed a tin dish, a spoon, two threadbare blankets, and resumed my wait in the passage—face to the wall.

By lunch time I was at last taken up to the third floor, and there placed into cell No. 328. About 15 feet by 15 feet, fourteen beds, double-deckers of course, some twenty-odd people (the number of occupants varied from 22 to 26), a wooden table, two benches, all rather dimly lit by what little light found its way in from the courtyard, dark in itself, through the two small and heavily barred windows just under the ceiling at the end opposite the thick iron door. I later learnt that this was one of the best prisons in Hungary with regard to washing and sanitary facilities and space, as each cell had a wash-basin with running water and a small walled-off space for the WC.[44] Also the ratio of beds to occupants was 2 : 3—while in most prisons there was only a tin basin and a can of water (usually empty) for washing, and a pail with a cover standing in one corner had to serve the purposes of a WC, emptied only once or twice a day, and often there were four to five

---

[42] This was actually the back side of the building, in Gyorskocsi utca: prisoners did not enter or leave by the main entrance in Fő utca. A marble plaque commemorating those whom the Gestapo had held there (whose number had included my uncle) was already affixed next the gate through which I entered; now there is also second plaque alongside it, commemorating those whom the ÁVH detained there in subsequent years.

[43] The form-filling had its funny moments. The forms were being typed, a procedure the official was not very good at, pecking at the keys with slow determination; moreover, he seemed to find it difficult to decide what colour to enter for my eyes, and needed some convincing that the location of the scar he noted was over my collar-bone, not shoulder-blade—both matters we had to discuss at length.

[44] It had been built before the First World War, when standards would appear to have been higher than after the Second.

times as many prisoners as beds. But I did not know all that at the time, so I was utterly depressed at the sight of it all.

With that day my actual prison-career in Communist Hungary, taking me through various prisons and forced-labour camps, commenced.

* * *

It was only after lying awake for hours the previous night that I succeeded in falling asleep, wedged in between two other prisoners. And now the clang of a bell, somewhere down the passage, roused me from my uneasy sleep. It was 6 a.m. Daily routine in the military prison of the Fő utca, Budapest, had began.

Twenty-odd prisoners were sorting out their belonging from amongst twenty-odd pairs of boots, trousers and jackets, scrambling into them in a space not fit for ten to move in. A queue had formed in front of the toilet and another one by the wash-basin. Why all this hurry? We had all day, hadn't we? No, we had not, we had to be ready, dressed, washed, the beds made and the cell cleaned by 6.30. Why, nobody could tell. It was a regulation.

At 6.30 the little window on the door opened, and we were handed our breakfast and daily allowance of bread. The breakfast: half a litre of some transparent brownish fluid, called "coffee". The daily allowance of bread: 40 decagrams (somewhat less than a pound) of hard, dry, dark brown something. Yet it was only with the greatest willpower that one could resist the temptation of eating it all for breakfast. By 7 a.m. we had finished our breakfast. Then we just sat about staring at the four walls or at each other, and waited for time to pass. At least those did who found a seat. For there were only two benches, seating but four–five at the most each. To sit on one's bed, let alone then lie, was strictly prohibited in the daytime.

Of course, if a new prisoner was in the cell, things were better.[45] He would have to tell all about his "case", and probably he had still been a free man only a few days ago, so he could tell a lot of interesting news of what was happening in the world without. For this was the only means of learning anything about events without the four walls of the cell. Then, as time proceeded things would get livelier. All the inhabitants of the third floor were still expecting their trial. So there were a few people every day who were taken down, either for trial, or to be interrogated, or to sign some official paper, or to see their solicitor. So each time the

---

[45] There was also an "initiation ceremony", at least in our cell. The newcomer would be warned about bullying Warder-Sergeant Csizmadia (meaning *Cobbler*), his habit of questioning new prisoners through the little window in the door, and the importance of giving truthful answers. Then, at some stage when the newcomer was not facing the door, the voice of Sergeant Csizmadia—actually a fellow-prisoner's, talking into a boot (whence the fictitious name) to disguise his voice and produce a slightly muffled effect— would order the newcomer to stand facing the wall, and then ask him a lot of very personal questions, demanding very detailed answers, to the great, if suppressed, hilarity of the cell. I remember being let off, and gaining house-points in the cell, when, on being asked "How do you counts fuck?", I replied "By shoving our prick up a cunt."

electric bell at the end of the passage rang, everyone turned expectantly to the door, and if it opened that was quite an event.

Being taken down for some reason or other was an exciting and good thing. It meant a break in the dull monotony of daily routine, also the off-chance of hearing some news and the possibility of a cigarette. There were many who just would not answer the questions of the prosecutor[46] investigating their case until they got a cigarette. And if they succeeded in getting a cigarette, it may also have meant a smoke for the whole community of the cell. The end of the cigarette was carefully hidden, and if nobody looked ashtrays were quickly emptied. Naturally everybody was carefully searched when handed over to the warder on duty on the third floor again. And yet, they may have been undressed completely in the passage, every square inch of their clothes may have been carefully gone through, but a few cigarette-ends would get in every day. The tobacco would be emptied on a piece of paper and screwed[47] into a new cigarette with toilet paper. But the cigarette so prepared still had to be lit, and unless one has seen it one cannot imagine how ingenious the human mind can be. Scrapings of a celluloid tooth-brush (nylon or plastic is no good for the purpose) mixed with iron-rust, wrapped in a piece of cotton wool, and rolled up and down on a hard surface under sufficient pressure and at sufficient speed, for instance, would if properly done begin to glow, and could be used to light a cigarette. If a small piece of flint, as used in lighters, was available, things were very much easier of course. A piece of cotton-wool blackened with shoe-polish would catch fire in an instant from a spark produced with flint and a bit of glass. Electric lights in the cell were used as well, but disliked, for they usually blew the fuse and so called attention to what was being done.

We had one piece of flint "built into" a small piece of the table leg that could be detached and replaced after use. Also, at one time there was a piece of flint in the stem[48] of the broom used for sweeping cobwebs on the ceiling. This piece was common property of the whole third floor, and very often it was one of the warders who would hand in the broom to "clear the cobwebs off the ceiling", not knowing that he was actually handing us the means of lighting a secret cigarette. Cotton wool was not a very common object in a prison cell either, of course, but could be replaced by picking at our blankets, and using the threads thus derived instead. (Women had it easier with cotton wool.)

The next event of the day was the "walk". Each cell on its own would be herded down to the courtyard, and spend 20–30 minutes solemnly and silently walking round and round beside the wall. All we saw of the world on these walks was

---

[46] In the Hungarian legal system, as in many continental ones, state-employed prosecutors are in charge of investigating criminal cases (although much of the initial groundwork may be done by the Police or—in those days—the ÁVH); my case was technically classified as a criminal one, and most of my cell-mates were charged with quite ordinary criminal or military offences.

[47] *Twisted* or *rolled* is meant.

[48] *Handle* is meant.

some eight stories of small barred windows upon small barred windows till there seemed to be no end to them, and at the top of this well turned upside-down a small quadrangle of blue or cloudy sky. After half an hour we were herded back to our cell on the third floor, and so meagre was our food that this "exercise" was enough to render us utterly exhausted. So then everybody began to talk of food, people would tell of their favourite dishes, give recipes for how to make a really good meal, and call up the memory of all the good meals they had had. The lack of sugar must have been the greatest in our diet, for I distinctly remember how I would spend evenings planning what candy-store I would go to if released and exactly what I would eat there—and so did the others too.[49]

If the Sun was shining we were lucky, for then we could tell the time by the progress of certain shadows on the wall opposite. And we would gather beneath the window to sniff the fumes rising from the kitchen directly beneath us and guess at what the lunch would be. It never varied much. Some sort of soup that tasted like dish-water and had a different name every day, and after it either beans, lentils, potatoes or cabbage cooked in salt water. Twice a week there was a tiny bit of horse-flesh in it, of well-nigh microscopic size.

But then there always was the fabulously wonderful possibility of getting a second helping. The food was distributed by prisoners, and they took good care to give less rather than more, to make sure the food would be enough for everybody. In consequence a few portions were always left and distributed according to the whim of the warder on duty. But he only decided which cell it should go to, within the cell the community decided upon the distribution. I do not know how it was in other cells, in ours we all had a number according to arrival in the cell (e.g. who had been there longest was number 1, and the last to have arrived had the highest number). So, if there was a second portion for the cell No. 1 would get it, if there were two No. 2 would get one too, etc. In this case No. 3 received a brass button, kept especially for this purpose, which meant that next time a second portion of food was handed in he would get it, passing the button to No. 4, etc. So it is needless to say how valuable the brass button was. There was a chance that it would mean cessation of hunger for an afternoon to its bearer.

Food ceased to be the main topic of conversation for an hour or two after lunch, only to crop up again in the afternoon. At 6 p.m. we got our supper, which was much the same as lunch only without soup. Then at 7.30 p.m. the command to get ready for the night was given. Beds were then pushed together, to make it possible for three to sleep on two beds, jackets and trousers neatly folded up and laid on the table in neat military order, last the boots, cleared of every speck of dust and smeared with the grease provided especially for this purpose, were lined up in the prescribed pattern, and, after the warder had inspected whether everything had

---

[49] Owing, no doubt, to our undernourished condition sex, a common topic in barrack rooms for instance, hardly ever a entered conversations or day-dreams.

been done according to regulations, the lights went out at 8 p.m. One more endless day had come to an end, to make place for an endless night, divided only by the flashes of the guards' reflector,[50] scaling row upon row of small barred windows from the depths of the dark courtyard up to the eighth floor at regular intervals...

A few days after Christmas I was informed that I would be tried on 30 December, and at the same time was given my indictment, which document proved the laughing stock of the prison for a few days, as in "the name of the Hungarian Peoples' Democracy", which had abolished all titles and class-distinction, the public prosecutor of the Hungarian People's Army's Air Force charged me as "Corporal Count Stephen Pálffy".[51]

On the morning of 30 December I was taken to the building of the Air Force Court-martial,[52] at the other end of town, guarded by two soldiers with tommyguns, but on crowded trams, so that they could hardly have used them had I tried to escape. On arriving I was told that my trial would not begin until 2 p.m. and ordered to stand beside the wall facing it. It was then 10 a.m., so I asked which paragraph of military or civilian law prescribed it that the accused spend several hours before his trial standing face to the wall, instead of preparing to defend himself. At this a young official in civilian clothes told me that "standing beside the wall was quite good enough for a count", but eventually they gave me a chair to sit on—still facing the wall, though. Of course, claiming the necessity to get prepared to defend myself was practically hardly more than a pretext, for defence was only theoretically possible. I had a lawyer to act as counsel for the defence, but was only allowed to meet him once before my trial, then only for ten minutes with a double wire-fence between us and in the presence of one guard on my side of the fence and one on his. This hardly made it possible for us to discuss either the case nor the line of defence to take in detail, particularly not with the guard having the right to stop us in the middle of a sentence merely because he (the guard) regarded what was just being said as not belonging to the case.

At 1 p.m. my mother arrived, and by some miracle of misunderstanding on the part of the officials was allowed to talk to me freely and without anyone else listening. It was then that I learnt how, after I had not arrived to Budapest on 30 November, nor the following day, she grew anxious (as I had wired her beforehand, telling her of my intended arrival) and sent me a wire, asking what had happened. She received a wire in reply, stating that nothing was wrong and she should

---

[50] *Spotlight* is meant.

[51] Skips over a **fudge.** I was allowed to read the documents attached to the indictment, which included (besides the "statement" I had signed after my interrogation) a Personnel Assessment from each of my immediate superiors during my service in the Air Force; that written by 2nd. Lt. Mészáros was predictably damning, but that written by the old-Communist captain at Kiskunlacháza made me sound fit for rapid further promotion—obviously nobody had bothered to tell him what purpose it had now been requested for.

[52] Military Court is meant.

not worry. My name was signed.[53] At the date of her receiving it I had been under arrest since five days.

Shortly after 2 p.m. I was escorted down a passage and entered the court. It was a small room, evidently designed for other purposes, a long table at one end, the professional judge and his two co-judges,[54] all three of them officers, sitting behind it, with the prosecutor on the right and the defence on the left. I was bade to take place facing them, and though there was a chair provided I spent most of the trial standing. The trial was public, but only my mother was present. A large red flag and the Communist coat-of-arms with the red star formed the background. The trial was a swift one. There were no witnesses, and all the evidence was a piece of paper I had signed at the time of being called up, which contained my personal data but no statement of the fact that I was a class-enemy—there was not even any space on the printed form for such a statement. After the judge had read out all the "facts" concerning my "crime" and asked a question or two, the prosecutor delivered his speech, then the defence delivered his, and at the end even I was given a chance to say a few words. Then the court adjourned for about 10 minutes, after which sentence was announced: two years imprisonment, loss of my rank,[55] and the loss of all political rights over a period of four years, to commence on the expiration of my term in prison. All this for the "forgery" I had committed in not declaring myself a class-enemy, and the blunder on the part of the "screening-committees" for not having spotted I was one. I appealed on the ground that the sentence was too heavy, the counsel for the defence on the ground that the wrong paragraph had been applied, mainly because the one he suggested should have been applied involved a much lower maximum limit of punishment. The appeal was accepted, but I had nonetheless to continue in prison.

Ten days after my trial I was put into a transport for a forced labour camp, and was regarded lucky for this by many of my fellow prisoners, as the labour camps were regarded with envy by those who were in prison, and many of my fellow prisoners had been in prison since months or years without succeeding in getting to a labour camp. Nobody knew of course which of the many camps we were going to, but rumours had spread that it would be one of the mines.

Crowded into a "rabó" (short in prison slang for "rabomobil",[56] the completely closed van for transport of prisoners, also called in Hungary somewhat ironically "fairy-tale car"), we were driven off early in the morning. The car, as said, was completely closed, save for a small, strongly barred, window at the back of it.

---

[53] But as *István*, not *Pista* (the diminutive of the former that I always used), so she knew it was a fake.

[54] *Lay assessors*, perhaps? The standard pattern of Hungarian Peoples' Courts, civil or military, of that period.

[55] In the mid-1990s I made a brief attempt, just for the hell of it, to have my corporal's rank restored, but the Personnel Section of the Ministry of Defence informed me that first I had to have the trial and sentence declared invalid; I could not be bothered to pursue the matter further.

[56] *Rab* means *prisoner*.

Peering out through this window we tried to guess by what little we saw of the road where we were being driven to. It was soon evident that we were driving toward the south or west of the "Dunántúl", the part of the country west of the Danube, and various places where we knew labour camps to be were suggested. Suddenly everybody seemed to know a lot about them, what the advantages and disadvantages of each were.

After some hours of driving a wooden guard-tower came into sight, then we saw masses of barbed wire and the car came to a halt. The doors were thrown open, and carrying what belongings we had, shivering from the cold in our thin linen suits, we were lined up in front of a low temporary building, in deep mud, a double barbed wire fence behind us. We could see some more wooden towers with guards in fur-lined overcoats, holding nasty looking little tommy-guns in their hands, reflectors all along the fence, and the roofs of some temporary barracks built on the sloping ground inside the fence.

After a long wait we were checked upon one by one, then led in beyond the fence through a gate that creaked unpleasantly on closing behind us. We were within the forced labour camp of Várpalota near Veszprém, where twelve-hundred prisoners, many of them sentenced to long terms for political offences, mined coal for the "socialist power station" of Inota[57]—naturally built by prisoners, like most large industrial plants in Hungary during the past ten years. Barbed wire, mud, guard-towers, low temporary buildings that looked damp and unhealthy, more barbed wire, a few prisoners in striped suits moving up slowly to have a look at us newcomers, the grey uniforms of guards moving outside the fence, the ferocious bark of some large dog on a chain somewhere behind the guards' quarters, the smoke of the power station at some miles distance, a bare hill on the other side of the valley, barbed wire again… that was the first impression as I carried my eyes around. It did not depress me, on the contrary: it almost gave me a feeling of freedom. The barbed wire was dozens of yards distant, the mud felt wonderfully soft underfoot after the stone floor of prison cells and passages, the buildings seemed lofty and spacious after the narrow cells, the prisoners moved about with their hands in their pockets and smoking cigarettes, the guards were at a distance where they could not hear what we were saying, the bark of the dog gave things a natural, almost home-like, touch and, most of all, the smoke of the power station rose to the unlimited sky above us, to the sky that also covered the hill opposite, to the sky on which the Sun would sometimes shine, under which birds flew and clouds of various colours and shapes would sail, the sky that was studded by the same silver stars at night for prisoner and free man alike. I took a deep breath and understood why people preferred labour camps to prisons.

---

[57] The main plant at Inota was an aluminium smelter, the power station an adjunct of this, but I was unaware of that at the time; I have tried to locate the site of the camp in recent years, but so far without success.

The inside of the barracks was no better than the outside. Brick floors, crowded with double-decker beds, clothes soaked with coal-dust and perspiration hung on strings to dry, a constant hum of human voices arguing, quarrelling or just making conversation, the smoke of cheap tobacco and the stove, thick layers of dust and dirt covering everything... There were better rooms, I later found out, this was just a transit-room for newcomers and the dregs of the camp, but it was my first impression, and whenever I think of Várpalota it is this room that appears before my mind's eye.

After a week or ten days of idling, which means peeling potatoes, sweeping the guards' quarters or collecting the litter of the camp to its collecting place, we new-comers were suddenly informed one morning that we were going down to the mine for the first time at noon. Rubber boots and miner's helmets were hurriedly distributed, the former leaky and the latter not fitting. Then we received a lamp[58] each, and down we went with the afternoon shift. (Needless to say, the price of every one of these items was later deducted from our wages.) The law prescribed that everyone working the first time in a mine must be given six days to learn his way about and to learn the security regulations, at full pay during them. The authorities of this mine pretended this meant six shifts, and by taking us down every second shift succeeded in reducing the time to four days.

I mentioned our wages above, which could create the impression that we were not so badly off after all, as we were paid for our labour. But this was only partly true. Officially we received the same wages as the civilian miners, but the whole system of wages was based on the "norma" in Hungary, i.e. a certain amount had to be produced in a given time, this was called "100 %". The only way for achieving 100% was by taking all the possible by-works[59] into account, yet as the lowest production price could be achieved by the lowest wages, by-works were hardly ever taken notice of when calculating the wages of a prisoner. He had no possibility of protesting, anyway. So the wages we received for our work were often only half of what a non-prisoner earned for the same work. But even from this already small amount a lot more was deducted. 30 per cent went to the Ministry of Justice. A further 5 per cent were deducted for income tax and old age insurance. Then of what was left 15 Forints per day were deducted for our food and keep. This meant roughly that out of 1000 Forints earned one received less than 200 at the end.

Várpalota was one of the larger forced labour camps. When we arrived there were some 1200 prisoners there, most of them political prisoners. People convicted for "conspiracy against the state", "war crimes', and charges of the kind, mostly "framed" against them because a Party Secretary or ÁVH officer or agent disliked them, or simply because they were "class enemies", former officers,

---

[58] These were open-flame carbide lamps; fortunately there was no gas in the mine.
[59] Something like *additional associated tasks* is meant.

professional people, and a few landowners. Any former officer who had partaken in the war in Russia—and naturally few regular officers had not—could any time expect to be charged with a "war crime", as they were called, on the ground for instance of having belonged to a regiment some members of which had shot Russian partisans. Few political prisoners had a sentence smaller than 10 years, the average sentence must have been 15 years, and quite a number were imprisoned for life. Many of them were in prison since 1945, having often actually spent one third of their life there.

Curiously enough, these people, whose life seemed the most wretched and hopeless, bore it with a relative cheerfulness one would not have expected. Some of them had spent years in Nazi concentration camps during the war, others had been prisoners of war in Russia for many years, and one would have thought they had lost all hope and belief in life by 1956. Yet it was not so. They were, besides working 8–10 hours down in the mine every day, all doing something else besides, learning languages, forming artistic groups for painting or acting, had chess and football competitions, etc. Of course, things were growing worse, they said: in 1951 they were still allowed to receive books from home, etc. all of which had gradually ceased since. (On one occasion while I was there, for instance, the complete works of Shakespeare were sent to somebody—in English. The same prison censorship which had allowed Cyrano de Bergerac in, in French, a few months earlier, now would not let Shakespeare pass. No reason was given.)

The guards themselves were seldom seen in this camp. They only entered once daily to count us. Every other official business was done through the camp leader and his clerk, both prisoners themselves. In principle they, like the room commanders, were elected by the other prisoners, to represent them. In fact they were nominated by the prison governor, to carry out his measures. They selected the people to do any special work, for instance, whether peeling potatoes or washing up the guards' quarters. Non-officially they also had a good deal of influence in deciding on the jobs people got, whether they should work underground in a bad place, or get better jobs just inside the mine, or one of the few "really good" jobs, like cooks, stokers in the baths, etc. And though they had no official power to punish, they could easily get somebody half a year's "deprival of privileges" or a fortnight in the "disciplinary cells". Apart from their few friends, who held the good positions, they were generally disliked, and often even hated. (The camp leader of Várpalota, who had begun his career in 1944 as a "nyilas"[60] youth organiser, had turned red in 1945 and become political major of the Hungarian red army, was later that year released after having spent only half his term. Unluckily for him another prisoner was also released the same day and met him at the railway station. On recognising him, he started

---

[60] "*Arrowcross*", a Hungarian version of Germany's Nazis, who came to power after Hungary's military occupation by Germany in 1944.

beating up the camp leader. Civilian miners interfered, but when they heard what it was all about they lent a hand at the beating up. He was—it is said— taken off by the ambulance.)

But every now and then one of the guards would find life dull, and come into the camp to "inspect". If he was in a particularly bad humour, which they usually were, an inspecting tour of half an hour could easily end in 20–30 people being punished for the slightest or for non-existent offences. (For the blanket on their bed being folded up, for it not being folded up; for wearing a cap, for not wearing it; for smoking in his presence, for throwing away their cigarette, etc.) Punishments would range from one day's special work to 20 days' disciplinary cells (less than 10 days was never inflicted). These cells were just beside the guardroom, small concrete chambers with no windows, only a heavily barred opening over the door. Some plank was thrust in at night to sleep upon, but taken out early in the morning again. A jug of water was provided, and a pail for other purposes. Half a pound of bread every day, and half a portion of hot food every second. It can be imagined what it meant to spend three weeks in them in a winter—like the winter 1955–1956 was—when we often had to dig our way out of the barracks in the morning so much snow fell at night, and often we had no water for days because the pipelines had burst in the frost—three feet under ground.[61] Being sent to these cells was equivalent to a frozen limb or two. There were six of them, with often three occupants each, yet there was usually a list of people waiting for their turn to commence their punishment.

But to be deprived of one's so-called privileges was hardly better. It meant: no visitors, no letters, no cigarettes, etc. for the period it lasted. Three months was in practice the minimum time; it often was inflicted for times[62] up to a year. All these things were scarce enough anyway. Visitors and letters every two, three or six months, depending upon the term.[63] (The scale was: up to one year, two years, five years, or above. All political prisoners automatically belonged to the "above five years" group with regard to "privileges".) Parcels only twice a year, unless one had an unusually high per cent at work.[64] These parcels could weigh 6 1/2 lbs. and only contain certain things, mostly food of a kind that was not a "luxury". By letters an open post-card is to be understood, with not more than 30 lines of writing. A visitor meant ten minutes to maximum one hour at two sides of a table, with guards walking up and down the whole time either side, watching that one should behave according to regulations (hands behind back, etc.) and listening to every word that was said. (One prisoners repeatedly smuggled out letters to his visitor by making a small bundle of the letter written on very fine paper, and pretending his face was swollen because of a sore tooth. He waited for a moment

---

[61] On reflection, they must have been nearer the surface.

[62] *Durations of* is meant.

[63] *of imprisonment*, to which one was sentenced.

[64] I.e. one's work achievement expressed as a percentage of the target 'norm'.

when the guard looked away for a few seconds, then literally spat his message at his visitor. It worked perfectly, he was never caught at it.)

On 6 February my case came up before the Court of Appeal, in my absence, as I was told I do not possess the money to pay for the journey for three people (myself and two guards). No one took the trouble to inform me what its decision was. Actually, as I found out later, the sentence had been annulled and the whole case sent back to the court that had tried me in the first instance—not because the Court of Appeal regarded it unjust, but because it just could not stand legally as it was. So they demanded further evidence. But of this I knew nothing at the time, it was quite in vain to try and find out from the prison officials, and the one letter I could receive in two months I had already received. So I lived in a state of suspense and strong nervous tension for the next month or so.

In the meantime I had been found medically unfit for underground work. (Várpalota was perhaps the only camp in Hungary where the mining company had the forced labourers examined by a doctor.[65] In the other ones the prisoners were just sent down to work after they arrived, and either they could stand it or not. If not, the worse for them.) Not being one of the camp leader's friends, I was incapable to get any overground job. This did not mean that I was left idle. The lodgings and offices of the guards had to be cleaned, heated, the garbage had to be carried out of the camp, and snow had to be cleared away in and around the camp—even if it was melting and would evidently disappear completely by the next morning. The aim was not only to do something useful, it was rather to keep everyone occupied at least 8 hours a day. But, for this kind of work one did not receive even a nominal fee.[66] Besides, the food was worse for—we were told—as we "are not working" we need less calories. On the same grounds, that we are not working, we could have no money[67] to buy cigarettes, soap, tooth-paste or some additional calories, nor were we allowed to receive any parcels.

Once, when very frustrated at this situation, I recklessly applied the expression "slave labour" to it. (Which, as is evident from the paragraph above, could have no resemblance to the truth, of course.) Needless to say that, though there were only a handful of prisoners about, I was called to the guard-room to report within half an hour. Small privileges can best be got by giving small informations concerning other prisoners. I was told to stand, face to the wall, at attention, and then a stream of abuse was poured at me, in the coarsest possible language and the loudest possible shout. I was to be glad of the privilege of being in a camp and not in a prison, that I was inciting an uprising, that I was a damned bastard of a class-enemy

---

[65] A **fudge:** while the medical examination was routine, the doctor in question, a prisoner too, was a fellow class-enemy (a Count Hoyos), and I suspect, although he never said so, that he aimed to do me a favour by declaring me unfit for work down the mine.

[66] *Wage* is meant.

[67] One was never handed cash, of course, but the price of such things would be deducted from whatever surplus one might have accumulated in one's wage-account.

(the other adjectives applied to me throughout cannot be repeated in print), etc. At last I was set to work on washing up the floor of the passage that ran down the building where the guard-room was.

I would never have thought that one can perspire in one's shirt-sleeves in winter while washing a floor, but then I learnt it. A guard stood over me with special orders to torment me. If I washed "too fast" then I was not "thorough enough", if "too thorough" then not "fast enough". If I stopped when somebody passed then I was lazy, if I did not then I was not showing due respect. If I said "yes" to a remark then I was mocking him, if I said "no" then contradicting, if I did not say anything then I was sullen. As the passage was long, and as people were coming in all the time with muddy boots, it was naturally dirty again by the time I had finished. This, too, was my fault, and I had to wash it over and over again.

Perhaps I would have continued washing that passage for the rest of my sentence, but luckily I was suddenly called back to the camp, and told to get ready to be transferred to another camp. This meant handing in all my "belongings" like blankets etc., only keeping what was on me. In consequence it was quickly accomplished, and we all stood, some 50 of us, with what little private belonging we had in the way of soap, tooth-brushes and the like tied up in a bundle, waiting to see what would happen next.

What happened next was that we were all carefully searched. Cold perspiration stood out on my brow, for I had in my pocket a portefeuille,[68] in itself a prohibited object, with some photographs, three envelopes, four post-cards and four stamps in it.[69] My pocket had up to then been the safest place for them, because though the rooms were thoroughly searched at regular intervals, for some unknown reason they never searched our pockets. And now it would prove to be my worst misfortune. But it was too late to do anything about it, I could not step out of line or drop them, all I could do was to depend upon my good luck. I stood silently, hands lifted over my head, while my pockets were being searched. Then the portefeuille was taken out of them with a frown. "Now—I thought—they will find the envelopes and postcards, and off I go to the cells." They opened the portefeuille, looked at each photograph carefully, cast one glance at the envelopes, folded in two with the post-card in them, then handed it all back with the remark that keeping photographs is prohibited and I should hand them in the moment we arrive at our destination. They had not recognised the envelopes as such. With a sigh of relief I promised everything as they began to search the next man.

Crowded into a truck we were driven to our destination, a small village not far off called Herend. It is generally known for its factory of china,[70] but lately coalfields had been found beside it, and it had been decided to mine them with forced

---

[68] *Wallet* is meant.
[69] All of this had been taken from me when I entered the Fő utca prison, but I had extracted them from the bundle of my personal belongings during our journey to Várpalota.
[70] Porcelain factory is meant.

labour—the coal was of poor quality, so it had to be got out of the earth in the cheapest possible way. So, while the preliminary work for starting the mine was being carried on, by civilian miners, a barbed-wire enclosure had been set up, within which a camp of barracks had to be erected by summer for the prisoners to mine the coal. At the time of our arrival there was one temporary barrack standing, its walls made of reeds, its roof of tarred paper. The food and drinking water had to be carried by hand from the mine's kitchen, ca. 1/2 mile away—for washing purposes we could melt snow, if there was any. The inside of the building was supposed to be heated, but no fuel was provided, so planks and other building material of wood disappeared with surprising speed. This, of course, was prohibited, but could not be stopped.

But before I could find out any more about the camp I was suddenly summoned to the guard-room, and told to get ready within 3/4 hour to travel to Budapest for trial. I could not understand, but they did not seem to know much more either, saying they had received orders by telephone, telling them that I should be in Budapest by 11 a.m. next morning. In the course of getting ready for the journey I lost my precious envelopes and stamps too. After being searched before our departure from Várpalota I had made a little slit in the lining of my coat and slipped them into it. Now I was ordered to get a new outfit, for the one I had was regarded too dirty to appear in court in. With a guard beside me all the time I could not do anything but hand in the old one, envelopes and all, in exchange for my new one. My hands were then chained together,[71] the chain fastened with a lock, and the barrel of a tommy-gun a few inches from my ribs I was marched off to the station.

After half an hour or so I got used to my chains and was no longer embarrassed by them, and began to enjoy our trip immensely. You must not forget, by then more than three months had elapsed since I had last been among people who were not dressed in striped suits, since I walked more than ten feet without seeing a barbed-wire fence or wall in front of me. Now I was sitting in a waiting room of a railway station, its walls covered with posters advising what tooth-paste to use, what to feed pigs on, or informing me of the by-laws and regulations of the railway. I once more learned that it was "strictly forbidden to spit on the floor", and heard all about the illness of a stout woman's mother-in-law.

At other times I hated all of this. But after three months' seclusion it was all novel again and savoured of life, nay: LIFE, as it is lived beyond barbed-wire fences and thick stone walls. When our train arrived we found an empty compartment, and had it all to ourselves till Budapest—people would just look in, see what was probably a dozenfold murderer, in his striped suit, chains and tommy-gun pointed at him, so they would move on in horror. The train was well heated, the seat seemed immensely comfortable, and the evening landscape as it rolled past the

---

[71] *Handcuffed* is meant.

window I found more beautiful than any I had ever seen. My guard was quite a good man, after some time he even went as far as offering me cigarettes, and discussing his difficulties in finding suitable lodgings for his family with me.

On arriving to the prison (a closed prison-van was expecting us at the station) I was placed into a solitary cell and, still not knowing what I would be tried for next morning, for the first time after quarter of a year once more enjoyed a bedroom of sorts all to myself. I was roused in the morning by the well-known clang of the bell somewhere down the passage and, as my cell had no wash-basin, soon one of the so-called "house-workers" appeared with a tin basin of water. I by this time was used to the relatively free life in camps and, recognising him as a former cell-companion, greeted him with all heartiness. But he only cast frightened glances towards the open door, while making frantic signs at me to lower my voice, and quickly retreated only saying that he would later return for the basin. Of course I had forgotten that we were prohibited to talk to each other, this was a prison. But later we succeeded in having a few words, and he was full of envy to hear of how "wonderful" life must be in a forced labour camp. In his view it was a privilege, and I remembered how I had wished to get to one as soon as possible while still in the prison, in the same way as I had wished to get to the prison as soon as possible while being interrogated by the Intelligence Department. Life's joys are very relative.

At about ten o'clock I was taken to a little room close to the courtroom, to await the commencement of my trial there. Someone had inscribed Dante's words "Lasciate ogni speranza..." over the door leading to the courtroom in crude letters, and meditating on those words I paced up and down. At last I was led into the courtroom, which was still completely empty. Then the solicitor defending me arrived, but hardly had I greeted him the guard in charge of me interrupted us, and informed me that I was not to talk to anyone. In vain did the lawyer try to persuade him to let us do so. So there we sat, he in one corner I in the other, and I still did not know what I was going to be tried for within a few minutes. Then my mother arrived, but all I could do was to nod her a distant greeting and give her the best I could manage in the way of a reassuring smile.

At last the judge, a captain, his two co-judges, two corporals, and the prosecutor, also a captain, arrived and the trial began. It was only in the course of the trial, which lasted less than an hour, that I learnt that the Court of Appeal had given my case back to the lower court because of lack of evidence, and I was going to be tried again on the same charge, with practically the same evidence. Needless to say, I was sentenced to exactly the same term of imprisonment again. I was given a chance to talk to my defence[72] during the trial at least, and we decided that there was no use appealing again—it would just be a waste of time and money. So I returned to Herend the next morning, chained.

---

[72] The lawyer defending me is meant.

After my second trial life settled down to a steady routine, no longer interrupted neither by the excitement of a trial, nor by the constant expectancy for something to happen to lessen my sentence. By the end of March the camp at Herend was overcrowded, three people to two beds; after long begging we were at last supplied with water, not drinkable though, as it came from one of the shafts of the mine, but for washing purposes at least; and as the days grew longer so did the working hours too. It was here, during this period, that I got my first real lesson in practical economics. I had of course learnt about laws of economics influencing prices and business in general, but at that time, at school, it all seemed very abstract and theoretical. I was now to find that these laws were everything but abstract and theoretical, nor were they arbitrary either.

Money, of course, did not circulate in the camp, but a different currency was used instead: cigarettes and tobacco. This was the first lesson, that money is not an artificial invention but a necessity. Cigarettes would buy anything from food to labour, from everyday needs to luxuries. There was no "official" difference in rate between different brands, but some had a decided tendency to be more favoured than others. The most solid currency was the cheap and strong "Kossuth" cigarette, that was always accepted by everybody in payment for anything, not only because most people liked it but also because (in a sense a vicious circle) everybody knew that it would always be accepted. Other cigarettes were of course also accepted in payment, but sometimes it was stipulated that payment be made in "Kossuth". On the other hand, "luxury" cigarettes, which would have cost two–three times as much "outside", were no better currency than any other; they had, at best, only a slight rarity-value, only taken notice of by collectors.

I made a sport out of watching the "market prices" and their changes, though unluckily of course I had no chance of making notes of my observations. But it was astounding the way these changes followed the laws I had learnt years earlier at school. Someone received a parcel with, say, 500 cigarettes. He did not invest them in anything, but being a strong smoker himself kept them for his own use. Yet, the next day the price of one portion of meat went up from 5 cigarettes to six. The presence of just so much more free capital in a completely closed market showed its effect. Businesses sprang up, some business-minded people started wholesale business in food, buying up all food for sale, and then selling it next day with profit.[73] Soon three or four people had the whole market in hand, and dictated the prices within reasonable limits. All of them people who had started this kind of transaction because they did not have any cigarettes (= capital) themselves, buying the first lot on credit.

What made all this business life so interesting a study was that the people who partook in it were in their majority completely uneducated and had never heard about economics. They just acted and dealt according to the natural laws of economics. Had someone told them that the mysterious word "stock exchange"

---

[73] There was also an enterprising prisoner who ran a laundry service for those who could afford it, and another made sandals, from conveyor belt material, for sale.

really covered nothing more or different than what they were doing, only on a larger scale, they would not have believed so.

Another interesting feature of this prison life was how much of a world of its own it is. If one is in it it is not, like when regarded from without, a small part of the world closed away from the rest, but an independent world that has some contact with that other world, generally known as the "outside world". It was a world with its own laws, its own connections, friendships and animosities, its own aspect of affairs, views on life and politics. A couple of dozen camps and a score of prisons strewn all over the country were parts of this world; the territory that lay beyond the barbed-wire fences and walls was strange and alien, inhabited by a different race of different morals and customs, a race with which one had some connection, some of whom one knew, but only vaguely, their problems and thoughts were different, their economies were different—much like the connection between two adjoining countries whose inhabitants are on the whole on friendly terms, but are of so different race and mentality that they can never really understand each other.[74] The things that went on in that outside world did not au fond affect one any more than would, for instance, the floods of the Yang-ze-Kiang affect the inhabitants of Canada. One took an aloof and distant interest in them, same as the Canadian would see the floods in China in the newsreel, probably even discussed them, but the things that really mattered were those that affected one's life directly: a cut in lunch-time, the reorganisation of the distribution of beds, who is to distribute the food, which guard was to be on duty on Sunday were really important affairs, in comparison with which all outside events were unimportant.

But there was one feature of outside life which could hold general interest: the question of a general pardon.[75] "Absolutely sure" information about when it would be issued and whom it would affect and to what extent was constantly to be had. Every possible event was good for an excuse to expect a general pardon. Some people knew for sure that there was a secret clause in the so-called Constitution of Hungary according to which a general pardon must be issued every three years. (Three years was not a random guess: the last pardon had been issued in summer 1953 when Imre Nagy first became prime minister, and it was then 1956.) Hardly had I arrived in prison, I already heard of a general pardon that was to be issued on 1 January 1956 (this was December 1955). It was quite sure, because Hungary had been accepted to the UNO, and the Charter of the UN made it compulsory for the government of every country newly joined to issue a general pardon. But it would also be issued because the second Five-year Plan begins then. Later the date changed to 15 February, 1 March, 4 April ("Liberation-day" of Hungary by the Red Army in 1945), 1 May, 16 May, and so on, the dates sometimes being connected with some event, sometimes chosen for some unaccountable reason.

---

[74] Many years after this was written Solzhenyitsin coined the term *Gulag Archipelago* for the phenomenon here described.

[75] *Amnesty* is meant.

There were of course sceptics who would not believe, but they were simply shouted down if they dared open their mouths to object against too high unreasonable hopes. There was a part who denied any belief in such rumours, but whose spirit yet showed the effects of them. And there were those who spent all their time gathering new information, elaborating it and then passing it on. People who had been in prison since 1946 said, though, that exactly the same rumours had been circulating then already, nor had they ever varied in the time between. But those, of course, everyone knew, had been mere rumours, not like the newest, which was based on undeniable facts.

Another thing that struck me as fantastic was the speed with which news concerning this "inside" world spread. Cut off almost completely from the outside world and practically hermetically form each other, yet people knew all about others and events in other camps and prisons. It was a question of a few weeks only before one heard that somebody had been unexpectedly released from a camp at the other end of the country, or that some prison had a new governor. Of course, time counted much less in a sense, a bit of news less than a month old counted as new. This did not, though, apply to events in the outside world. We knew of the uprising in Poznań[76] a couple of days after it had happened, and of the nationalisation of the Suez Canal the next day.[77]

The building of the camp was urgent, forced labour in the mine should have started by May, so at least some of the buildings had to be ready by then to accommodate the miners.[78] In consequence Sunday as a day of rest was dropped. From the beginning of April till the middle of July we literally worked non-stop, from 6 a.m. till 7 p.m. every day, with one hour lunch-time. This meant in practice that work began a good deal sooner than 6 a.m. (on the excuse that so much precious time of work is lost by settling down to and getting ready for work), and usually it was found at 7 p.m. that there still was some very urgent work to do that day, which in the end lasted till it grew dark—and in that part of the year it does not grow dark much before 8 p.m. We received no wages for these plus-hours, nor did we get paid for work done on Sunday, it all went "to raise our production" we were told if we tried to complain. This was to be understood, as the Governor and the guards received bonuses on the production/time spent on it. The more was produced in the lesser time, the greater the bonus.

---

[76] In summer 1956.

[77] This sentence conceals a **fudge:** for a while we had a wireless set. A prisoner who was a trained electrician was repairing it for one of the guards (who was bending the rules to save the cost of taking it to a proper repair shop); the prisoner saw to it that its reparation proved "uncommonly difficult", so that for a considerable period the set was always "still not working properly" when the guard came to enquire about progress, but then sprung to life when no guards were around.

[78] One positive side-effect of this haste was that, to overcome the shortage of bricklayers, one could volunteer to be trained as a bricklayer. I too did so, and was accepted: not only was laying bricks more fun than just lugging them, but during the initial training period one had to achieve only one half of the standard production quota to qualify for "100%" productivity, the criterion for all "privileges".

The quality of the food had also dropped sharply in April,[79] and it is beyond me to understand to this day how we all survived in good health. For if I say "non-stop work" I mean it. Not only was the lunch-time considerably shorter than the prescribed one hour, partly because we began it later and ended it sooner than we should have done, but also because in this camp the guards had a mania for counting us. Which would have been all right if they could have counted. But they could not. To count two hundred people standing in rows of five took them a quarter of an hour or so. Three of them would count us one after the other, then they would compare their results and find that something was wrong. So all they could do was to start anew. The effect of all this was that if one stood at the end of the queue for food, by the time one got one's portion one hardly had the time to gobble it down and was already called to work again. But besides the lunch time being thus shortened, one just could not stop for a moment while working. Guards walking about took good care that one should not, and if one stopped to light a cigarette or blow one's nose, one would be sure to appear behind one's back and start making a row.

Nor did one have enough sleep and rest. It was often after 11 p.m. before one could get into bed, because before that we had to be counted again (after being counted at work's end), and perhaps the book the guard on duty was reading was interesting, or he was chatting with another guard, and just did not come to count us. All this time we had to stand lined up in front of our beds, waiting for them to come.[80] In the morning, on the other hand, the guard on duty was tired with lack of events, so he awoke us 1/2–1 hour earlier, just to make the camp look livelier. People were so exhausted that they simply fell asleep in almost any position the moment they got a chance to do so. That's the way to build Socialism.

The building of the mining camp at Herend went on at the forced top speed, as above described, till the middle of July, though the arrival of the first miners in May had been cancelled until some uncertain future date.[81] Of course, we had heard of certain political changes in the outside world, and everybody was trying to guess

---

[79] Initially there were too few of us to justify a separate kitchen, and we received our food from the civilian miners' canteen; by April a separate kitchen dedicated to feeding the prisoners had been set up.

[80] The evening count was sometimes also combined with an *ad hoc* kit inspection. On one such occasion the duty sergeant (Hasznos by name, which means, of all things, *Useful*), bawled at me: "Your mess tin is filthy! what would your mother have said, had one of your servants made such a bad job of washing up?", smiling broadly at his witticism; "I believe"—it slipped out of me—"that my mother neither knew nor cared who, when or how did the washing up." At this, looking up at me (he was a short squat man), he came out with: "Of course, being a fucking count you look down on others!", to which I could not but reply "Only if they are shorter than I am." The room tittered, he moved on looking perplexed (he was not very bright) but, curiously, from that day on he stopped vexing me, even tried to seem friendly.

[81] This had the incidental advantage that we builders were moved into the already completed brick barracks from our temporary shed; the camp Governor used this occasion to separate those in prison for "political" crimes, only a score or so in this camp, from the common criminals, and we were placed in a room of our own. Not that we did not get on with the others or they with us—*honour among thieves* is a true saying (only gipsy prisoners were insufferable, because dirty, quarrelsome and thieving)—but presumably because we were considered "a bad influence" on mere thieves and the like.

what their consequences would be for us. We knew that in the end the events would have some effect on our future, but could never find out for certain how or what. To illustrate a method of getting information: when we received visitors, once every two months, for 10–15 minutes, guards were standing about on either side of the table across which we talked, listening carefully to every word that was said. But their attention would slacken every now and then for a few seconds or minutes, then it perhaps succeeded to say a few words of "prohibited" information (we were not supposed to be allowed to talk about anything else than "family affairs"), possibly in some foreign language. But, I being a "class-enemy", special care was taken that I should get even less chance for that than the others. Yet it was possible to pass on some information in the following manner (I quote from memory):

My mother, to the officer in charge: "May I hand over the newspaper with Comrade Rákosi's speech in it to my son?" (So I knew there had been such a speech.)
Officer: "No! No newspapers are allowed into the camp."
My mother: "May I tell him what it was about?"
Officer: "No, you are only allowed to talk of family affairs!"
My mother: "But the release of my son is a family affair for us!" (So I knew there was something concerning prisoners, or something concerning "class-enemies" in it, or both.)
Officer: "No!"

Of course my mother knew all the time that she would not be allowed to hand in the paper, or tell me details about what it contained, but by asking those questions she could give me some information she could give me in no other manner.

The first effect that we actually felt, beyond vague rumours that commissions were visiting all camps and prisons, interrogating[82] prisoners, and that many were suddenly released before their term ended, was a sudden cut in working hours. We just could not believe at first when we were told that there would be no work on the following Sunday, but there wasn't any.[83] The incessant nagging of the guards who watched over our work also ceased, and unless somebody was too obviously doing nothing they did not bother how much he worked. Something had changed in the whole atmosphere.

---

[82] *Questioning* is probably meant.
[83] But Sunday did not become a day of rest: the governor took to coming on an inspection tour of the camp soon after lunch, to check that both the building site and the barrack rooms were spotlessly clean and tidy. Thus the morning had to be spent ensuring this, nor could the beds be lain on and crumpled until after the inspection. Moreover, if dissatisfied he'd return before supper was distributed, to verify that matters he had objected to had been put right, so the afternoon was no more restful than the morning had been. However, on some notable occasions we 'politicals'—apparently better able to scrub, clean and tidy without squabbling over who does what than the others—were let off the hook, even held up as an example to the rest of the camp: "Go, look at the room of the politicals, and emulate their standard! They can dismiss now; the rest I'll inspect again later."

It had been, in principle, always possible to be released conditionally after the half, two-thirds, three quarters or seven-eighths of one's term had expired, but usually not more than one or two in a hundred were granted this favour, though of course everybody always applied. Now suddenly twenty-five out of thirty applicants were released.

But further miracles were to happen: one day it was suddenly announced that there would be a cinema performance in one of the half-built barracks next Saturday evening. Hardly had we time to understand the meaning of it, when one of the guards turned up with paper and pencil, and asked who wanted to subscribe to the "Művelt Nép" and/or the "Élet és Tudomány"? (The first being a "cultural" weekly, on questions of art, literature, music, etc., the second a popular scientific and technical weekly.) Perhaps, he half implied, later on we would also be allowed to subscribe to some daily paper—a thing that had been allowed up to 1953 or so, and then stopped abruptly without any explanation.

In the meantime I had succeeded in building out a route for contact with my mother through some people in the village of Herend.[84] This did not, of course, mean that I could correspond with her as if I were free, but occasional letters were this way smuggled out and in, also a few parcels—food, cigarettes, vitamin tablets. Unluckily, after not much more than perhaps six weeks some other people, who were using a different route for similar purposes, had a row about some cigarettes one of them had received and the other also claimed, and the second one did the worst thing possible for a convict to do: in anger and rage at not getting the cigarettes from his opponent he gave information to the prison officials. So there was a raid for illegal parcels etc. one morning, and quite a number were caught at it. I actually had received one just the day before, but got scent of the raid just in time to hide away its contents. But that was the end of any illegal contact with the outside world.

Life would have been a good deal easier now, for also the food had grown better again, mainly in consequence of the Governor allowing us to buy supplementary food for five florins per day on all days we worked more than 8 hours—which still meant six days of the week. The five florins covered something like half a pound of white bread plus some bacon, or cheese, or jam, or sugar etc. and some fruit each day. This, though it might seem little, was just enough to provide us with the extra calories which distinguish between starvation and healthy hunger.

But, the general circumstances growing easier, I had at the same time the ill-luck of the engineer who had the technical side of the building[85] in hand to take a strong dislike to me for some inconceivable reason. Actually, there was one

---

[84] Alas! memory fails and I can no longer un-fudge the details: all I remember is that the contact my end was a civilian who, for some reason connected with the construction works, visited the building site regularly; I think, but may be wrong, that I never knew the name of the people who acted as postal go-between in the village. Nor can I recall how I established this route.

[85] *Construction* is meant.

engineer who belonged to the Ministry of the Interior, that had all prison affairs in hand, who was officially responsible for the work, but there was also a convict engineer who did all the actual work instead of him. And though it was the civilian engineer who took all the decisions, the influence of the convict was predominant. It was he whose antipathy I had roused, and in a quiet fashion he did his best to make my anyway difficult situation even more so.

So, after a harassed month, during which I was shifted from one job to another almost every day, when a transport of prisoners was taken away from the camp to some unknown (for us) destination, it was but natural that I was one of the transported. Some 18 of us crowded into a hermetically closed van, designed for ten or twelve at the most, we journeyed across the Dunántúl to arrive, after travelling 7-8 hours and 300 kilometres, to the southwest of the country, the city of Pécs, known for the uranium mines in its neighbourhood. But it was not there that we were to work: a block of flats had to be erected in the middle of the city for ÁVH officers, and it was our job to do so.[86]

After spending the night in the County Prison we were next morning taken to the camp. An empty building-site in the middle of the city, flanked on three sides by streets and a public park, by another empty site on the fourth side, and the back-walls of some houses there. Our site was surrounded by the obligatory barbed-wire fence, wooden towers for the guards at the four corners. There were also two further wooden towers, one each on the longer sides of the fence, but these were always unoccupied till the last days of my stay in that camp—which were also the last days of the camp, in October. But at the time of our arrival it was only the end of September.

The change of atmosphere, as compared with what it had been half a year earlier, showed most distinctly on the food-question here. There was a kitchen attached to the camp and the food they served us, after being reasonable both in quality and quantity at the beginning, soon grew worse and worse and less and less. But while all we could do about it a few months earlier, at Herend, was to grumble amongst ourselves and try to complain—here we went on hunger-strike. One evening, after a rather strenuous day, when the end of work had been pushed out by more than an hour, on the excuse that some concrete foundations had to be made still that day, both the quantity and quality of the supper was below even the usual standard. But this time, instead of just eating what little it was and going to bed hungry, we refused to let it be distributed and, instead of queuing up for it in the usual place, all lay on our beds.

Within less than an hour the governor of the County Prison, under whose jurisdiction we belonged, arrived with some officers, and actually almost pleaded with us to accept the food, promising improvement of the food, the accommodation,

---

[86] A row of ugly apartment blocks stands on the site, in Semmelweiss utca, to this day; who their inhabitants were or are I have no idea.

the supply of clean underwear, promising in short to better everything we complained about. It was near midnight by the time we acquiesced to accept our supper, and the kitchen had in the meantime almost doubled it. It was the first victory of convicts over their gaolers that I experienced since I was in prison.

The population of the town was completely on our part,[87] that could be seen by the way they threw cigarettes, fruit and other articles in to us through the fence. The small children were the best, they just did not take any notice of the guards shouting at them, but walked up to the outside of the fence and brought us whatever they had to give. The guards, of course, were in an impossible situation, because they could not very well start shooting up children of eight or ten, who ran about around their towers and pulled faces at them, jeering and mocking all the time as they did so—much to our amusement.

All the guards could do was to search the ground near the fence carefully every morning before we went out to work, and pick up articles thrown in there. This they did, and also took every other precaution to cut us off from the free world, from which only a few feet and a barbed-wire fence divided us. But they were on the whole quite good at it, our information concerning events outside were much worse than they had been at Herend.

So we had not the faintest notion why the guards were suddenly doubled on Sunday, 21 October. There was a faint rumour that something was brewing up, Poland was mentioned too, but nobody seemed to know anything. Work went on like usual on Monday, besides[88] the fact that the double guards were still on. We were awakened at the usual time on Tuesday, the 23rd,[89] and breakfast was distributed like normal. After breakfast there was suddenly some stirring among the guards, and we were ordered to get ready to leave the camp for the day, with our tin saucepans,[90] spoons and our daily ration of bread. No explanation was given.

That the decision was a hurried and sudden one could be judged by the fact that, in discordance[91] with all previous experience, we were crowded on board of an open truck instead of a closed prison van, and driven through the streets of the town in that. The atmosphere was tense throughout the city, silent figures muffled up in their coats and scarves hurried along the streets with expressionless faces, while loudspeakers kept bawling out sinister message, only part of which we could understand as the truck rushed along the streets and squares of Pécs with us. But what little we did understand made us wonder what was going on: snatches of orders prohibiting all meetings and gatherings, prohibiting the inhabitants of the town to move on the streets without special permits after dusk, orders calling

---

[87] *Our side* is meant.

[88] *Apart from* is meant.

[89] On reflection, this must have been the next day, 24: the Budapest events only occurred on the evening of the 23rd.

[90] *Mess tins* is meant.

[91] Not in accord with is meant.

everybody's attention to the necessity of keeping up order under all circumstances, and admonishing everybody not to withstand[92] the police or other official authorities. It was 7 a.m. on Tuesday, 23 October 1956.[93]

* * *

We soon arrived at the gates of the County Prison[94] and were herded into a cell on the second floor. There were 12–14 beds in it for the twenty of us,[95] no blankets or anything, just the straw sacks.[96] It was evident that it must have been emptied in a hurry, only a short time ago, to make place for us. Some of the woman prisoners, of whom there were nearly two hundred at the time, of the County Prison of Pécs had occupied it before us, and having nothing else to do, we searched the cell thoroughly, finding cigarette-ends and even whole cigarettes hidden away, and torn bits of paper, which must have been "black"[97] letters written to each other inside the prison. The fact that all these things were still about also pointed towards the cell having been emptied in a great hurry. Its windows opened onto the street, and through them we could see away over the roofs and housetops of Pécs to one or two distant villages to the south.[98] If we climbed up to the window and pressed our face against the bars we could just see the pavement of the street on the opposite side. But a guard with a tommy-gun was patrolling up and down there, and if he noticed anyone in a window, he shouted in abusive language for him to draw back.

The sky, covered by heavy grey clouds in the morning, cleared by noon and the Sun shone in through the bars. After weeks and months of constant hard work we enjoyed lying idly on our backs and, as in the hurry of getting us in no one had thought of searching us, we still had some cigarettes, which we smoked openly while discussing the possible reason for the last few hours' events. The sounds filtering in from the city beneath us gave us no clue whatsoever, they sounded quite normal and everyday, beyond the constant low drone of the loudspeakers, the words of which, try as we would, we could not understand.

At noon our lunch was brought, from the kitchen in the camp, not from the prison kitchen—the latter being even worse. The afternoon passed almost as eventlessly as the morning, but for the fact that towards the evening our blankets were brought into the prison from the camp, and we were told that possibly we would

---

[92] *Resist* is meant.

[93] But see earlier footnote as to date: it was probably 24 October 1956.

[94] According to a plaque on its wall a listed building *(műemlék)*, which says more for its age than comfort.

[95] Fallible memory keeps insisting that there had been more than twenty convicts in the camp, working on the building site: we must have been split up at some point, for transport or on arrival.

[96] Neither in the Air Force nor in any prison or camp did we ever have matraces to sleep on, only bed-size bags of sacking material stuffed full of straw—if there is an English term for these, I am ignorant of it.

[97] Illicit, illegal, as in black market.

[98] The prison building stands on a hillside, on the north and above most of the sloping old town of Pécs.

have to spend a couple more days in there before returning to work again. No explanation was given this time either.

In the evening, towards nine o'clock, we heard what must have been a huge crowd shouting slogans, also as if somebody had been making a speech over the loudspeakers, but could not discern any details, only single words here and there, which in themselves did not explain anything. Towards midnight sound died down, and we tried to sleep. For my part this was the last night for a long time to come which I slept through.

The next day, Wednesday, was completely eventless again. The guards behaved, on the whole, with a tentative friendliness, but gave no explanations. This was also the last time we got a meal from the camp kitchen. We tried to judge by the sounds we heard from the town what was happening, but they sounded as if ordinary life were going on as usual.

Then in the evening we heard the shouts and cheers of what must have been a mass demonstration somewhere in the town, and this time we could half make out some of the slogans; "Ruszkik haza!" (= "Russians go home") was the most common among them. Then it seemed as if the sounds would be coming nearer, and actually, a few minutes later a crowd, carrying red-white-and-green national banners appeared in front of the prison. With unbounded enthusiasm they shouted the latest news to us, who were crowded in the small space of the windows: there had been a revolution, Imre Nagy was prime minister, they were demanding that the Russians leave the country, that Hungary be independent and neutral, general pardon for all political prisoners and a supervision[99] of all non-political cases; there had been fights in Budapest and elsewhere in the country, but now the revolutionary forces had taken over power; here in Pécs, the army, the police and even the ÁVH had taken their side, we should be quiet, a Commission of the Revolutionary Council was coming to the prison next morning and would start releasing all those who were innocent and in prison for false charges. After all had been said the crowd on the street started singing the Hungarian National Anthem,[100] and by the second line of it the whole prison had joined.

I think I shall never forget those minutes, the crowd deep below us in the street, carrying national banners, singing the National Anthem, and we standing on top of our beds in striped prison suits, joining in whole-heartedly, and the well-known melody of it streaming from all windows of the prison, rolling down its dark passages, breaking through the bars—tears stood out in our eyes and we still could not quite believe that what we had all been awaiting since ten years and more was now coming true.

---

[99] *Review* is meant.

[100] Introduced in the first half of the nineteenth century to replace the Habsburg-centric *Gott erhalte unsern Kaiser* (who was, in any case, king, not emperor, in Hungary) its words are those of a poem that asks God to bless and protect Hungary and her people, its melody slow and solemn; not even the Communists dared to abolish or change it (Rákosi did try once, but neither Kodály nor any other composer was willing).

Then the crowd below marched away, telling us they still had to go to the uranium mines that night, to guard them against any possible Russian attack. Next some of the guards, amongst them one or two well-known in the whole prison for their ruthless brutality, appeared at the little window in the door, and showed us their caps, from which the red star,[101] for years hated symbol of Russian oppression, had been taken off. The same guards who had, a day or two earlier, inflicted every punishment within their means onto a prisoner found with cigarettes in his possession within his cell now handed us in cigarettes by the dozen, told us everything would be all right, and treated us almost like equals. Pessimist began to doubt their behaviour, and said there must be something fishy about it—unluckily they proved right for the time being. Hardly had we settled down half-ways for the night, though none of us could sleep, when the little window on the door opened again, and we were informed, still in the former friendly tone, that undisciplined gangs of criminals were trying to make the best of the events, and having got some arms were at large near the city. It was to be expected that they would try to attack the prison, so whatever we hear, we should be quiet and should not excite ourselves—this did not alter the fact that next morning a Commission would release all those who deserved it.

After this announcement there was sinister silence on the passage for a time. Then we heard shuffling feet and movement outside the door. Next the sound of sharp, metallic, clicks reached out ears, a sound unmistakable to anyone who had ever handled firearms: the clicking of the lock after the firearm is loaded. Then infinitely long moments of expectant silence passed, suddenly broken by the fast tuck-tuck-tuck of tommy-guns echoing along the passage. A hysterical female voice was heard to shout "Murderers! they are killing us…" and then deadly silence settled on the whole building for a few minutes. This silence again was broken, by the brutal and coarse shouts of guards, the sound of a heavy body being dragged down the stairs, a painful moan or two. Hardly had we recovered from all of this, which took place within a few minutes, I think, but seemed an eternity at the time, when the door flew open, the lights were switched on, and the figure of the prison's deputy-governor, red in the face with rage, the red star, evidently re-fixed in a hurry, askew on his cap, appeared, two armed guards behind him, his hand on his open revolver-bag.

From his lips poured a flow of abuse, coarse, blasphemous and brutal language the like of which I never heard before or after—and I had heard quite a good deal of it by then. The names we were called and the adjectives applied to us are irreproducible, and the sum of it all was that we were dirty scoundrels,

---

[101] Hungary's Constitutional Court has just (May 2000) upheld the constitutional legality of a new section of the Criminal Law Code, which forbids the public use of symbols associated with oppressive ideologies such as, and explicitly mentioning, the Nazi swastika as well as the Communist red star and hammer-and-sickle.

that we thought we could do anything, that we would just walk out of the prison, that we had soiled the National Anthem by taking it onto our dirty lips and afterwards behaving like so many dastardly cut-throats, etc. etc. But he would see to it that we noticed what a mistake we had made, and we would spend the rest of our prison term regretting this evening. After he had finished shouting all this at us the door was slammed to, and we were left in the darkness of our cell to ponder: what had happened?

The week that followed is but a hazy blur in my memory. I remember that we were transferred to another cell, opening onto the courtyard, the next morning. Then one day cigarettes, lighters, matches, pencils, etc. were taken away from us. Then again we were given cigarettes. At times we heard shouts outside and in the prison's yard. The food was meagre and grew less every day. The guards sometimes had red starts on their caps, then they had not again. There were extra guards patrolling in the yard, reinforced by ÁVH men. They also at times had red stars, at others had not. Nobody had slept more than an hour or two at a stretch since that memorable night, the atmosphere was tense and irate. We were tired, hungry, and did not know what was going on outside.

By those inexplicable channels which can never be quite hermetically stopped some news sickered into the prison. Fighting was going on throughout the country. Thousands had been killed in Budapest. Budapest looked worse than it had after its two-month siege in 1945.[102] Russian tanks had stamped into crowds of women and children. Children were blowing up Russian tanks. And then came the hopes: the West was intervening, the UNO had sent a police force to stop the fighting, Yugoslavia was sending troops to restore peace. Rákosi, Gerő, Farkas and the rest were being tried for treason. But one could never check on anything, one could never find out how much was true and how much was exaggeration and fantasy. We could not eat any more, we could not sleep, we could not sit in one place, we could not stand each other's presence, people were quarrelling over the merest trifles, and each time we heard steps approach the door we all looked towards it expectantly, to see what we could read off the face of the guard.

The guards also were taking special precautions. Not more than two prisoners were let out of the cells at a time, to fill the water jugs at the tap and empty the pails which served a different purpose. And while they were out an armed guard walked beside them, while another one stood on the corner, whence he could cover the whole of the passage with his tommy-gun.

Then suddenly, as lunch was being distributed on 1 November, the whispered news passed along the whole prison that a Commission was here, to supervise all cases and release all innocently imprisoned. Ears glued to the door we listened as names were being shouted somewhere and we heard the rattle of keys, the opening and closing of doors, as one by one the prisoners called for were being led up.

---

[102] Actually almost three months, from December 1944 to 13 February, 1945.

Nerves grew even tenser, if that was still possible. They started calling the names in alphabetic order, then they jumped a few letters, then jumped back to the beginning of the alphabet again. Slowly they proceeded down the alphabet, and it grew evident that some names had been completely skipped. Every now and then somebody called up would return to the cell door with a guard, and we would hand out his belongings, but it was impossible to exchange a single word with them.

M, then N. Next O—I never knew there were so many names beginning with O. At last! P! My heart beat so wildly, I could hardly walk. Up to the third floor. Suddenly I found myself in an office. At the far end a table, three civilians, with red-white-and-green badges in their buttonholes, on one side of it, two or three indistinguishable grey uniforms of guards on the other. A check on name and personal data. I could hardly talk for excitement[103]—I knew my fate would be decided in a few moments. Then I was asked why I was in prison. I am incapable to recount how I managed to tell them—but I must have done, for after I finished they (the three civilians) looked at each other, a silent nod, and "Cell No. 23" was the verdict. Cell No. 23! that was the cell for those to be released…

The longest night of my life followed, it seemed interminable. Crowded in quarter the space necessary we sat about all night in the dark, part already in civilian clothes, the others still in their striped suits, waiting for the pale light of dawn. But dawn came, and morning came, and nothing happened. Then, at last, around ten o'clock, the three civilians of the previous day appeared in the cell, one of them held a little speech, explained to us what had happened in the past week, then after a further hour or so elapsed at last they began to release us in groups of five to ten. At 3 p.m. on 2 November 1956, after spending eleven months and two days in prison, I at last crossed the prison gates again, without an armed guard behind me, to do exactly as I chose.

Next morning I succeeded in finding a truck going to Budapest,[104] and by noon I was in Hungary's capital again. I was too exhausted to do anything beyond having a bath, a light supper, and after deciding that on Monday the 5th I would start

---

[103] Yet, how familiar that routine was! Name? Number? Date and place of birth? Mother's maiden name?

[104] A final **fudge.** When I stepped out of prison, in my Air Force uniform and great-coat (earlier deprived of their corporal's stripes), I was possessed of one day's cold rations—half a kilogram of bread, a quarter of bacon and processed cheese—and cash to the exact amount of a single railway fare to Budapest. There were, however, no trains running.

So I decided to blow my railway fare on cigarettes, matches, some newspapers, and several cups of decent coffee in the principal café of Pécs. Here I got talking to some young men at a neighbouring table, who proved to be members of the county's Revolutionary Committee and filled me in on what had been happening, while I told them about myself and my wish to get to Budapest to find out what had become of my mother there. They then took me along to the Town Hall, where the Revolutionary Committee had established itself (a late-nineteenth century gothick pile, full of soldiers with red-white-and-green armbands and fixed bayonets at every turn of stairs and passages), and issued me a pass, which I still have and treasure, that entitled me to come and go at will in order to enquire about transport possibilities. It was thanks to them that I found myself on a truck heading for Budapest early the following morning.

at last a free life in a free and independent country, I took half a dozen sleeping pills and fell asleep. I was roused next morning, on Sunday, the 4th, by the booming of Russian tank-guns. And that was the end of freedom for Hungary again.

Epilogue

We actually lingered on in Budapest for a while after 4 November 1956, hoping against hope that by some miracle "the West", the United Nations, or somebody with a vestige of a conscience, would do *something*—at least send observers—to put a brake on the re-Sovietisation of Hungary and give it a chance to revert to being a country one could live in.

During these weeks the late Peter Kemp tracked us down in Budapest (on the suggestion of a distant cousin of my mother's, Tony Apponyi, who knew Peter from the London club they both belonged to). Having been parachuted into Poland as an SOE officer towards the end of the war, having there been arrested as a "spy" by the advancing Red Army, and having then been held in an NKVD prison in Moscow until the wartime British Military Mission there got wind of this and extricated him (with some difficulty), he was no friend of the Soviets; in 1956 he had obtained journalistic accreditation from, I think, the Daily Express to enable him to come to Hungary and see for himself what was happening there. He had no Hungarian and I gladly assisted him in his fact finding, translating and interpreting as best I could.

However, it was becoming apparent that I would be well advised to leave the country before too long. Just then nobody was looking for me, yet, but I had no personal identity documents: as a national serviceman I had had no civilian ID Card, on being arrested my military ID Card had been taken from me. All I had was the document setting me at liberty, issued by the Revolutionary Committee of County Baranya: this had been an excellent identification until 4 November, but became a most incriminating one thereafter. I thus ran the risk of being "pulled in" for further investigation should I run into a cordon of pro-Soviet Workers' Militia, who were checking the identities of passers-by on the streets of Budapest with increasing frequency. It would, in any case, have been impossible to survive for long without some proper ID document, which I had no means of obtaining: such were issued by the Police, whom I had no wish to contact.

My mother declared that if I was leaving she was coming too, otherwise she would never see me again, a plausible fear the way the situation was then developing. On being told that we were about to leave, Peter Kemp suggested that on getting to Vienna I contact his friend Mr Hitchcok, then head of the British Council there: they talked on the telephone most days, and he would thus learn of our safe arrival. The next morning, having heard that railwaymen were running one train a day on all main lines, we went to the Keleti Station, from which most trains going west of Budapest departed. Here we found an already crowded train which, we were told, might eventually leave in the direction of Hegyeshalom, the border-station with Austria, and settled into it; later in the day an engine was attached and we rolled off westwards.

Somewhere between Győr and Mosonmagyaróvár the train stopped at a level crossing, and the guard came along to inform passengers that Soviet security forces were checking ID documents on the station platform at Mosonmagyaróvár. By the time he was in the next coach virtually all occupants of ours were making for the doors: looking up and down the train, as we dropped to the ground, we saw passengers scrambling down from all other coaches too.

Walking along the road in a westerly direction, under a grey wintry sky, by dusk we got to the village of Jánossomorja. Here, by a process I no longer remember, we finished up in a hay-loft, together with several others patently also heading for the Austria. The farmer assured us that later that night somebody would guide us to the border, and we waited, tense and ill at ease. However, eventually some men did appear to lead us out of the village by back alleys, and then towards the border along dirt tracks and, finally, across ploughed fields.

By now the sky had cleared and it was freezing hard, so we could confirm from the stars that we were, indeed, trudging in a westerly direction, nor was the going as heavy as it night have been had the fields been soft mud. Our guides assured us that there were no physical barriers at the border—unlike a few years before, and then again for many years to come, when barbed-wire fences, trip-wires, mine-fields and permanently manned watch-towers with search-lights marked the border—nor any Hungarian border guards in evidence of late; occasional Russian patrols along the border were the only risk we had to face. This too we had heard in Budapest already, and I carried a bottle of vodka—never known to have been refused by a Russian soldier—in my haversack for the eventuality of a meeting; that apart it contained a sponge-bag and pair of pyjamas only: we had decided to travel light.

After a while our guides stopped and informed us that we were at the border. They received everybody's remaining Hungarian currency, warned us against deviating to the south or north, since we stood at the tip of a salient of Austrian territory that jutted into Hungary, said good-bye, and turned back. Soon the group that had that far kept together scattered, and we continued across further fields on a bearing that, we hoped, would keep us in Austria and eventually lead us to some inhabited place. In time this brought us to a metalled road, roughly perpendicular to our direction of advance.

While we were discussing whether to continue walking across the fields beyond the road or to follow it to the right or left, an approaching car appeared from the north and stopped a few yards from us. Caught in its headlights like dazzled rabbits, we could make out no detail of the car or its occupants until a man in civilian clothes emerged from the driver's seat, followed by a Hungarian policeman from the back of the car. Our hearts sank: clearly, we *had* deviated too far north or south from our westerly course, and were now back in Hungary.

However, it soon transpired that the civilian was a Belgian who was driving his car up and down along the Austrian side of the border to pick up refugees, and that the policeman had simply not bothered to change out of his uniform before crossing into Austria. Relieved we piled into the car, and were driven to the Reception Centre at Andau, a few miles down the road. During the drive, being able to communicate with our Belgian in French, we learnt that, following registration at Andau, the Austrian authorities moved refugees to temporary holding camps. Yet another camp was most certainly not what we had left Hungary for, and by the time we got to Andau he had agreed to take us to Vienna when he himself returned there in the morning. So we accepted a hot drink at the Reception Centre, but did not register.

Shortly after first daylight we were ringing the door-bell of our Kálnoky cousins in Vienna, who offered breakfast, baths, and beds, and then saw to it that when we did register as refugees we could continue with them rather than going to a camp. I telephoned Mr Hitchcock, who passed on the news to Peter Kemp, asked me to dinner (with J. B. Priestley, coincidentally in Vienna for some previously arranged British Council do), and suggested that, since I appeared to have some English, I might help out at the British Council which, linguistically quite unprepared for the task, was trying to cope with interviewing hundreds of Hungarian refugee students who hoped to continue their studies in Britain.

After a week or two of this I was told to bring all my kit the next day, since I too was, presumably, interested in a scholarship: final decisions about these were taken in London, and a plane-load of prospective candidates was being flown out in the morning. So on 10 December a "whispering giant" Comet took me to London courtesy of BOAC, which wined us, dined us, and even presented us with packets of "555" cigarettes. At Heathrow—in those days a large Nissen hut, at least the part we were taken to after landing—the good ladies of the WVS pressed mugs of sweet, milky tea on us, as though we had just braved the Channel from Dunkirk rather than enjoyed BOAC's hospitality. A coach then took us into London—and I began to feel like turning back as we rolled past mile upon mile of near-identical semi-detached housing, drenched in wintry drizzle and the orange glow of sodium lamps, along the Great West Road.

Placed in a student hostel on Tavistock Square, some days later I too was invited to attend an interview in Senate House. Once again I faced a table with three men behind it, who asked me questions. Of what passed between us I remember only that I kept telling them, in whatever words, that to the best of my knowledge England had two universities, and that I had no particular preference between these two. I was thanked politely, and the next candidate called.

Not long after—all of this happened in the space of a fortnight, between 10 December and Christmas—I received a letter inviting me to call on the Senior Tutor of Trinity Hall, Cambridge, the late Charles Crawley. On the appointed day I duly arrived in his rooms and, after brief initial pleasantries, he asked me how I was related to "*the* General Pálffy". Lost as to whom he might mean, I replied that over the centuries there had been many soldiers in the family, and quite a few had made it to general, but I did not have a clue beyond this. Only after he had shown me a passage in a book taken from his shelves did I realise that he meant my great-grandfather Maurice (who had played a prominent, if not entirely laudable, role in Hungary in the 1850s).

That settled, we talked some more about history in general and family connections (a mid-nineteenth century Austro-Hungarian Ambassador to the Court of St James, related on my mother's side, in particular), until Charles Crawley told me that just then he could not find my papers, but had arranged with his wife that I was to join them for lunch. So we walked across the Backs to Maddingley Road, Mrs Crawley received me kindly, and I enjoyed a relaxed family lunch with them (the Christmas vacation having begun, all the young Crawleys, roughly my age, were at home too). Music, and its condition in Hungary was, as I recall, a topic of the conversation.

After coffee had been served Charles Crawley looked at his watch and, rising, said that he had to leave if he was not to be late for a college meeting. "That's it!" I thought "But at least I've had a pleasant lunch." However, to my surprise he added that, since Full Term started on 14 January I had best come up on the 12th, to stay with them until further arrangements had been made. And thus did I come to be *in statu pupillari* at Trinity Hall, Cambridge, by the Lent Term of 1957— as far as I then knew.

For—as I learnt a few years later from Bob Runcie, at the time Dean of the college and subsequently Archbishop of Canterbury—the foregoing had had a prelude a week or so earlier. The Fellows had met to pick a Hungarian refugee to admit and support (all colleges were at the time taking in and supporting one or two Hungarian refugees). As the names of candidates were being read out Louis Clarke, one of the oldest Fellows of the college (elected long before a compulsory retiring age was introduced), was, as was his wont, apparently half dozing near the end of the table. However, when they got to my name he perked up, although generally given to being stone-deaf, and spoke: "Pálffy? Pálffy, did you say? Went shooting with a Pálffy once—1910 was it? or 1911? can't remember. Excellent shot, though. Must have this one!" So, rather than stick a pin in the list of candidates, the Fellows agreed to my admission, subject to a satisfactory interview with the Senior Tutor.

The genealogy

Schematic overview
1. The purported mediæval descent (10–14th century)
2. Konth to Pálffy to Pálffy ab Erdőd (15–16th century)
3.a The baronial line (16–17th century)
3.b The main line (16–17th century)
4.a The Pauline line (17th century)
4.b The main line (17–18th century)
5. The junior or Királyfa line (18–20th century)
6. The senior line—Malaczka, then princely, branch (18–20th century)
7. The senior line—Stomfa, then Pálffy-Daun, branch (18–20th century)
8. The senior line—Vöröskő branch (18–19th century)
9. The senior line—Vöröskő branch—eldest sub-branch (18–21st century)
10. The senior line—Vöröskő branch—second sub-branch (18–20th century)
11. The senior line—Vöröskő branch—third sub-branch (18–20th century)
12. The senior line—Vöröskő branch—fourth sub-branch (18–21st century)

In some cases I have been unable, so far, to establish the year of birth or death from the sources at my disposal. Symbols used in the tables: = married, ✗ killed fighting as a soldier (incl. died of wounds later); those from whom we all descend, down to Rudolph (1750–1801), are shown in **bold.**

Genealogical statistics
1. Numbers in the family during the 15th to 20th centuries
2. Christian names given between c. 1360 and 2000
3. Violent deaths
4. Golden Fleece

Schematic overview

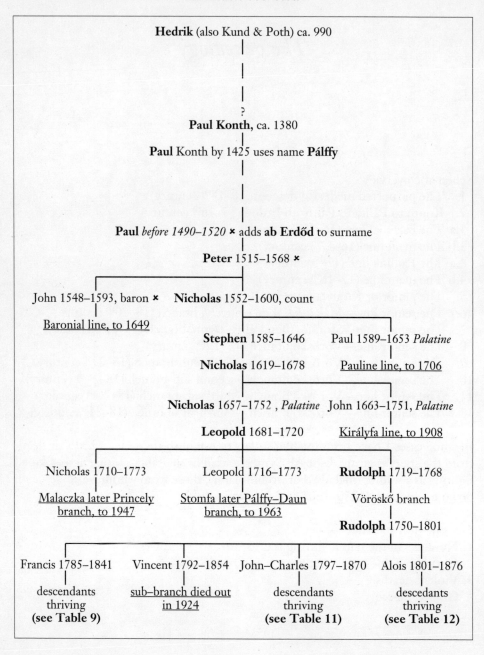

Hedrik (also Kund & Poth) ca. 990

?

Paul Konth, ca. 1380

Paul Konth by 1425 uses name Pálffy

Paul *before 1490–1520* ✕ adds **ab Erdőd** to surname

Peter 1515–1568 ✕

John 1548–1593, baron ✕   Nicholas 1552–1600, count

Baronial line, to 1649

Stephen 1585–1646   Paul 1589–1653 *Palatine*

Nicholas 1619–1678   Pauline line, to 1706

Nicholas 1657–1752 , *Palatine*   John 1663–1751, *Palatine*

Leopold 1681–1720   Királyfa line, to 1908

Nicholas 1710–1773   Leopold 1716–1773   Rudolph 1719–1768

Malaczka later Princely branch, to 1947   Stomfa later Pálffy–Daun branch, to 1963   Vöröskő branch

Rudolph 1750–1801

| Francis 1785–1841 | Vincent 1792–1854 | John–Charles 1797–1870 | Alois 1801–1876 |
| descendants thriving **(see Table 9)** | sub–branch died out in 1924 | descendants thriving **(see Table 11)** | descendants thriving **(see Table 12)** |

1. The purported mediæval descent (10ᵗʰ–14ᵗʰ century)

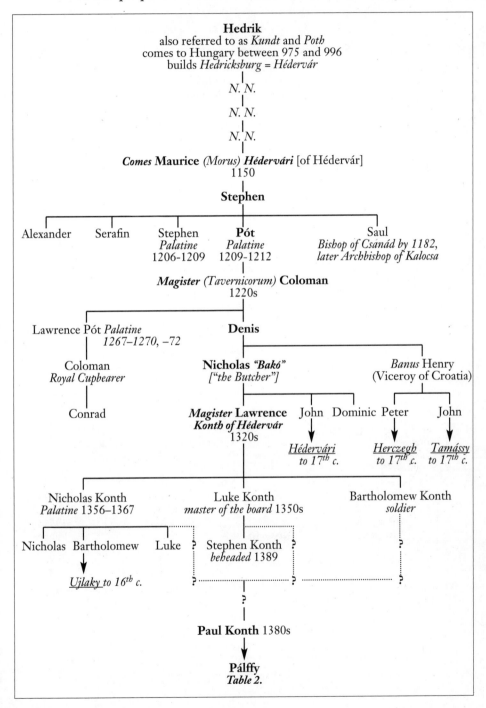

Hedrik
also referred to as *Kundt* and *Poth*
comes to Hungary between 975 and 996
builds *Hedricksburg = Hédervár*

N. N.

N. N.

N. N.

Comes Maurice *(Morus)* **Hédervári** [of Hédervár]
1150

Stephen

Alexander   Serafin   Stephen
Palatine
1206-1209

Pót
Palatine
1209-1212

Saul
*Bishop of Csanád by 1182,
later Archbishop of Kalocsa*

Magister (Tavernicorum) **Coloman**
1220s

Lawrence Pót *Palatine*
1267–1270, –72

Denis

Coloman
Royal Cupbearer

Nicholas *"Bakó"*
["the Butcher"]

Banus Henry
(Viceroy of Croatia)

Conrad

Magister **Lawrence
Konth of Hédervár**
1320s

John Dominic Peter   John

*Hédervári
to 17ᵗʰ c.*

*Herczegh
to 17ᵗʰ c.*

*Tamássy
to 17ᵗʰ c.*

Nicholas Konth
Palatine 1356–1367

Luke Konth
master of the board 1350s

Bartholomew Konth
soldier

Nicholas Bartholomew Luke ? Stephen Konth
beheaded 1389
?   ?

Ujlaky to 16ᵗʰ c.   ?   ?

?

Paul Konth 1380s

Pálffy
Table 2.

2. Konth to Pálffy to Pálffy ab Erdőd (15ᵗʰ–16ᵗʰ century)

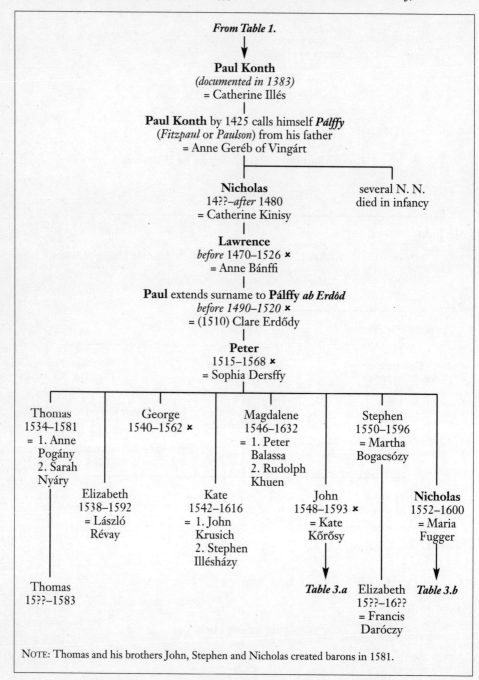

From Table 1.

Paul Konth
(documented in 1383)
= Catherine Illés

Paul Konth by 1425 calls himself *Pálffy*
(*Fitzpaul* or *Paulson*) from his father
= Anne Geréb of Vingárt

Nicholas
14??–*after* 1480
= Catherine Kinisy

several N. N.
died in infancy

Lawrence
before 1470–1526 ✖
= Anne Bánffi

Paul extends surname to **Pálffy** *ab Erdőd*
before 1490–1520 ✖
= (1510) Clare Erdődy

Peter
1515–1568 ✖
= Sophia Dersffy

Thomas
1534–1581
= 1. Anne
Pogány
2. Sarah
Nyáry

George
1540–1562 ✖

Magdalene
1546–1632
= 1. Peter
Balassa
2. Rudolph
Khuen

Stephen
1550–1596
= Martha
Bogacsózy

Elizabeth
1538–1592
= László
Révay

Kate
1542–1616
= 1. John
Krusich
2. Stephen
Illésházy

John
1548–1593 ✖
= Kate
Kőrősy

Nicholas
1552–1600
= Maria
Fugger

Thomas
15??–1583

Table 3.a

Elizabeth
15??–16??
= Francis
Daróczy

Table 3.b

NOTE: Thomas and his brothers John, Stephen and Nicholas created barons in 1581.

3.a The baronial line (16th–17th century)

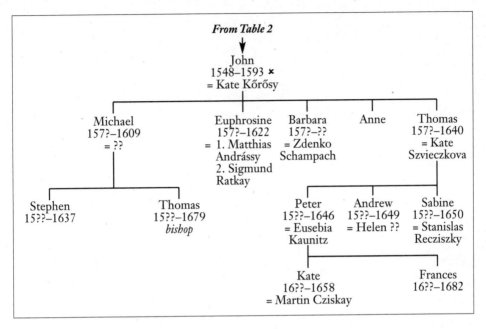

3.b The main line (16th–17th century)

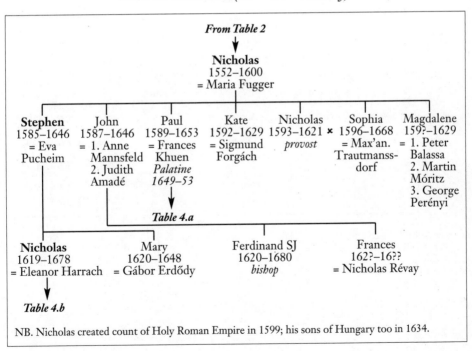

4.a The Pauline line (17th century)

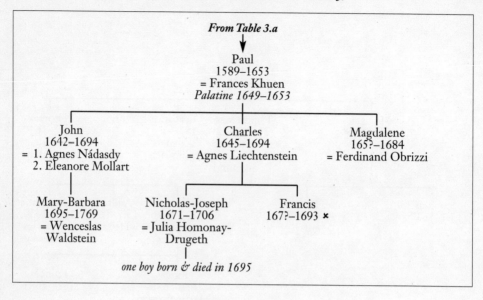

From Table 3.a

Paul
1589–1653
= Frances Khuen
Palatine 1649–1653

John
1642–1694
= 1. Agnes Nádasdy
2. Eleanore Mollart

Charles
1645–1694
= Agnes Liechtenstein

Magdalene
165?–1684
= Ferdinand Obrizzi

Mary-Barbara
1695–1769
= Wenceslas
Waldstein

Nicholas-Joseph
1671–1706
= Julia Homonay-
Drugeth

Francis
167?–1693 ✕

one boy born & died in 1695

4.b The main line (17th–18th century)

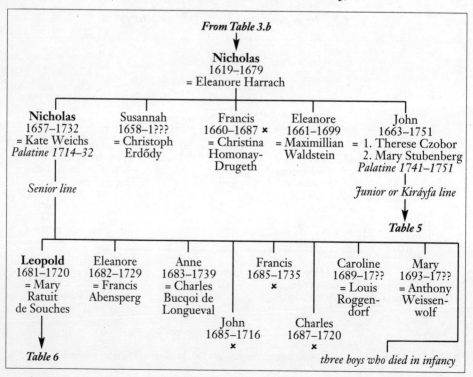

From Table 3.b

Nicholas
1619–1679
= Eleanore Harrach

Nicholas
1657–1732
= Kate Weichs
Palatine 1714–32

Senior line

Susannah
1658–1???
= Christoph
Erdődy

Francis
1660–1687 ✕
= Christina
Homonay-
Drugeth

Eleanore
1661–1699
= Maximillian
Waldstein

John
1663–1751
= 1. Therese Czobor
2. Mary Stubenberg
Palatine 1741–1751

Junior or Kiráyfa line

Table 5

Leopold
1681–1720
= Mary
Ratuit
de Souches

Eleanore
1682–1729
= Francis
Abensperg

Anne
1683–1739
= Charles
Bucqoi de
Longueval

Francis
1685–1735
✕

Caroline
1689–17??
= Louis
Roggen-
dorf

Mary
1693–17??
= Anthony
Weissen-
wolf

John
1685–1716
✕

Charles
1687–1720
✕

Table 6

three boys who died in infancy

216

5. *The junior or Királyfa line (18–20th century)*

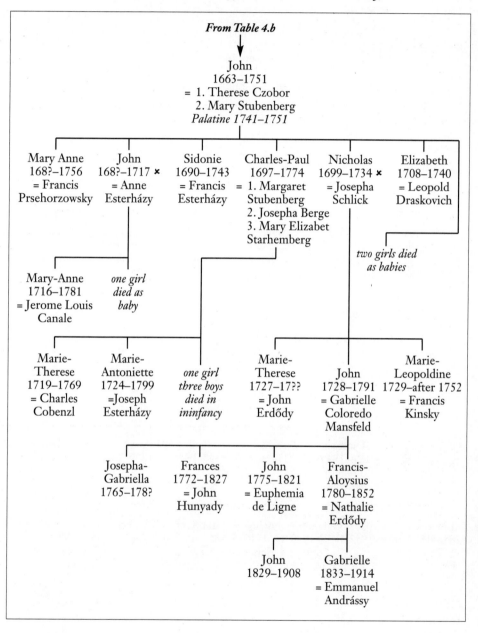

From Table 4.b

John
1663–1751
= 1. Therese Czobor
   2. Mary Stubenberg
   Palatine 1741–1751

| Mary Anne 168?–1756 = Francis Prsehorzowsky | John 168?–1717 × = Anne Esterházy | Sidonie 1690–1743 = Francis Esterházy | Charles-Paul 1697–1774 = 1. Margaret Stubenberg 2. Josepha Berge 3. Mary Elizabet Starhemberg | Nicholas 1699–1734 × = Josepha Schlick | Elizabeth 1708–1740 = Leopold Draskovich |

two girls died as babies

| Mary-Anne 1716–1781 = Jerome Louis Canale | *one girl died as baby* |

| Marie-Therese 1719–1769 = Charles Cobenzl | Marie-Antoniette 1724–1799 =Joseph Esterházy | *one girl three boys died in ininfancy* | Marie-Therese 1727–17?? = John Erdődy | John 1728–1791 = Gabrielle Coloredo Mansfeld | Marie-Leopoldine 1729–after 1752 = Francis Kinsky |

| Josepha-Gabriella 1765–178? | Frances 1772–1827 = John Hunyady | John 1775–1821 = Euphemia de Ligne | Francis-Aloysius 1780–1852 = Nathalie Erdődy |

| John 1829–1908 | Gabrielle 1833–1914 = Emmanuel Andrássy |

6. The senior line–Malaczka, then Princely, branch (18–20th century)

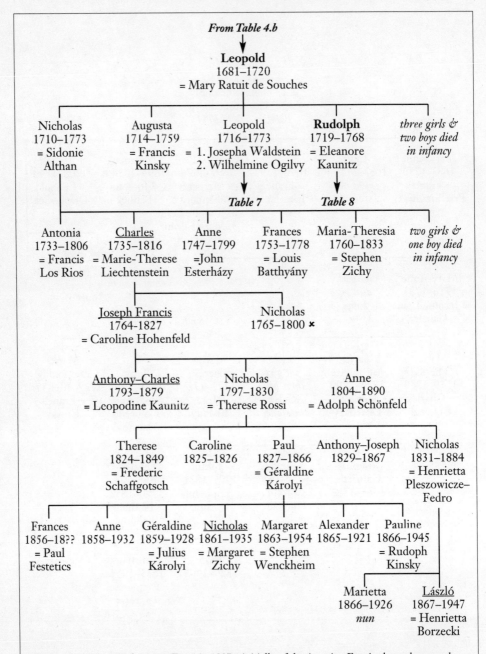

From Table 4.b

Leopold
1681–1720
= Mary Ratuit de Souches

Nicholas	Augusta	Leopold	**Rudolph**	*three girls &*
1710–1773	1714–1759	1716–1773	1719–1768	*two boys died*
= Sidonie	= Francis	= 1. Josepha Waldstein	= Eleanore	*in infancy*
Althan	Kinsky	2. Wilhelmine Ogilvy	Kaunitz	

Table 7   *Table 8*

Antonia	Charles	Anne	Frances	Maria-Theresia	*two girls &*
1733–1806	1735–1816	1747–1799	1753–1778	1760–1833	*one boy died*
= Francis	= Marie-Therese	=John	= Louis	= Stephen	*in infancy*
Los Rios	Liechtenstein	Esterházy	Batthyány	Zichy	

Joseph Francis	Nicholas
1764-1827	1765–1800 ✗
= Caroline Hohenfeld	

Anthony–Charles	Nicholas	Anne
1793–1879	1797–1830	1804–1890
= Leopodine Kaunitz	= Therese Rossi	= Adolph Schönfeld

Therese	Caroline	Paul	Anthony–Joseph	Nicholas
1824–1849	1825–1826	1827–1866	1829–1867	1831–1884
= Frederic		= Géraldine		= Henrietta
Schaffgotsch		Károlyi		Pleszowicze–
				Fedro

Frances	Anne	Géraldine	Nicholas	Margaret	Alexander	Pauline
1856–18??	1858–1932	1859–1928	1861–1935	1863–1954	1865–1921	1866–1945
= Paul		= Julius	= Margaret	= Stephen		= Rudoph
Festetics		Károlyi	Zichy	Wenckheim		Kinsky

Marietta	László
1866–1926	1867–1947
nun	= Henrietta
	Borzecki

NB. Charles was created prince *(Fürst)* in 1807—initially of the Austrian Empire but subsequently granted recognition in the Kingdom of Hungary too—the title to pass on by primogeniture in the male line; those who bore the title are underlined in the table above.

7. The senior line–Stomfa, then Pálffy-Daun, branch (18–20ᵗʰ century)

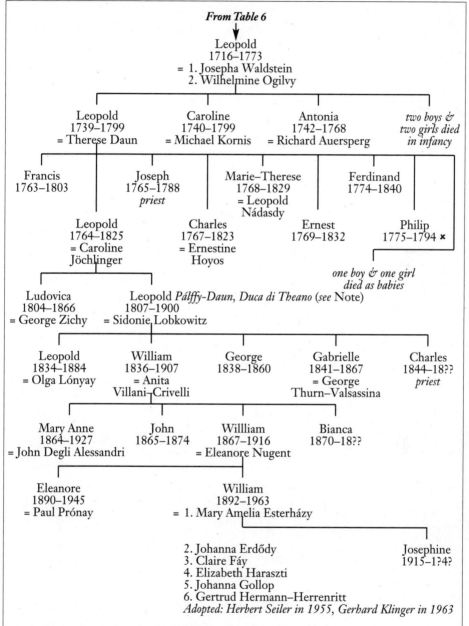

From Table 6

Leopold
1716–1773
= 1. Josepha Waldstein
2. Wilhelmine Ogilvy

Leopold
1739–1799
= Therese Daun

Caroline
1740–1799
= Michael Kornis

Antonia
1742–1768
= Richard Auersperg

*two boys &
two girls died
in infancy*

Francis
1763–1803

Joseph
1765–1788
priest

Marie–Therese
1768–1829
= Leopold
Nádasdy

Ferdinand
1774–1840

Leopold
1764–1825
= Caroline
Jöchlinger

Charles
1767–1823
= Ernestine
Hoyos

Ernest
1769–1832

Philip
1775–1794 ✕

*one boy & one girl
died as babies*

Ludovica
1804–1866
= George Zichy

Leopold *Pálffy-Daun, Duca di Theano* (*see* Note)
1807–1900
= Sidonie Lobkowitz

Leopold
1834–1884
= Olga Lónyay

William
1836–1907
= Anita
Villani–Crivelli

George
1838–1860

Gabrielle
1841–1867
= George
Thurn–Valsassina

Charles
1844–18??
priest

Mary Anne
1864–1927
= John Degli Alessandri

John
1865–1874

Willliam
1867–1916
= Eleanore Nugent

Bianca
1870–18??

Eleanore
1890–1945
= Paul Prónay

William
1892–1963
= 1. Mary Amelia Esterházy

2. Johanna Erdődy
3. Claire Fáy
4. Elizabeth Haraszti
5. Johanna Gollop
6. Gertrud Hermann–Herrenritt
Adopted: Herbert Seiler in 1955, Gerhard Klinger in 1963

Josephine
1915–1?4?

NOTE: In 1853 Leopold (1807–1900) added his grandmother' surname, whose family had just died out, to his: he and his descendants were since known as Pálffy-Daun; in 1876 the Italian title *Duca di Theano*, which had been granted his grandmother's grandfather, was also transferred to him and his descendants by primogeniture in the male line.

8. The senior line–Vöröskő branch (18–19th century)

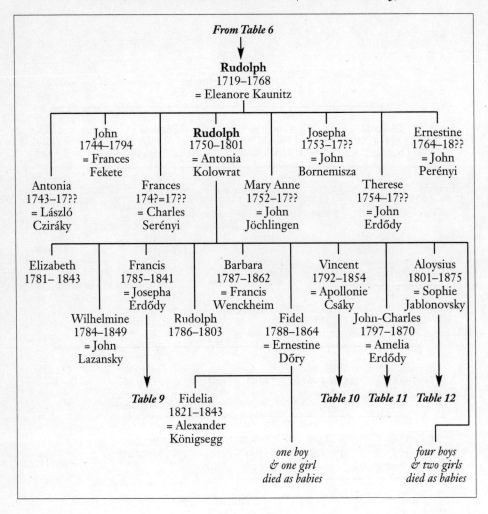

From Table 6

Rudolph
1719–1768
= Eleanore Kaunitz

John
1744–1794
= Frances
Fekete

Rudolph
1750–1801
= Antonia
Kolowrat

Josepha
1753–17??
= John
Bornemisza

Ernestine
1764–18??
= John
Perényi

Antonia
1743–17??
= László
Cziráky

Frances
174?=17??
= Charles
Serényi

Mary Anne
1752–17??
= John
Jöchlingen

Therese
1754–17??
= John
Erdődy

Elizabeth
1781– 1843

Francis
1785–1841
= Josepha
Erdődy

Barbara
1787–1862
= Francis
Wenckheim

Vincent
1792–1854
= Apollonie
Csáky

Aloysius
1801–1875
= Sophie
Jablonovsky

Wilhelmine
1784–1849
= John
Lazansky

Rudolph
1786–1803

Fidel
1788–1864
= Ernestine
Dőry

John-Charles
1797–1870
= Amelia
Erdődy

Table 9 Fidelia
1821–1843
= Alexander
Königsegg

Table 10 *Table 11* *Table 12*

*one boy
& one girl
died as babies*

*four boys
& two girls
died as babies*

9. The senior line–Vöröskő branch–eldest sub–branch (19–21st century)

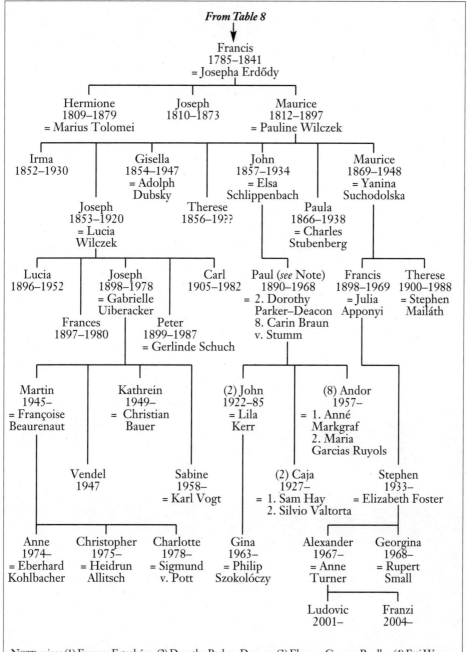

From Table 8

Francis
1785–1841
= Josepha Erdődy

Hermione
1809–1879
= Marius Tolomei

Joseph
1810–1873

Maurice
1812–1897
= Pauline Wilczek

Irma
1852–1930

Gisella
1854–1947
= Adolph
Dubsky

John
1857–1934
= Elsa
Schlippenbach

Maurice
1869–1948
= Yanina
Suchodolska

Joseph
1853–1920
= Lucia
Wilczek

Therese
1856–19??

Paula
1866–1938
= Charles
Stubenberg

Lucia
1896–1952

Joseph
1898–1978
= Gabrielle
Uiberacker

Carl
1905–1982

Paul (see Note)
1890–1968
= 2. Dorothy
Parker–Deacon
8. Carin Braun
v. Stumm

Francis
1898–1969
= Julia
Apponyi

Therese
1900–1988
= Stephen
Mailáth

Frances
1897–1980

Peter
1899–1987
= Gerlinde Schuch

Martin
1945–
= Françoise
Beaurenaut

Kathrein
1949–
= Christian
Bauer

(2) John
1922–85
= Lila
Kerr

(8) Andor
1957–
= 1. Anné
Markgraf
2. Maria
Garcias Ruyols

Vendel
1947

Sabine
1958–
= Karl Vogt

(2) Caja
1927–
= 1. Sam Hay
2. Silvio Valtorta

Stephen
1933–
= Elizabeth Foster

Anne
1974–
= Eberhard
Kohlbacher

Christopher
1975–
= Heidrun
Allitsch

Charlotte
1978–
= Sigmund
v. Pott

Gina
1963–
= Philip
Szokolóczy

Alexander
1967–
= Anne
Turner

Georgina
1968–
= Rupert
Small

Ludovic
2001–

Franzi
2004–

NOTE: wives (1) Frances Esterházy, (2) Dorothy Parker–Deacon, (3) Eleanor Greene-Roelke, (4) Etti Wurmbrand, (5) Louise de Vilmorin, (6) Edith Hoch, (7) Marie-Therese Herberstein, (8) Carin Braun v Stumm.

10. The senior line–Vöröskő branch–second sub–branch (18–20th century)

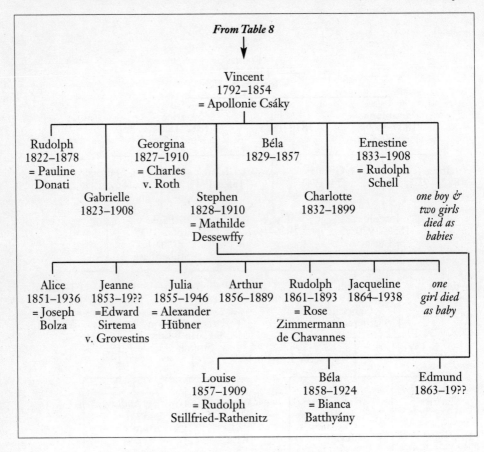

11. The senior line–Vöröskő branch–third sub–branch (18th–20ᵗʰ century)

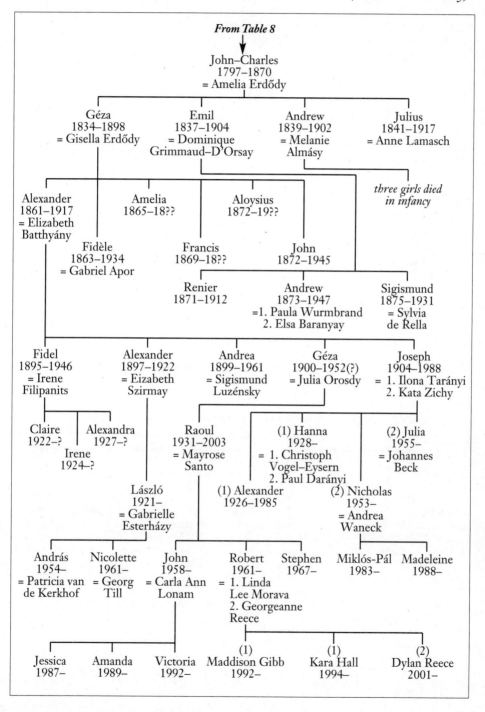

From Table 8

John–Charles
1797–1870
= Amelia Erdődy

Géza
1834–1898
= Gisella Erdődy

Emil
1837–1904
= Dominique
Grimmaud–D'Orsay

Andrew
1839–1902
= Melanie
Almásy

Julius
1841–1917
= Anne Lamasch

*three girls died
in infancy*

Alexander
1861–1917
= Elizabeth
Batthyány

Amelia
1865–18??

Aloysius
1872–19??

Fidèle
1863–1934
= Gabriel Apor

Francis
1869–18??

John
1872–1945

Renier
1871–1912

Andrew
1873–1947
=1. Paula Wurmbrand
2. Elsa Baranyay

Sigismund
1875–1931
= Sylvia
de Rella

Fidel
1895–1946
= Irene
Filipanits

Alexander
1897–1922
= Eizabeth
Szirmay

Andrea
1899–1961
= Sigismund
Luzénsky

Géza
1900–1952(?)
= Julia Orosdy

Joseph
1904–1988
= 1. Ilona Tarányi
2. Kata Zichy

Claire
1922–?

Alexandra
1927–?

Irene
1924–?

Raoul
1931–2003
= Mayrose
Santo

(1) Hanna
1928–
= 1. Christoph
Vogel–Eysern
2. Paul Darányi

(2) Julia
1955–
= Johannes
Beck

László
1921–
= Gabrielle
Esterházy

(1) Alexander
1926–1985

(2) Nicholas
1953–
= Andrea
Waneck

András
1954–
= Patricia van
de Kerkhof

Nicolette
1961–
= Georg
Till

John
1958–
= Carla Ann
Lonam

Robert
1961–
= 1. Linda
Lee Morava
2. Georgeanne
Reece

Stephen
1967–

Miklós–Pál
1983–

Madeleine
1988–

Jessica
1987–

Amanda
1989–

Victoria
1992–

(1)
Maddison Gibb
1992–

(1)
Kara Hall
1994–

(2)
Dylan Reece
2001–

12. *The senior line–Vöröskő branch–fourth sub-branch (18th–21st century)*

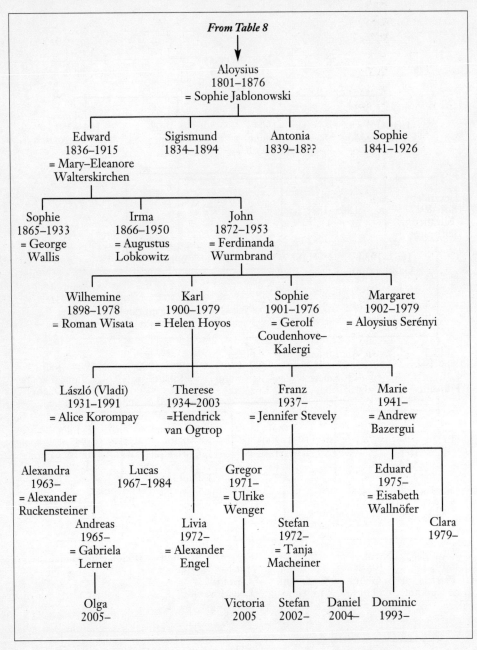

From Table 8

Aloysius
1801–1876
= Sophie Jablonowski

Edward
1836–1915
= Mary–Eleanore
Walterskirchen

Sigismund
1834–1894

Antonia
1839–18??

Sophie
1841–1926

Sophie
1865–1933
= George
Wallis

Irma
1866–1950
= Augustus
Lobkowitz

John
1872–1953
= Ferdinanda
Wurmbrand

Wilhemine
1898–1978
= Roman Wisata

Karl
1900–1979
= Helen Hoyos

Sophie
1901–1976
= Gerolf
Coudenhove–
Kalergi

Margaret
1902–1979
= Aloysius Serényi

László (Vladi)
1931–1991
= Alice Korompay

Therese
1934–2003
=Hendrick
van Ogtrop

Franz
1937–
= Jennifer Stevely

Marie
1941–
= Andrew
Bazergui

Alexandra
1963–
= Alexander
Ruckensteiner

Lucas
1967–1984

Gregor
1971–
= Ulrike
Wenger

Eduard
1975–
= Eisabeth
Wallnöfer

Andreas
1965–
= Gabriela
Lerner

Livia
1972–
= Alexander
Engel

Stefan
1972–
= Tanja
Macheiner

Clara
1979–

Olga
2005–

Victoria
2005

Stefan
2002–

Daniel
2004–

Dominic
1993–

1. Numbers in the family during the 15th to 20th centuries

The family's size, the number of its members generation by generation from that of Paul Konth (the 1st, at the top) down to the 18th from him—the last probably "complete" generation, in that it is most unlikely to grow, all of whose members were born in the twentieth century—is shown graphically below. Note that the mapping to centuries is approximate: within a single generation by descent age-differences of 30–40 years are not uncommon, and in any case even the lives of individuals often straddle successive centuries.

Each person who attained full adulthood is represented by ■ and each who died before that by ■—infant mortality would appear to have been most prevalent in the eighteenth to early nineteenth centuries, but it is doubtless vastly understated for earlier times when infant deaths were not recorded meticulously. Similarly, until the second half of the sixteenth century the number of women is doubtless also severely understated: the main source of information for periods earlier than that is official documents, which rarely mention women.

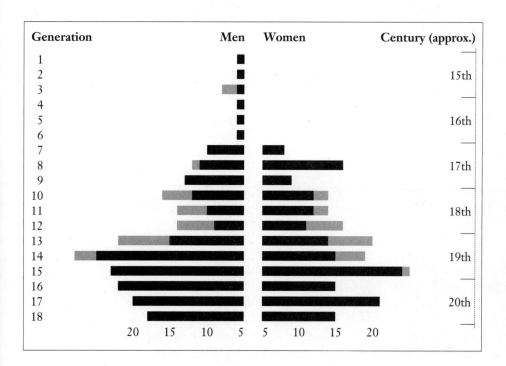

The 19th generation—which at the time of writing consists of six boys and six girls (and also one girl who died immediately after birth), all born in the last years of the twentieth and first of the twenty-first century—is not included above since it is likely to grow further.

2. *Christian name given in the family between ca. 1360 and 2000*

Variations on names that are essentially the same—e.g. Andrew/Andor/Andreas, or Kate/Catherine—have been grouped together. The names of those who died in early infancy not included, because in most cases not known.

Boys

Alphabetic		By frequency	
Alexander	4	John	16
Aloys	2	Nicholas	13
Andrew	5	Charles	10
Anthony	2	Francis	8
Arthur	1	Stephen	7
Béla	2	Joseph	6
Charles	10	Leopold	6
Christopher	1	Andrew	5
Edmund	1	Paul	5
Edward	2	Rudolph	5
Emil	1	Alexander	4
Ernest	1	Thomas	4
Ferdinand	2	László	3
Fidel	2	Peter	3
Francis	8	William	3
George	2	Aloys	2
Géza	2	Anthony	2
Gregor	1	Béla	2
John	16	Edward	2
Joseph	6	Ferdinand	2
Julius	1	Fidel	2
László	3	George	2
Lawrence	1	Géza	2
Leopold	6	Maurice	2
Luke	1	Sigismund	2
Mark	1	Arthur	1
Martin	1	Christopher	1
Maurice	2	Edmund	1
Michael	1	Emil	1
Nicholas	13	Ernest	1
Paul	5	Gregor	1
Peter	3	Julius	1
Philip	1	Lawrence	1
Raoul	1	Luke	1
Renier	1	Mark	1
Robert	1	Martin	1
Rudolph	5	Michael	1
Sigismund	2	Philip	1
Stephen	7	Raoul	1
Thomas	4	Renier	1
Vincent	1	Robert	1
William	3	Vincent	1

Girls

Alphabetic		By frequency		Alphabetic (cont.) ..cont'd		By frequency ..cont'd	
Alexandra	2	Frances	7	Irma	2	Margaret	2
Alice	1	Therese	6	Jacqueline	1	Sabine	2
Amelia	2	Antonia	5	Jeanne/Johanna	2	Wilhelmine	2
Andrea	1	Marie-Therese	5	Josepha/Josephine	3	Alice	1
Anne	4	Mary-Anne	5	Julia	2	Andrea	1
Antonia	5	Anne	4	Kate	4	Augusta	1
Augusta	1	Barbara	4	Leopoldine	1	Bianca	1
Barbara	4	Elizabeth	4	Livia	1	Caja	1
Bianca	1	Kate	4	Louise	1	Euphemia	1
Caja	1	Sophie	4	Lucia	1	Euphrosine	1
Caroline	3	Caroline	3	Ludovica	1	Geraldine	1
Charlotte	2	Eleanore	3	Magdalene	3	Gina	1
Claire	2	Gabrielle	3	Margaret	2	Gisella	1
Eleanore	3	Josepha/Josephine	3	Marie-Antoinette	1	Hermione	1
Elizabeth	4	Magdalene	3	Marie-Therese	5	Irene	1
Ernestine	2	Mary	3	Marietta	1	Jacqueline	1
Euphemia	1	Pauline	3	Mary	3	Leopoldine	1
Euphrosine	1	Alexandra	2	Mary-Anne	5	Livia	1
Fidelia	2	Amelia	2	Nicolette	1	Louise	1
Frances	7	Charlotte	2	Pauline	3	Lucia	1
Gabrielle	3	Claire	2	Sabine	2	Ludovica	1
Georgina	2	Ernestine	2	Sidonie	1	Marie-Antoinette	1
Geraldine	1	Fidelia	2	Sophie 3	4	Marietta	1
Gina	1	Georgina	2	Susannah	1	Nicolette	1
Gisella	1	Irma	2	Therese	6	Sidonie	1
Hermione	1	Jeanne/Johanna	2	Wilhelmine	2	Susannah	1
Irene	1	Julia	2				

3. Violent deaths

Note: *Fell in battle* includes those who died afterwards of wounds received.

Name	Year	Age	Place	
Fell in battle				*fighting against*
Paul	1520	30+	Kocsina (Croatia?)	Turks
Lawrence	1526	50+	Mohács	Turks
George	1562	22	Temesvár	Turks
Peter	1568	53	Velicza (Slavonia)	Turks
John	1593	45	Somoskő	Turks
Nicholas	1621	28	Fülek	Gábor Bethlen
Francis	1687	27	Eszék	Turks
Francis	1693	20	Pignarolla, Italy	French
John	1716	30	Pétervárad	Turks
John	1717	~30	Belgrade	Turks
Charles(-Joseph)	1720	40	Belgrade	Turks
Nicholas	1734	35	Parma, Italy	French
Francis	1735	50	Parma, Italy	French
Philip	1794	19	Landrecy, France	French
Nicholas	1800	35	Verragio, Italy	French
Killed in duel				*with*
George	1860	20	Viterbo	a prince Odescalchi
Died in accident				*its nature*
Nicholas	1830	33		out shooting
Lucas	1984	16		skiing
Executed				*sentenced by*
Fidel	1945	50	Budapest	Peoples' Court
Other				*What?*
Géza	1952 ?	52	Soviet Gulag	abducted by NKVD

4. Golden Fleece

Name	Lived	Remarks
Paul	1589–1653	Palatine; from king of Spain
Nicholas	1657–1732	Palatine; from Charles III
John	1663–1751	Palatine; from Charles III
Nicholas	1710–1773	Hungarian chancellor; from Maria-Theresia
Charles, first prince	1735–1816	Hungarian chancellor; from Joseph II
Joseph-Francis, pr.	1764–1827	From Francis I
Fidel	1788–1864	Hungarian chancellor, from Ferdinand V
Anthony-Charles	1793–1879	diplomat; from Francis I
Maurice	1812–1897	Field Marshal; from Francis-Joseph
Nicholas, pr.	1865–1935	From Francis-Joseph

Vöröskő, and other Pálffy estates in Counties Pressburg & Nyitra

History of Vöröskő

The earliest recorded castle on the site—known variously as Vöröskő in Hungarian, Cerveni Kamen (which means 'red crag' as well) in Slovak, and Biebersburg ('beavercastle') in German—was apparently raised in the 1230s for Constance, grand-daughter of King Béla IV and queen of King Ottokar of Bohemia, following whose death it became a royal castle. As such it was in 1271 besieged, but not taken, by Ottokar of Bohemia, and a decade or so later by rebellious barons.

However, by the end of the thirteenth century, a period of baronial power and infighting, the castle had become the joint property of one Thomas, son of *comes* Tiburch, and Martin Eimech deputy Justice of the Realm; the latter sold it to one Mathew, Lord Lieutenant of Pressburg and Master of the Horse, for 200 marks and a suit of armour. Within a decade it then fell into the hands of Matthew Csák, for a period undisputed master of northern Hungary, but on his death King Charles reclaimed it as a royal property.

In 1350 his son King Louis donated the castle, to which fourteen villages were then attached, to a German military commander in his service, one Ulrich Wolfarth. From the latter's widow it eventually passed into the hands of George of Bazin & Szentgyörgy[1] who in 1441 settled it on his wife. However, later in the century, George of Bazin & Szentgyörgy having joined a conspiracy against King Matthias, Vöröskő was confiscated into royal hands; only after 1501 was it again owned by his descendant, Peter, who repeatedly pawned[2] it to raise money, on the last occasion to John Szapolyai—who in 1526 after Mohács made himself King John—in 1515.

Following that Peter's death in 1516 Szapolyai pawned Vöröskő on; at some point it must have became a royal property again, for in 1522 King Louis donated

---

[1] His family took its name from two estates near Pressburg that were later much coveted, and in the eighteenth century finally acquired, by the Pálffy family.

[2] Technically inherited landed estates were inalienable, but this was regularly got round by formally merely "pawning" them (frequently giving rise, often one or more generations later, to complex lawsuits).

it to yet another, younger, Peter of Bazin & Szentgyörgy on condition that, should he die without issue, it was to revert to Queen Mary. He did, and in the following year she donated it to the Thurzó brothers, who in 1535 sold it to their business partners the Fuggers of Augsburg.

Starting in 1580 Nicholas Pálffy then bought the castle, and the by now fifteen villages that went with it, from the several Fuggers who owned it jointly, paying altogether almost eighty-thousand Rhineland Florins for it. This process must have been completed by 1592, for in that year his full and exclusive rights in the property were confirmed by a royal patent.

From then until 1945 Vöröskő remained in Pálffy hands.

Pálffy estates in Counties Pressburg & Nyitra ca. 1905

Villages in these counties where in about 1905 the landowner, principal or of a substantial estate, was a Pálffy; there were of course Pálffy estates elsewhere, in other counties, too.

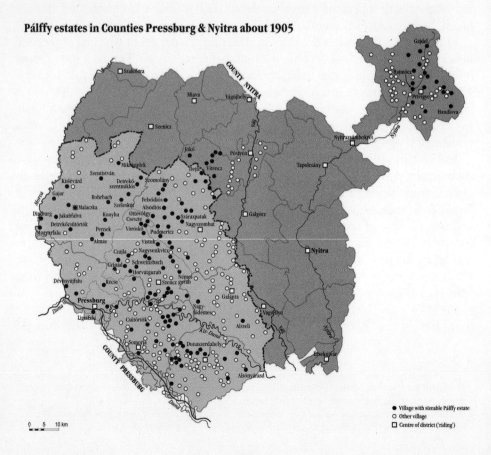

Pálffy estates in Counties Pressburg & Nyitra about 1905

230

Who	*In County Pressburg* (pop.)	*In County Nyitra* (pop.)
"Hans" Pálffy	Pudmericz *(1,627)*	
Béla Pálffy	Bélvatta *(308)*	
	Illésháza *(593)*	
	Tonkháza *(238)*	
	Vajasvatta *(165)*	
Cts. Alexander Pálffy	Csölösztő *(226)*	
Cts. Béla Pálffy	Csenke *(314)*	
	Kismagyar *(512)*	
	Nagymagyar *(1,353)*	
	Tönye *(372)*	
	Újhelyjókai *(391)*	
Francis Pálffy	Kosolna *(552)*	
John Pálffy	Alsódiós *(1,199)*	Bajmócz *(1,183)*
	Alsónyárasd *(1,616)*	Brezan *(555)*
	Alszeli *(2,266)*	Brusznó *(387)*
	Bogdány *(748)*	Chrenócz *(304)*
	Csütörtök *(1,118)*	Chvojnicza *(627)*
	Czajla *(1,322)*	Czigel *(578)*
	Dubova *(772)*	Gajdel *(1,833)*
	Dunaújfalu *(1,293)*	Kós *(850)*
	Egyházfa *(349)*	Nedozser *(683)*
	Grinád *(1,190)*	Poruba *(581)*
	Harangfalva *(483)*	Rásztocsnó *(764)*
	Horvátgurab *(1,174)*	Tuzsina *(2,242)*
	Jánostelek *(511)*	
	Kápolna *(414)*	
	Királyfa *(948)*	
	Kissenkvicz *(327)*	
	Kürt *(772)*	
	Limbach *(895)*	
	Nagysenkvicz *(1,109)*	
	Németgurab *(1,374)*	
	Neustift *(458)*	
	Ottóvölgy *(1,158)*	
	Pénteksúr *(171)*	
	Sáp *(327)*	
	Selpőcz *(493)*	
	Szárazpatak *(1,161)*	
	Vámosfalu *(693)*	
	Vistuk *(1,228)*	
	Vök *(213)*	

Who	In County Pressburg (pop.)	In County Nyitra (pop.)
Joseph Pálffy	Dejte (1,251)	Lancsár (182)
	Felsődiós (1,696)	Lopasó (823)
	Felsődombó (398)	Nizsna (447)
	Kátlócz (937)	Radosócz (410)
	Losoncz (687)	Strusz (530)
	Szomolány (1,413)	Vitencz (1,631)
	Pagyerócz (266)	Kocsin (211)
Pálffy (?John? "Hans"?)	Jánosháza (189)	
Pálffy, unspecified	Bögölypatony (329)	Jókő (1,024)
	Diósförgepatony (732)	Chach (882)
	Fenyves (398)	Dubnicza (199)
	Gocznód (196)	Handlova (3,506)
	Igrám (628)	Kis-Csaucsa (526)
	Jaszlócz (537)	Neczpál (327)
	Kispaka (158)	
	Nagyfödémes (2,706)	
	Ógelle (240)	
	Papkörmösd (338)	
	Pósfa (220)	
	Sárfő (1,351)	
	Tótgurab (985)	
	Tótújfalu (498)	
The senior's entail	Beketfa (123)	
	Benkepatony (285)	
	Csécsénypatony (341)	
	Egyházgelle (195)	
	Főrév (965)	
	Kislucs (213)	
	Ligetfalu (1,805)	
	Lőgérpatony (464)	
	Maczháza (158)	
	Nagybodak (692)	
	Sikabony (750)	
	Verekny (599)	
	Zoncz (233)	
Pálffy-Daun	Almás (1,126)	
The prince	Detrekőcsütörtök (1,286)	
	Detrekőszentmiklós (1,108)	
	Detrekőszentpéter (632)	
	Detrekőváralja (691)	
	Dévényújfalu (2,900)	

Who	*In County Pressburg* (pop.)	*In County Nyitra* (pop.)
	Dimburg *(1,805)*	
	Gajar *(4,252)*	
	Hidegkút *(831)*	
	Jakabfalva *(1,150)*	
	Kiripolcz *(977)*	
	Kislévárd *(1,522)*	
	Konyha *(1,804)*	
	Magyarfalu *(2,369)*	
	Malaczka *(5,053)*	
	Miklóstelek *(318)*	
	Pernek *(1,107)*	
	Récse *(3,843)*	
	Rohrbach *(1,326)*	
	Széleskút *(1,261)*	
	Szentistván *(1,798)*	
Stephen Pálffy	Vistuk *(1,228)*	
John & Stephen Pálffy	Vöröskő (3/8th–5/8th), *with*	
	Cseszte *(1,813)*	
	Halmos *(520)*	
	Hosszúfalu *(598)*	
	Istvánfalu *(407)*	
	Istvánlak *(452)*	
	Pila *(306)*	
	Schweinsbach *(1,370)*	
	Torcs *(251)*	

This was 106 villages out of 293, i.e. 36%, in County Pressburg and 25 out of 430, i.e. 6%, in County Nyitra; my source (the relevant volumes of *Magyarország várm-egyéi és városai [Hungary's Counties & Towns]*, a kind of latter-day Hungarian Dooms-day Book)—whose village by village entries are, alas, far from uniform—also uses phrases such as *for long a Pálffy property* about numerous further villages, especial-ly in County Nyitra, but unless current (at the time of publication in the first decade of the twentieth century) Pálffy ownership is made explicit these have not been included in the list above.

The names of the villages are not, incidentally, as weird as they may look—many of them contain one or more of the following simple roots:

al(só)	*low(er)*	hely	*place*	ó	*old*
dió	*walnut*	horvát	*croat*	pap	*priest*
domb	*(low) hill*	hosszú	*long*	patak	*brook*
egyház(a)	*church*	kis	*little/small*	sár	*mud*
fa	*tree*	kő	*rock/crag*	telek	*tenement*
falu/falva	*village*	kút	*well*	tót	*slovak*
fel(ső)	*up(per)*	lak	*dwelling*	új	*new*
halom	*hillock*	magyar	*hungarian*	vám(os)	*toll*
harang	*bell*	nagy	*great/large*	völgy	*valley*
ház(a)	*house*	nyár	*poplar*	széles	*broad*
hegy	*hill*	német	*german*	szent	*saint*

Glossary of terms and concepts

Archduke, *Archidux, Erzherzog,* title invented by the Habsburgs for all members of their own family and in the 15th c. confirmed by an imperial decree issued by *Emperor* (q.v.) Frederic III, himself a Habsburg, to set them above all other ruling families (much as archangels outrank angels).

Barones regni was long the collective designation of the holders of the dozen or so—the number fluctuated slightly—most senior offices of state (who all received handsome emoluments while in office, from the earliest times), **not** a reference to holders of a *hereditary title* (q.v.); it gradually fell into disuse following the introduction of the latter.

Chancellery, evolved by late 12th c. to manage all royal paperwork, up to then entrusted to the Archbishop of Esztergom (but the Chancellors for long continued to be bishops). In the 16th c. Ferdinand I transferred it to Vienna, when it became known as the **Hungarian Chancellery** to distinguish it from other ones also there. By the 18th c. and to 1848—the Chancellors by now lay *magnates* (q.v.)—royal policy for Hungary was formulated in the Chancellery, which also became the main conduit between the king and the *Lieutenancy Council* (q.v.). In 1848 on the formation of a ministry answerable to Parliament it was abolished (the last Chancellor, up to that date, was my great-grandfather, Count George Apponyi).

Comes was used from early mediæval times to designate the governors—Lord Lieutenant in the mediæval sense might be the nearest English equivalent—of *counties* (q.v.), **not** a *hereditary title* (q.v.); later it was also applied to the governors of some specific regions (of one or more counties). King St Stephen is known to have still appointed persons of lowly origins to such positions, but by the 12th c. at the latest only men of some standing were so appointed. In more modern times the (effectively untranslatable) term *főispán* was applied to those appointed by the Crown to supervise a county, until the office—from the late 19th c. comparable to that of a French *préfet*—was abolished after 1945.

Counties *(comitates, vármegye),* to begin with administrative units of the vast royal possessions and as such managed by a *comes* (q.v.) appointed by the Crown, soon became the administrative subunits of the country as a whole. Importantly, from the last decades of the 13th c. they evolved self-government by officials and justices elected by the county's *nobles* (q.v.) at county assemblies; in formal terms the erstwhile *comes* (q.v.), now *főispán*, merely presided at these, and in general sought to ensure that the elected officials acted in accordance with royal directives. Elected officials were replaced by salaried ones in the late 19th c.

Crown Guardians, two in number, first appointed in the late 15th c. to be responsible for the safety of the *Holy Crown* (q.v.) and other regalia; legislation of 1608 laid down that *Parliament* (q.v.) was to elect one Catholic and one Protestant to this office, which only ceased after 1945, when crown and regalia fell into the hands of the US army in Germany.

Emperor, *Holy Roman of the German Nation,* from Otto *the Great* in 970 (emulating Charlemagne) to Francis I, who unilaterally abolished the title in 1806 (having in 1804 made himself hereditary Emperor of Austria). Initially in effect hereditary, by the 13th c. it became elective, the College of Electors (from the 14th c.) being the Archbishops of Trier, Mainz and Köln, and the rulers of Saxony, the Palatinate, Brandenburg, and Bohemia; in the 17th c. those of Bavaria, Brunswick-Lüneburg and Hanover were added. From Frederick III in the 15th c. on all Emperors were Habsburgs, with the brief exceptions of a Wittelsbach and then Francis of Lorraine, consort of Maria Theresia, in the late 18th c.

Golden Bull, charter of the liberties of freemen issued by King Andrew II—under popular pressure and most reluctantly—in 1222; in many respects similar to the English King John's Magna Carta of 1215. Enacted as a statute by Parliament in 1351 (if with some slight modifications), until 1848 it remained the touchstone for *noble* (q.v.) privileges.

Golden fleece, *toisson d'or,* order of chivalry founded by Duke Philip *the Good* of Burgundy in 1429 and initially limited to 24 members; by the 16th c. the Habsburgs, having acquired Burgundy by marriage, took it over as the highest distinction they awarded (comparable in this to the Garter in England), but first extended, then completely abolished the limit on numbers. It remained in the gift of the (senior) Spanish branch of the House of Habsburg until its extinction in 1700, thereafter of the (junior) Austrian branch; but on acquiring the throne of Spain the Bourbons also claimed the right to award it. In principle membership of the order was restricted to titled Catholics, but exceptions were made (notably by the Bourbons of Spain), e.g. the Duke of Wellington received it following Napoleon's defeat. No Habsburg has sat on any throne since 1918, but all *archdukes* (q.v.) still receive and wear it, and Otto the head of the Habsburg family still awards it to other individuals who in his view merit this.

Gotha, Almanach de, was three series of genealogical handbooks of European titled nobility (limited to those alive at the time of publication, and the immediately preceding generations), published annually from the early 1800s by Justus Perthes of Gotha, hence the popular name; a new series, published elsewhere, has been started since the Second Word War. Inclusion was subject to presenting reliable documentary proof for titles claimed, to filter out false ones. The three series, each bound in a different colour, were: the *Hofkaländer* (Court

Calendar) devoted to sovereign (of however small a territory) ruling houses, past and present, as well as ducal and princely families; the green-bound *Gräfliches Taschenbuch* (Pocketbook of Counts) for counts, as also marquesses and viscounts, subdivided between titles that antedate 1500 (in even years) and later ones (in odd years); finally the *Freiherrliches Taschenbuch* for barons.

Hereditary Lands, *Erbländer,* the collective term for the several archduchies, duchies, principalities, counties and other territories the Habsburgs ruled by hereditary right; following the Battle of the White Mountain (1620) the Kingdom of Bohemia was for all practical purposes also treated as one of these. In 1804, to match Napoleon's new title, Francis I renamed the whole lot collectively **Austria**—historically Austria, Upper- and Lower-, had been two marquisates, later duchies, and finally archduchies along the Danube between Bavaria and Hungary—and made himself its hereditary Emperor.

Hereditary titles were only introduced into Hungary in the 16th c. by the Habsburgs, modelled on the pattern prevalent in the Empire, i.e. **all** legitimate descendants of the original grantee inherit the title. The only Hungarian ones granted were **baron** (seven-pointed coronet) and **count** (nine-pointed coronet); however, foreigners who acquired estates in Hungary could gain recognition of their existing foreign titles by *indigenatus* (which involved an Act of Parliament and payment of a fee), thus **marques** and *prince* (q.v.) came to be introduced too. Of the six Hungarian families some members of which bore the title *prince* (q.v.) that of three (Batthyány, Esterházy, Grassalkovich) was imperial, of two (Festetics, Pálffy) Austrian, and only one Hungarian (Lónyay, received in 1917 when he married the widow of the late heir Archduke Rudolph). Hereditary titles were last granted in 1916/17 by Charles IV; their official use was abolished by legislation of 1946.

Hofkriegsrath, *Court Military Council,* during the 16th to early 19th c. the supreme military planning and decision-making body of the Habsburgs; on the argument that Empire and *Hereditary Lands* (q.v.) did or might contribute to fighting the Ottomans in Hungary, from the mid-16th c. all military activity in the country was subordinated to it.

Holy Crown [of Saint Stephen], believed to be (but probably not) the actual crown used at the coronation of Stephen in the year 1000; by the 12th c. it had become established that only a coronation performed with this crown, by the Archbishop of Esztergom Primate of Hungary, was valid. Further regalia include a cope—probably actually embroidered, in part at least, by Saint Stephen's queen Gisela—as well as a later sword of state and orb. From the late 15th c. to 1945 two *Crown Guardians* (q.v.) were responsible for their safekeeping (at Visegrád, Pressburg, finally Buda). Last used for their appointed purpose in 1916, in the winter of 1944/45 crown and regalia were taken to Germany and eventually fell into the hands of US forces; returned to Hungary in 1978 they were put on show in the National Museum, but since 2000 the Holy Crown itself—symbol of Hungary's statehood (and as such also depicted over the present Republic's coat of arms)—is on display in the central lobby of the Parliament building.

Justice of the Realm, *Iudex Regni, országbíró,* emerged in the late 12^(th) c. to take over virtually all the judicial functions of the *Palatine* (q.v.), with a seat in the king's inner council. With the passage of time the office came to be primarily political, the Justice of the Realm standing in for the Palatine if this office was vacant or its holder incapacitated. During the 16^(th) to 18^(th) c. in particular this made it a key office: there was frequently no Palatine because, *inter alia,* a *Parliament* (q.v.) had to be called to elect one, while the Justice of the Realm was merely appointed by the Crown. In 1881 the office was formally merged into the Presidency of the Curia, the country' senior court.

Knights of Malta, strictly of the *Sovereign Military Order of Knights Hospitaler of St John:* founded in Jerusalem in the 12^(th) c. to care for the sick and fight the infidel, later forced to move via Rhodes to the island of Malta by which name it is since generally know (it remained there until Napoleonic days; the Order's headquarters are now at Rome). All aspirants have to show noble descent (the number of *quarterings* (q.v.) required varies from country to country) to join the Order: full or *professed knights* take wows of obedience, personal poverty and celibacy like monks do, *knights of honour* are excused the second two. These days the Order—still recognised as sovereign, i.e. issuing passports etc, by some countries—is devoted exclusively to works of charity, principally in the medical field.

Lieutenancy Council, *Consilium Regium Locumtenentiale Hungaricum, Helytartótanács,* body set up in 1723 with the approval of *Parliament* (q.v.) to govern Hungary on behalf of the (perennially absent) king—excepting only taxation and military affairs, in which the king had to act with Parliament—presided over by the *Palatine* (q.v.) or, if there was none or he was unable to do so, the *Justice of the Realm* (q.v.); it consisted of 22 members appointed by the Crown who acted like a cabinet, each being allocated responsibility for some one specific area of government while decisions were taken collectively by majority vote. It was dissolved in 1848 when that year's legislation created a responsible ministry answerable to Parliament (although no such ministry was in office between 1849 and 1867).

Magister tavernicorum, *Master of the Treasury, tárnokmester*—often referred to as just *magister* (much as in England the Chancellor of the Exchequer is often referred to as just *the Chancellor*)—was the third-ranking great office of state, created in the early 13^(th) c. to manage royal finances. Ranking immediately after the *Palatine* (q.v.) and *Justice of the Realm* (q.v.), the *magister* performed a number of their key functions if both those offices were vacant.

Magnates, *magnates regni,* generic term by the 15^(th)–16^(th) c. applied to all those—generally of significant wealth—who held or had held senior offices of state or court dignities as also, it would seem, to all those too who, although holding no office or dignity, were invited to attend the Greater Royal Council (which eventually evolved into the Upper Chamber of *Parliament* (q.v.)); from the late

15th c., even before the introduction of *hereditary titles* (q.v.), they were styled *magnificus*. Later **magnate** came to be used as shorthand for members of the wealthy and titled landed aristocracy.

Neoacquistica commissio, body set up, exempt from Hungarian law, by Leopold I in 1690 to administer all land retaken from the Turks in Hungary, which he wished to treat as ownerless *(terra nullius)* conquest and thus entirely at his disposal. However, many whose families had fled the Turkish occupation a century or more earlier had good inherited claims to land in those regions: the *neoacquistica commissio* could not entirely disregard these but, making up its own rules, made it as difficult as possible to regain land by inherited right, demanding documentary evidence to standards often difficult to meet (many archives had perished) and then requesting payment in cash of a "war-indemnity tax" based on the estate's assessed value. Only in 1715 were such matters transferred to the King's Bench Court, which applied Hungarian law; the return of estates was then accelerated by legislation in 1723. The commission was finally dissolved in 1741.

Noble Guard, Royal Hungarian, created at Maria Theresia's initiative by legislation of 1764 to accompany and guard the sovereign at all times, each *county* (q.v.) to nominate young men of suitable background to serve in it for five years: 100 from Hungary and 20 from Transylvania. Its privates were subalterns, NCOs captains or majors, subalterns colonels, and the Captain commanding it a full general, his deputy a major-general. By the 19th c. those serving in it were also often entrusted with carrying important messages, especially to embassies abroad (like English king's/queen's messengers). After their five-year stint many transferred to regular cavalry regiments. It was dissolved in 1848.

Nobles, *nobiles* (H. *nemes*, from *nem* = Latin *gens*[1] i.e. something between "family" and "clan"), was the term increasingly applied from the late 13th c. to the country's freemen; from the 13th c. kings were also granting patents of nobility as rewards for services rendered, thus it was at all times possible to rise to this status, inherited by all legitimate descendants. Nobles were usually, but not necessarily, granted a coat-of-arms (if so, depicted with a five-pointed coronet) and also came to be distinguished from others by a qualifier, usually territorial, to their surname (i.e. *Surname of Someplace*). By the *Golden Bull* (q.v.) of 1222 and subsequent legislation nobles were exempt from all direct taxes (initially in recognition of their duty to join the king's army whenever called to do so), were entitled to own freehold land, and were enfranchised (besides a number of lesser privileges). Nobles constituted approximately five per cent of the population, and most—two thirds to three quarters—farmed holdings of 40–50 acres or less, or owned no land at all, but in law all nobles, from the landless poorest to the wealthiest *magnates* (q.v.), were equal: in a sense their status might be

---

[1] According to the Oxford Dictionary also the ultimate source, via French *gentilhomme*, of the English term *gentleman*.

compared, very roughly, to that of a *civis romanus* in ancient Rome. Their special status and privileges were abolished by legislation of 1848.

Palatine, *Comes Palatinus, nádorispán,* office under the Hungarian crown created in the 11th c. initially to run all royal estates including judicial functions in these; by the 12th c. evolved into the head of the king's government and in the king's absence from the country his deputy there, retaining some judicial appeal functions. To the 15th c. appointed and dismissed by the king at his pleasure, but thereafter *Parliament* (q.v.) demanded a say in this and from 1608 formally elected him from amongst those (two Catholics and two Protestants) proposed by the Crown. Habsburg kings often left the office vacant, especially during the 16th c., and consistently tried to reduce its role until Charles III in 1723 set up the *Lieutenancy Council* (q.v.) presided over by the Palatine. In 1790 Leopold II hit on the idea of an *archduke* (q.v.) filling the office, and the last three were such. None were nominated after 1848.

Parliament, Hungarian—pre-1848 usually called the *Diet*—had its beginnings in a spontaneous coming together of elected representatives of the *nobles* (q.v.) of all *counties* (q.v.) in the second half of the 13th c. and began to take shape when the Crown invited such to join the bishops and *magnates* (q.v.) in their deliberations later that century. Infrequently called in the 14th c. it took off in the 15th, by now enlarged with representatives of the *Royal Free Cities* (q.v.) too (whose voice was, however, by the 18th c. whittled down to a single collective vote). From 1608 it was formally divided into an Upper Chamber (bishops, holders of *hereditary titles* (q.v.) and a selection of *ex officio* members), and a Lower Chamber of Members elected by the nobles of the counties (by the 17th–18th c. two per county) who had to speak and vote as instructed by their county assembly. Most Habsburg kings were loath to call Parliaments, but kept being forced to do so: no tax was recognised as legal unless approved, usually for a limited number of years only, by Parliament, nor could soldiers be raised without its consent. From 1848 (with a gap to 1867: there was no Parliament from 1849) the franchise was tied to property, income and educational qualifications; general adult suffrage had to wait until the inter-war years. The Upper Chamber was reformed in 1885, abolished in 1920, then resuscitated in modified form, and in 1945 finally vanished.

Prince is a confusing *hereditary title* (q.v.). Until the coming of the Habsburgs it was in Hungary applied exclusively to the direct descendants of a king but thereafter the practice prevalent in the Empire came to be recognised here too. Members of the House of Habsburg were all *archdukes* (q.v.), but the heads of a number of German—what later became Austria (*see* under *Hereditary Lands*) was part of Germany—families had the title **Fürst,** always followed by the family's surname (members of the family other than its head were styled variously prinz or count, followed by Christian and surname, depending on the terms of the original grant); in Latin, Italian and French Fürst has always been rendered *princeps, principe* and *prince.* This is different from the imperial title **Herzog,** only accorded to the heads of families that were sovereign rulers of a territory (however small) under the *Emperor* (q.v.), generally rendered into English as *duke*.

Quarterings, heraldic technical term for the number of preceding generations whose noble descent is shown, from the now defunct practice of *quartering* coats of arms with (i.e. including in them) the arms of both parents, and then so on for further generations back: four quarterings means up to grandparents, eight to great-grandparents, sixteen to great-great-grandparents, and so on.

Royal Free Cities, *regiæ liberæque civitas, szabad kiráyi város*, emerged in the Middle Ages; by 1500 there were fifteen of them. Technically the "property" of the king or queen, hence "royal", they (unlike market towns) were not subject to the administrative control of the *county* (q.v.) in which they were situated, and were governed by their own Councils, elected by the weightier of their burghers, hence "free"; besides local self-government their charters—which tended to be modelled upon those of towns in Germany, whence many of their burghers had immigrated to Hungary—granted them the right to hold, and tax, regular fairs and, in many instances, staple-rights too. First enfranchised by King Sigismund early in the 15th c., legislation of 1608 conferred collective *noble* (q.v.) status on each, all attendant rights and privileges pertaining to the Royal Free City as a whole; however, their voice in *Parliament* (q.v.) was soon whittled down to a single vote between them. Legislation of 1867 abolished their special standing.

Saint Stephen, Order of, founded by Maria Theresia in 1764—on the occasion of her son Joseph II becoming *Emperor* (q.v.)—specifically for Hungary. It was limited to 20 Grand Crosses, 30 Commanders, and 50 Members, all of whom had to show at least four noble *quarterings* (q.v.), although this last requirement was on occasion disregarded; until the 1880s those awarded the Grand Cross could petition to be made privy councillors, commanders barons or, if already that, counts, members barons (in this like the military Maria Theresia Order).

Tied peasants, *jobbágy* (from *jobb = better*), evolved from the servants working landed estates in the early Middle Ages; by the late 13—early 14th c. they had gained a measure of economic well-being and personal liberty, if always subject to tithes, taxes and payments in produce or cash to the *nobles* (q.v.) who owned the land they worked. During the 15th c.—almost continuous war with the Turks, some civil wars, and repeated periods of weak central government—their condition began to deteriorate sharply as state and landowners exacted ever more from them; in 1514 this resulted in a major peasants' revolt (known from its leader as the Dózsa Rebellion), which was put down cruelly and led to punitive legislation that increased their burdens, notably the *corvé*, and decreased their rights sharply, in particular tying them to their village and landowner "in perpetuity" (although this last was soon eased). The Turkish wars of the 16–17th c. provided an unofficial escape route into soldiering, but from the early 18th c. their burdens, the *corvé* in particular, kept being increased again. Typically a tied peasant farmed 25–50 acres of the noble landowner's land, and had the use of a plot of about one acre for house, outbuildings and garden, from none of which he could be evicted (short of committing a serious criminal offence) and all of which passed on to his sons, but he had to obtain the landowner's, and the county's, agreement to move away, and for minor offences was subject to the jurisdiction of the "manorial court"; much, therefore, depended upon the attitudes and behaviour of the landowner or, in the case of larger estates, his estate managers. He was not a "serf" in the sense that of those in Russia, literally owned by the landowners, were but nor was he a free tenant farmer—and of course he could never own freehold land (although enterprising tied peasants did lease land to have it worked by others). The status of tied peasant was abolished by legislation of 1848.

Transylvania, Governor of *(voyvode, vajda)* one of the very earliest great offices of state: King Saint Stephen, having defeated his uncle who had been undisputed master there, appointed the first *voyvode* in 1008 to run Transylvania on his behalf in place of the defeated uncle. Transylvania being remote, rich (mineral and, crucially, salt mines), strategically important, and geographically self-contained, such governors were thereafter appointed until the Turkish conquest of central Hungary cut it off from the rest of the kingdom (at which stage it became an autonomous principality, its prince, *fejedelem*, elected for life).

Viceroy of Croatia [& Slavonia], *banus Croatiae, horvát bán*. The first was Prince Álmos, younger brother of King Coloman *the Bookish* who had in 1105 formally united the Crowns of Croatia-Slavonia with that of Hungary. Never a sinecure—in the Middle Ages because of Dalmatia and access to the Adriatic (disputed by Byzantium and then Venice), from the 15th to the 18th c. because in the front line facing the Ottoman Empire, in the 19th c. and until the First World War because of pan-Slav unrest fomented by adjacent Serbia—holders of this office, which lasted until 1918 (albeit by then just the official title of a cabinet minister), ranked among the most senior dignitaries of the Hungarian Crown.

Selected bibliography

Includes only the most important reference works consulted that have a **specific** bearing on the family's history, or concern particular aspects of Hungarian institutions and offices.

A Pálffyak [The Pálffys]
   Reiszig Ede dr. ifj., pp 47, Légrády Testvérek, Budapest, *n.d.* [ca. 1900]
Adatok erdődi báró Pálffy Miklós életrajza és korához [Data for a biography and the age of Baron Nicholas Pálffy of Erdőd]
   Jedlicska Pál, pp 820, Érseki Lyceum Könyvnyomdája, Eger, 1897
Erdődi gróf Pálffy János nádor [Palatine Count John Pálffy of Erdőd]
   Málnási Ödön dr. vitéz, pp 39, Greif Druck, München, 1961
Erdődi Pálffy Tamás [Thomas Pálffy ab Erdőd]
   Takáts Sándor, pp 85—118 in **Hadtörténelmi Közlemények** [Military History Communications] Vol. XVI, Pts. 1–2, 1915, Magyar Tudományos Akadémia, Budapest
Eredeti részletek Gróf-Pálffy család okmánytárához s Gróf Pálffyak életrajzi vázlatai [Original excerpts of the Count Pálffy family archives & biographical sketches of Counts Pálffy]
   Jedlicska Pál, pp 760, Stephaneum Nyomda Rt, Budapest, 1916
Gräfliches Taschenbuch ["Almanach de Gotha" — Counts]
   Justus Perthes, Gotha, 1939
Magyar alkotmány- és jogtörténet [Hungarian constitution- and law-history]
   Eckhart Ferenc, pp. 482, Osiris Kiadó, Budapest, 2000
Magyarország családai [Families of Hungary]
   Nagy Iván, XII + 1 vols, Ráth Mór, Pest, 1857–1868
   (facsimile edition ed. *Szakály Ferenc*, Helikon Kiadó, Budapest, 1987)
Magyarország történeti kronológiája [Hungary's historical chronology]
   ed. *Benda Kálmán*, IV vols, Akadémia Kiadó, Budapest, 1981–1982

Magyarország vármegyéi és városai (Magyarország monográfiája) [Hungary's counties and towns (Monograph of Hungary)]
ed. central & county-by-county committees, Apollo Irodalmi Társaság, Budapest, *n. d.* [successive vols. between c. 1900–1910]
– **Nyitra Vármegye,** pp 736
– **Pozsony Vármegye,** pp. 754
Pálffy Pál nádor levelei (1644–1653) ... Batthyány Ádámhoz és Borbálához [Letters of Palatine Paul Pálffy (1644–1653) ... to Adam and Barbara Batthyány]
Collected, edited and introduction by *Éva S. Lauter*, pp. 222 (Vol. 1 of the series **Régi Magyar Történelmi Források** [Old Hungarian Historical Sources]), Budapest 1989
Révay Nagylexicon [Révay Great Encyclopedia]
Originally published in vols. I–XX before 1914, but updated with supplementary vols. in the inter-war years; Woodstone CD-ROM edition, 1999

Index

Since the text is about Pálffys in Hungary, neither they nor it have been indexed. Kings of Hungary are shown in the form '**Andrew I**' (also so indexed if mentioned in the text before on the throne); where the serial number of a Habsburg as King of Hungary differs from that which he used as (Holy Roman or Austrian) Emperor a cross-reference of the form '**Charles VI,** Emperor *See* **Charles III**' is given; rulers of other nations are shown in the form '**Louis XIV** of France'.

Historic (c. 1000 to 1920) Hungary

Cracow

Olmütz

Lőcs

Trencsén

Besztercebánya

H I G H L A

Vöröskő

Vág

Nagyszombat

Selmecbánya

Pu

Danube

Vienna Pressburg

Nyitra

L O W E R
A U S T R I A

Érsekújvár

E

Magyaróvár Komárom

Esztergom

Sopron

Győr

Vác

Tata

Tisz

Kőszeg

T R A N S D A N U B I A

Pápa

Buda Pest

S T Y R I A

Szombathely

Rába

Várpalota Székesfehérvár

Körmend

Veszprém

Szolnok

Szentgotthárd

Balaton

Egerszeg

Simontornya

C E N T R A L

Kanizsa

Kalocsa

Varasd

Szekszárd

Szeged

Szigetvár Pécs

Körös

Mohács

C R O A T I A

S L A V O N I A

Dráva

Zagreb

Eszék

Száva

B O S N I A

Belgrade